The BBC Proms Guide to Great Orchestral Works

Nicholas Kenyon has been Director of the BBC Proms since 1996. He was a music critic for *The New Yorker*, *The Times*, and the *Observer*, and was Controller, BBC Radio 3, from 1992 to 1998, responsible for the award-winning Radio 3 seasons 'Fairest Isle' and 'Sounding the Century'. He wrote the history of the BBC Symphony Orchestra and edited the influential volume *Authenticity and Early Music*. In 2001 he wrote a new edition of his biography of Simon Rattle. He is now Controller, BBC Proms, Live Events and Television Classical Music, and was appointed a CBE in 2001.

in the same series

THE BBC PROMS GUIDE TO GREAT CHORAL WORKS
edited by Nicholas Kenyon

THE BBC PROMS GUIDE TO GREAT CONCERTOS
edited by Nicholas Kenyon

THE BBC PROMS GUIDE TO GREAT SYMPHONIES
edited by Nicholas Kenyon

THE BBC PROMS GUIDE TO

Great Orchestral Works

edited by Nicholas Kenyon

ff

faber and faber

First published in 2004
by Faber and Faber Limited
3 Queen Square London WC1N 3AU

Typeset by Faber and Faber Limited
Printed in England by Bookmarque Ltd, Croydon

A CIP record for this book
is available from the British Library

ISBN 0-571-22097-5

10 9 8 7 6 5 4 3 2 1

Contents

List of Contributors

Andrew Achenbach 185
Brendan Beales 222
Julian Budden 195
Anthony Burton 39, 41, 44, 76, 115, 120, 140, 169, 207
Piers Burton-Page 21, 29, 37, 80
David Cairns 14
David Cox 255
Misha Donat 10, 12, 180
David Fanning 237
David Gutman 86
James Harding 50
Malcolm Hayes 215, 256
Andrew Huth 133, 144, 234
Adrian Jack 52, 56, 70, 192, 230
Stephen Johnson 187, 242
Lindsay Kemp 94, 126
Peter Kemp 200, 201, 202
Tess Knighton 79, 111, 155, 164, 223
Gerald Larner 154, 157
Malcolm MacDonald 1, 3, 6, 65, 72, 96, 99, 159, 239
Colin Matthews 104
David Matthews 32, 166
Robert Maycock 16, 17, 18, 20, 47, 82, 83, 106, 119, 137, 148, 150, 151, 177
Diana McVeagh 113
Barry Millington 203, 246, 247, 249, 251, 253
David Nice 189
Roger Nichols 173
Geoffrey Norris 131
Bayan Northcott 153
Hugh Ottaway 77
John Pickard 188, 191
Eric Roseberry 183

Introduction

Is there any more thrilling sound than that of a massive orchestra in full flight? Whether your taste is for Stravinsky's *Rite of Spring* or Strauss's *Don Juan*, for Ravel's *La valse* or Janáček's Sinfonietta, this book brings together some of the most inspiring pieces ever written for the orchestra and provides an accessible and authoritative guide to their riches. Designed to complement the *BBC Proms Guides* to *Great Symphonies* and *Great Concertos*, this collection of notes does not include those two major categories of orchestral music, but samples many other forms: overtures, suites, tone poems, symphonic poems, ballets, and just some of the vast number of orchestral extracts from operas that were so popular in concert programmes of the past. If you want to understand more about what makes these orchestral pieces so fascinating and compelling, this is the place to start.

The symphony orchestra will surely be seen as one of the most distinctive products of late Western civilisation. Its combination of human involvement and technical sophistication is unique: the balance between inspired individual effort and top-flight instrumental technology, under the direction of that ambiguous but mythically powerfully figure, the conductor, provides one of the iconic images of our time. Yet like all other cultural institutions that reached their present form in the nineteenth century, there have been many challenges to its existence and there is much questioning of its current role.

Musicians have always played together: but when did a collection of instruments become an orchestra? The first great British musical historian, Dr Charles Burney, believed that the orchestra began in 1607 when Claudio Monteverdi assembled thirty-three instruments and created a richly varied palette for his opera *Orfeo*. More recently, scholars have suggested that the concept of an orchestra really dates from the second half of the seventeenth century in France, when the institutions of the French court, the *petite bande* and *grande bande*, were assembled to play the music of Lully and his contemporaries. The orchestra as we know it evolved between the last decades of the seventeenth and the first decades of the eighteenth century, and was ready to find its leading role in the music of the classical period – Haydn, Mozart and Beethoven. Still, many of the combinations of instruments assembled during the eighteenth century in the centres of music-making around Europe might well have surprised us, and it was not until the growth of public concerts and the vast developments in instrument-making in the early nineteenth century that what we would recognise as the modern symphony orchestra came into being.

What is clear is that for three hundred years, orchestras have been created to serve the vanity of patrons, the political ambitions of monarchs, and increasingly, the musical needs of the growing middle-class audience for public concerts. More recently the needs of recording and broadcasting have stimulated the creation of remarkable ensembles from the NBC Symphony to the BBC's orchestras in this country. And there is one other group which has been extremely influential in the creation of orchestras: the musicians themselves, either rebelling against the constraints with which they were controlled (as in the formation of the London Symphony Orchestra by a group of players a century ago), or sensing the opportunities for entrepreneurial activity in a world that still needs orchestral music for films, adverts, and classical spectaculars.

So the story of the orchestra is on the one hand the story of its musical repertory, which is explored in this book, but it is also the story of the remarkable institutions that it has created along the way: the Royal Philharmonic Society in London, the Leipzig Gewandhaus, the Vienna Philharmonic, and the great American orchestras funded largely by private endowments – some of which seemed so impregnable but are now subject to economic turmoil. One of the key developments in our musical life over recent decades has been the challenge to the centrality of the symphony orchestra. This challenge originated years ago, in the emergence of the 'chamber orchestra' as a more appropriate model for the performance of Baroque and some Classical repertory, but has been renewed in the last thirty years by the development of specialist contemporary-music ensembles like the London Sinfonietta and Ensemble Modern, and the huge growth of period-instrument ensembles such as the English Concert, Academy of Ancient Music and the Orchestra of the Age of Enlightenment. The orchestra has had to react to the potential narrowing of its remit, and it has responded by changing both its role and its playing techniques.

Today the orchestra is at a turning point: will it become, as Ernest Fleischmann who ran the Los Angeles Philharmonic once suggested, a 'community of musicians', from which can be derived contemporary-music groups, early-music groups, jazz bands, world-music ensembles and educational resources, as well as a full orchestra who will come together to play the great masterpieces? Pierre Boulez perhaps put it best when he said that an orchestra should be 'an ensemble of possibilities that excludes nothing'. Whatever happens, the twenty-first century will be a testing time for the orchestra as an institution, a time in which it must shed some of its massive encumbrances and regain something of the flexibility and adaptability of earlier centuries.

Just as the orchestra has changed and evolved continuously, so too has public taste altered. In this selection of works we have been firmly led by those pieces likely to be encountered in the orchestral repertory today – those most often included in concert performances, radio broadcasts and recordings. Over half the works in the book were written in the now-completed twentieth century, though it is a reflection on the current repertory that the selection is heavily weighted towards the first half of the century, with too few works written after the Second World War: we have started with the unquestioned classics and will hopefully expand in the future to include the most successful pieces by living composers.

However, in putting this collection together we are faithfully reflecting the current taste of orchestras and audiences alike. Nowadays it is rare for a BBC Proms season to pass without including – as this book includes – Stravinsky's three great ballets, Debussy's *La mer* or Holst's *Planets* suite. In the past it was very different, because of the dominance of operatic extracts and shorter pieces, especially overtures, which were almost indispensable in past programmes. For the record, the most frequently played single work at the Proms (even including the ritual pieces of the Last Night) is Wagner's overture to *Tannhäuser*, which has been heard over 280 times – often more than once a season in the early years under Sir Henry Wood. Several other Wagner orchestral extracts were popular: then we come to Berlioz's 'Hungarian March' from *The Damnation of Faust*, Grieg's *Peer Gynt* suite no. 1 and Rossini's overture to *William Tell*, all of which exceeded 150 performances, mainly in the first half of the Proms' life. But these are by no means the most familiar works of the present-day Proms, where Debussy's *Prélude à 'L'après-midi d'un faune'*, Wagner's 'Prelude and Liebestod' from *Tristan and Isolde*, Gershwin's *American in Paris* and Bernstein's 'Symphonic Dances' from *West Side Story* jostle for attention alongside more recent music. There is a fascinating story to be researched and written here about the interaction of changing audience tastes, changing fashions in programme-building, and the changing priorities of conductors and orchestras.

We hope that these high-quality programme notes which have been provided for audiences in the Royal Albert Hall during recent BBC Proms seasons will be equally valuable in book form, as a complement to radio and CD listening, and concert-going. Each note is designed to be consulted and read separately, so there is some inevitable repetition between different notes.

Acknowledgements

I would like to thank Edward Bhesania for his expert help in the preparation of this volume, and for writing the new composer biographies. Mark Pappenheim, who originally commissioned many of these notes for BBC Proms Publications, has had much input into their shape and consistency, and gave advice on the content of the volume. Sarah Breeden oversaw the project for BBC Proms Publications, and Hannah Rowley has tirelessly assembled the notes and contacted authors. We are especially grateful to the many outstanding authors who have allowed their work to be reprinted in this new format, and to Belinda Matthews at Faber, who was so responsive to the idea that these notes could be collected in book form, and whose team has worked tirelessly to assemble the book against the unforgiving deadlines of a Proms season.

Nicholas Kenyon
Director, BBC Proms

Samuel Barber (1910–81)

Among the leading twentieth-century American composers, Samuel Barber, in spite of his European outlook, wrote in a largely conservative idiom. At fourteen, Barber began studies at the Curtis Institute, Philadelphia, producing notable early works such as the song cycle *Dover Beach* and the Cello Sonata. He then travelled to Vienna and Rome (while his compatriots Copland and Carter gravitated to Paris) and secured his reputation as a composer with his First String Quartet and First Symphony. The Adagio for Strings (1938), arranged from his First String Quartet, has become an enduring symbol of American music. He taught at the Curtis Institute from 1939 to 1942 before returning to Europe, where he wrote the Cello Concerto and the nostalgic *Knoxville: Summer of 1915*. His Pulitzer prize-winning opera *Vanessa* (1958) was followed by the less successful *Antony and Cleopatra* (1966), written for opening of the Metropolitan Opera's new house in Lincoln Center.

Adagio for Strings, Op. 11 (1936; arr. 1938)

In 1936, studying at the American Academy in Rome on a Pulitzer fellowship, Samuel Barber composed his String Quartet, Op. 11: a curiously balanced piece in two movements. Upon a hectic Allegro movement in B minor follows a large-scale Molto adagio in B flat minor, with a brief recall of the Allegro tacked on as a final coda. The previous summer Barber's friend and fellow composer Gian Carlo Menotti had introduced him to Arturo Toscanini and it was the great conductor who suggested that Barber should rescore the quartet's Adagio as a concert item for full string orchestra.

Toscanini conducted the NBC Symphony Orchestra in the premiere of this arrangement on 5 November 1938, in New York. With many ensuing performances, it was Barber's first music to reach a wide audience; over sixty years later, the Adagio for Strings remains not only his best-known piece, but one of the most famous American works of all time.

The Adagio well deserves its popularity for its intrinsic qualities alone. Yet it also owes much to the events of 1939–45. Though the piece's entire orientation is surely personal and romantic, performances multiplied as it answered a public mood of nostalgia, and fulfilled a need for solemn, dignified American music to honour the USA's war dead. By 1945 it seemed the natural choice for the memorial service for President Roosevelt. In 1967 Barber, accepting perhaps the vicarious quasi-religious associations which had long accrued to his piece, arranged it for chorus (with or without organ), setting the Latin text of the Agnus Dei. In the cinema, this all-American Adagio creates a disturbing counterpoint to the most horrific sequences of Oliver Stone's Vietnam War film, *Platoon*.

The restrained but profound lyricism of the opening bars sets a mood which is impressively sustained and amplified in cleanly flowing counterpoint that owes less to Mahler than to Bach and Sibelius. The predominant even-crotchet motion propels the music with grave inevitability in a long, shapely architectural curve to an eloquent (and very Sibelian) climax and an elegiac dying fall.

Béla Bartók (1881–1945)

Bartók, along with his contemporary Kodály, built up a Hungarian national art music that drew heavily on the country's rich folk tradition. After studying piano and composition at the Budapest Academy he embarked with Kodály on a series of tours to collect folk song: they recorded, transcribed and classified music from Hungary, Transylvania, North Africa and Turkey. Folk and folk-like material became central to his style, though Liszt and Strauss had been early influences, as, later, had Debussy; but it was the ballets of Stravinsky that led Bartók to his own ballets, *The Wooden Prince* (1914–17), and *The Miraculous Mandarin* (1917). From 1907 to 1934 Bartók taught piano at the Budapest Academy, during which time he developed a major career as a pianist, performing regularly in Hungary and abroad. Following investigations into Bartók's Aryanism under Horthy's pro-Nazi regime, he fled to the USA in 1940. Here, suffering from financial and health problems, he wrote his *Concerto for Orchestra*, the sonata for solo violin and the (incomplete) Third Piano Concerto and Viola Concerto.

Concerto for Orchestra (1943)

1 Introduzione
2 Giuoco delle coppie
3 Elegia
4 Intermezzo interrotto
5 Finale

In 1940, fearing the capitulation of his homeland to the Nazis, Bartók left Hungary for exile in the USA. For three years he wrote almost nothing new; he gave concerts and worked on the folk music of Asia Minor. By 1943 funds to support his research had dried up, and he was too ill to accept engagements as a pianist.

At this point Serge Koussevitzky, acting on the suggestion of the violinist Joseph Szigeti and the conductor Fritz Reiner, came to Bartók as he lay ill in hospital to commission a major score for the Boston Symphony Orchestra – a gesture that contributed greatly to Bartók's recovery of the will to compose. Premiered in Boston on 1 December 1944, the Concerto for Orchestra was the greatest public success of Bartók's career, and the beginning of his establishment as a popular 'repertoire' composer. It remains perhaps his most performed orchestral work, and is typical of the comparatively straightforward style of his final 'American' period (though it displays all the masterly contrapuntal technique of his earlier scores).

The 'concerto for orchestra' had already been established as a genre before Bartók wrote his: Hindemith seems to have been the first to use the term, in 1925, and subsequently such distinguished figures as Walter Piston, Goffredo Petrassi, and – most importantly, in 1939 – Bartók's lifelong friend Kodály wrote works with that title. But for them the term signified something akin to the Baroque concerto grosso, and their works sometimes went as far as to incorporate the contrasting 'concertino' and 'ripieno' groups of instruments. And although Ralph Hawkes, Bartók's new publisher, may have planted the seed by suggesting in 1942 that he should compose a series of works along the lines of Bach's Brandenburg Concertos, Bartók instead linked the form with the idea that opportunities for solo display should be afforded equally to all members of the orchestra, and with that of an ultimate orchestral showpiece. Morever, his Concerto is much larger than any of the previous examples – built on almost symphonic lines, as if a brilliant study for the series of symphonies he was apparently planning to write, if death spared him for a few more years.

In his programme note for the first performance Bartók commented: 'The general mood of the work represents – apart from the jesting second movement – a gradual transition from the sternness of the first movement and the lugubrious death-song of the third movement to the life-assertion of the last one.' This kind of emotional progression is by its nature more suited to expression in symphonic form than in any busy re-creation of Baroque manners.

The first movement, entitled 'Introduzione', itself includes a slow introduction to the vigorous Allegro vivace that occupies most of it. This introduction contains four distinct ideas, of which the first – a mysterious theme built out of a chain of rising and falling fourths – and the last (a threatening scale-fragment covering the interval of a tritone) are combined to produce the wiry, tensile first subject of the sonata-form Allegro proper. A hesitant, lyrical second subject heard first on solo oboe hints at nostalgia for Hungarian landscapes, but the bulk of the movement is taken up with robust contrapuntal arguments over the first subject – including a splendid canonic stretto, with some of the parts in inversion, for the full brass.

Bartók originally called the second movement, which is a chain of linked dances, 'Presentando le coppie' ('Presenting the Pairs'), a more accurate description of his compositional strategy than the published title 'Giuoco delle coppie' ('Game of the Pairs'). The tempo indication and metronome mark were garbled in publication, and only in 1993 did a revised edition reinstate the true Allegro that Bartók intended. A side drum establishes the underlying rhythm, and brings on a succession of instrumental 'pairs' on the principle of 'the animals went in two by two': bassoons in sixths, oboes in thirds, clarinets in sevenths, flutes in fifths, muted trumpets in major seconds, each refashioning the basic scrap of tune to their own liking. Their procession is intercepted and sanctified by a smoothly glowing brass chorale, then the pairs return in the same order, reinforced this time by contributions from other instruments of their own or related families. The side drum has the last word, as it had the first.

The deeply felt 'Elegia' returns to the material of the first movement's introduction, the various elements now being developed darkly, impassionedly, in a glittering, impressionistic scoring that puts this movement among Bartók's most characteristic 'night music' inspirations.

The fourth movement's 'Intermezzo', which alternates two graceful and teasingly flexible folk-like tunes, is 'interrupted' by a mocking reminiscence – begun by clarinet – of the over-repetitious march tune from Shostakovich's 'Leningrad' Symphony (all the rage while Bartók was composing his work, and Shostakovich was a great favourite of Koussevitzky). This interloper provokes the rest of the orchestra to disbelieving mirth before the intermezzo tunes return.

A brief horn signal sets the Finale off on a brilliant perpetuum mobile dash down the home straight. Several themes are brought to light in passing in the welter of activity: the last and most important of these is a declamatory tune first heard on solo trumpet, harking back to the chain of fourths of the first movement. A slackening of pace brings an extensive fugal development of the trumpet theme and then a briefer recall of the earlier perpetuum mobile music, which leads into unexpected tranquillo stillness. Out of this emerges a ghostly, swirling music on the strings, through which hints of themes glint forth on brass and woodwind; the sound-complex assumes more and more solid shape until the trumpet theme, vastly augmented, returns on full brass to crown the proceedings with peremptory grandeur. The rest is a sprint for the finishing line.

Music for Strings, Percussion and Celesta (1936)

1 Andante tranquillo
2 Allegro
3 Adagio
4 Allegro molto

Bartók composed his Music for Strings, Percussion and Celesta in 1936 in Budapest, answering a commission from the Swiss conductor and modern-music champion Paul Sacher to write something for the tenth anniversary of his

Basle Chamber Orchestra. Sacher conducted the world premiere in Basle on 21 January 1937. During a career with the orchestra that lasted some seventy years, Sacher was eventually responsible for bringing into being a respectable proportion of the twentieth century's least dispensable repertoire, but among his legion of important commissions, Bartók's Music for Strings, Percussion and Celesta stands in the very highest rank – for intensity of expression, originality of design and sheer musical quality.

The non-committal title ('Music for . . .') signals Bartók's awareness that his piece had no clear formal antecedents. It is not, however, any mere assemblage of disparate movements; it has a convincingly organic form, and an elegantly balanced tonal argument centred on the key of A minor/major. To some extent it belongs to the genre – actively promoted by many during the 1920s and 1930s – of modern revivals of the Baroque concerto grosso form. Here, however, if there is a soloistic element in the ensemble, it is provided by the (mainly pitched) percussion. Yet, in its concern with structural symmetries, chromatic exploration, stylised folk-dance rhythms and fantastic colours, the piece has little in common with the various 'Back to Bach' movements of its time. (It might be more realistically thought of as a direct successor to Bartók's Fourth and Fifth String Quartets, written upwards and outwards for a bigger body and a more colourful palette.)

Even the title's list of instruments ('. . . strings, percussion and celesta') is less than forthcoming about the scoring. Among the 'percussion' are a harp and a piano, whose role is in fact more extensive than that of the celesta. Timpani and xylophone also make significant, often soloistic contributions. And the strings are disposed antiphonally in two groups, as a double string orchestra, with inevitably enhanced opportunities for echo effects and massed polyphony. This unusual ensemble proved to be the ideal vehicle for Bartók's mature musical language at its most developed and refined. Nor was it slow to spawn a line of (mostly distinguished) quasi-imitations, such as Martinů's Concerto for Double

String Orchestra, Piano and Timpani and Frank Martin's *Petite symphonie concertante* for double string orchestra, piano, harp and harpsichord (both, incidentally, written for Sacher and his orchestra).

Bartók's work begins with a ghostly fugue (all the more eerie for its 'tranquillo' marking) scored almost entirely for the strings. The fugue subject's sinuous, desolate melodic arch does not merely rise and fall: the ascending phrases leave gaps in the chromatic scale which are filled in by the descending ones, so that within the span of each phrase no semitone is left untouched, adding to the atmosphere of constriction and grief. At first muted, the strings gradually take off their mutes and the dynamics steadily increase. The entries begin orthodoxly enough, but gradually steer the music round to E flat, the opposite end of the tonal spectrum from the initial A. This coincides with the fortississimo peak of the dynamic curve and a brief entry of cymbals and timpani. From this climactic point (not the movement's centre: E flat appears about two thirds of the way through, at the mathematical 'Golden Section') the fugue literally unwinds, the subject being heard in reverse and melting into a coda with a tremulous flurry of celesta figuration.

The fugue subject is varied throughout the remaining movements. The second – one of Bartók's most brilliant inventions – is a furious, extended scherzo in sonata form, featuring the whole ensemble, the two string bodies frequently 'shadowing' each other in close imitation and coming together to stress irregular motoric rhythms. Piano and timpani function as virtual soloists. In the recapitulation, the 2/4 time of the opening is tautened into 3/8, with a sense of hectic stretto.

The slow third movement is a phantasmagoric nocturne in six sections, these sections separated by phrases of the first-movement fugue subject. It begins with the skeletal ticking of the xylophone in dialogue with timpani glissandos and a recitative-like viola melody. Celesta and piano then add a sheen to more flowing melodies of the strings; reinforced by harp, together with string tremolandos, they next create a tremulous impressionistic shimmering. In complete contrast, a percussive, gauntly stalking episode in bare octaves intervenes, and then the elements of the second and third sections – the flowing string melodies and the shimmering figuration – are combined. The movement ends as it began, only in reverse, with timpani and violas, and xylophone tapping away into silence.

The finale is a joyous (if occasionally rather fevered) rondo, its main theme an extended version of the original fugue subject, now adapted to the Lydian mode and a Bulgarian dance rhythm. The accents of East European folk music can clearly be heard, especially in the episode-tunes but also in the strumming pizzicato chords of the string orchestra, the cimbalom effects of the percussion and the references to solo fiddling. A whirlwind acceleration climaxes in a Prestissimo strepitoso blizzard of string tremolandos, in whose wake a great assuaging song-like tune arises – a majestic 'diatonicisation' of the chromatic fugue theme – before the final decisive cadence into A major.

Ludwig van Beethoven (1770–1827)

Beethoven left his native Bonn in his early twenties for Vienna, where he became established in fashionable circles as a composer, piano virtuoso and improviser of considerable ability. His 'early' works developed the classical models of Haydn and Mozart. As early as 1796, he recognised signs of his impending deafness, and his subsequent suffering and alienation, as well as his creative resolve, were disclosed in his 'Heiligenstadt Testament' of 1802. His 'middle period' was characterised by a broadening of form and an extension of harmonic language which reflects his proto-Romantic expressive tendencies; this period produced the Symphonies Nos 2 to 8, notable piano sonatas, several string quartets and his only opera, *Fidelio*. From 1812 to 1818 he produced little music, but his last years saw the mould-breaking 'Choral' Symphony, and an exploration of increasing profundity in the more intimate genres of the string quartet and piano sonata.

Overture, *Egmont*, from Op. 84 (1810)

It isn't hard to see why Goethe's historical drama *Egmont* struck a sympathetic chord in Beethoven, whose own opera, *Fidelio*, is a passionate indictment of political oppression. Goethe's play is set in sixteenth-century Flanders, then under the rule of the Spanish Inquisition. Count Egmont, the governor of the province, is in love with Clärchen, and through her comes to sympathise with the just cause of the people. After failing in his attempt to persuade Philip II of Spain to relax his regime, Egmont is arrested and condemned to death. Clärchen poisons herself, and Egmont goes to the scaffold convinced that his sacrifice will inspire the people to rise up against their oppressors.

Beethoven composed his incidental music to Goethe's drama for a revival that took place in the summer of 1810. The previous year Vienna had been occupied by Napoleon's troops, and it surely wasn't by chance that the Kärntnertor Theatre chose at that time to mount a new production of Schiller's *Don Carlos* – another play dealing with Philip II's rule in the Netherlands – and that the theatre's 1810 repertoire included, besides *Egmont*, Schiller's *William Tell*. According to Beethoven's pupil Carl Czerny:

> When it was decided to perform Schiller's *Tell* and Goethe's *Egmont*, the question arose as to who should compose the music. Beethoven and [Adalbert] Gyrowetz were chosen. Beethoven wanted very much to have *Tell*; but intrigues were at once set on foot to have *Egmont*, supposedly less adaptable to music, assigned to him. It turned out, however, that he could make masterly music for this drama also, and he applied the full power of his genius to it.

For his part, Beethoven declared that he composed the *Egmont* music 'purely out of love for the poet'.

Of the nine numbers that Beethoven wrote for Goethe's play (they include four entr'actes, a melodrama, and a 'Victory Symphony'), only the overture has remained at all well known. Its slow introduction begins with the fatalistic tread of a strongly defined rhythmic motif in the strings, answered by the woodwinds with gentle supplicatory phrases. These two ideas, and the strong expressive contrast they embody, foreshadow the second subject of the overture's main Allegro section. At the end of the Allegro the rhythmic motif is given out in a still more forceful form, with the support of trumpets and timpani, before the music is abruptly cut off. The moment of silence that ensues symbolises Egmont's death; and perhaps we may hear the quiet, sustained woodwind chords that follow as a representation of his spirit leaving his body. Finally, the music turns to the major, for a 'Victory Symphony' in which Beethoven introduces the shrill sound of the piccolo.

Overture, *Leonore* no. 3, from Op. 72 (1806)

Beethoven began work on his 'rescue opera' *Leonore* (later retitled *Fidelio*) in 1804, and over the next three years was to produce not only two versions of the opera itself, but also no fewer than three overtures. The opera's premiere, on 20 November 1805, was prefaced by the overture known as '*Leonore* no. 2', while no. 3 formed part of Beethoven's first revision of the stage work, produced in March 1806. As for '*Leonore* no. 1', it was probably not the first, but the last of the three, and seems never to have been used in the theatre (Beethoven may have designed it for a projected revival of *Leonore* in Prague, in 1807).

The three *Leonore* overtures have two things in common: they are all in C major and they all make use of the melody of the Act 2 aria, 'In des Lebens Frühlingstagen' ('In the springtime of my life'), in which, from the depths of his dungeon cell, the unjustly imprisoned Florestan recalls his young love for Leonore, the faithful wife who, unbeknown to him, has infiltrated the gaol in male disguise, intent on freeing her husband at any cost.

Leonore no. 3 is the greatest and most frequently heard of the three – at once more condensed and more expansive than no. 2. More condensed, because Beethoven compresses the material of the earlier overture's introduction into scarcely more than half the number of bars; more expansive, because he provides the Allegro with the full-scale recapitulation that had been so noticeably absent before. In both overtures, though, the climax of the development coincides with the startling entry of the off-stage trumpet call which, in the opera, announces the long-awaited arrival of the Minister, Don Fernando, and with it Florestan's salvation. In *Leonore* no. 3, the newly recomposed trumpet call is approached in the manner of a cadenza, and the bars that lead up to it are curiously similar to those preceding the cadenza in the finale of the Fourth Piano Concerto, on which Beethoven had been working at the same time.

Why, in view of the dramatic effectiveness of *Leonore* no. 3, did Beethoven compose an entirely new – and much shorter – overture for the familiar final version of his opera in 1814? By then, he had realised that his previous attempts had been too self-sufficient to serve as the prologue to an opera, and threatened to overshadow its opening scenes. Although Mahler's questionable custom of inserting *Leonore* no. 3 between the two scenes of *Fidelio*'s second act has been followed by a few conductors since (notably Furtwängler and Klemperer), the piece rightly belongs in the concert hall, not the opera house.

Hector Berlioz (1803–69)

One of the most imaginative and individual composers of the nineteenth century, Berlioz inherited a French love of instrumental colour and put it at the service of his vivid imagination. Indeed Berlioz encapsulated the essence of the Romantic artist: headstrong, with a turbulent emotional life, he was strongly drawn to literature; his music was inspired by Shakespeare (*Romeo and Juliet*, *Beatrice and Benedict*, as well as his overture *King Lear*), Goethe (*The Damnation of Faust*), and Byron (*Harold in Italy*). His epic opera *The Trojans*, based on Virgil's *Aeneid*, represents the pinnacle of the French grand opera tradition. He was one of the leading conductors of his day and published much vivid musical criticism. Among his writings is a famous and influential treatise on orchestration.

Overture, *Le corsaire*, Op. 21 (1844; rev. 1852)

Berlioz's exuberant seascape dates from the early autumn of 1844. In its original form it was composed in Nice, where Berlioz had gone for a holiday after an exhausting summer organising and conducting concerts in Paris. Unlike the recent *Roman Carnival*, which had close links with the opera *Benvenuto Cellini*, it was a wholly independent concert overture; but the proximity of the earlier overture (Berlioz had performed *Roman Carnival* several times that year) clearly influenced the shape of the new work. Like *Roman Carnival*, it begins with a flourish, a swift-moving digest of what is to come, which then gives way to a slow lyrical theme that itself returns later to play an important part in the main (Allegro) section of the work; and, like *Roman Carnival*, the overture is remarkable for its rhythmic verve and energy.

This time, however, the rhythms suggest not the pulse of the dance but the play of wind and sea and the exhilaration of the 'young light-hearted masters of the wave'. At first Berlioz entitled his overture *La tour de Nice*, after the tower high up on the Ponchettes rock, looking far out over the Mediterranean, where he wrote the work; and it was first performed under that name in January 1845. Later it was called *Le corsaire rouge* (the title of the French translation of James Fenimore Cooper's novel, *The Red Rover*), and finally, by the time of its publication in revised form in 1852, *Le corsaire* – linking it, by further association, with Byron's poem 'The Corsair'.

Under whatever title, the music celebrates the dangers and excitements of the imagined life of the privateer. The pirate or brigand as free man, in contrast to the citizen of bourgeois society hemmed in by convention and the daily cares of profit and loss, was a favourite Romantic theme. Perhaps, too, Berlioz projected himself imaginatively into the sea-adventurer's existence the more eagerly because of the frustrations of his own professional and domestic existence in this period.

The music is marked from the beginning by an enormous zest, as rapid fortissimo violin scales in C major are answered by excited woodwind in syncopation. When the violins reply, it is in A flat major. A flat is the key of the ensuing Adagio, a beautiful extended melody underpinned by a booming D flat on cellos and basses.

After this lyrical interlude, a vivid crescendo leads to a return of the rushing scale passages, and from now on the pace is unflagging. When the Adagio theme returns, it is bandied about between different instruments, a fact which, together with continual changes in key, dynamics and accent, increases still further the sense of speed and irresistible momentum. At the climax, the arpeggio opening of the main theme is proclaimed majestically by the brass against a swirl of rising string scales, followed by a stridently defiant statement of the full theme, first in C, then in D, at which point it disappears in a welter of syncopations. The effect is of an upheaval of sea and sky, the musical equivalent of a Turner storm at sea. At the end there is a last reminder of A flat, before the final blaze of C major.

'Hungarian March', from *The Damnation of Faust*, Op. 24 (1846)

The story of Faust and the nation of Hungary had nothing in common until this march brought them together. It is a typically quirky example of Berlioz's determination to keep a good piece alive when circumstances were against it. For the *Rákóczy-indulo*, as it was first known, came into being as a strictly occasional one-off.

Berlioz was due in Pest to conduct concerts in February 1846, and had been asked to orchestrate a national march for his programme. Being Berlioz, he decided to do a little more than arrange the tune. Also being Berlioz, he had not realised the effect it would have. When a quietly booming bass drum entered, it was taken to represent distant gunfire, a symbol of rebellion by the suppressed Hungarians against the Austrian empire, given to them by a composer from the most revolutionary of all nations. By the end, cheering had turned into a major demonstration, and Berlioz into a local hero.

That could have been all there was to it, except that he was writing a large-scale work based on Goethe's version of the Faust legend and needed a vigorous episode to offset the opening's meditative atmosphere. His dramatic instincts told him he had just composed the very thing. There was a snag: the location. Given the tune, it could only be one place. Unfortunately, Goethe hadn't thought to send Faust there. Little daunted by such niceties, though a touch apologetic about his effrontery, Berlioz simply thought up a new scene. Faust was whisked off to the Hungarian plains and had his smouldering ennui set on fire by the rousing sight of an army with a cause to fight for.

What Berlioz did not foresee was that the wheel would turn full circle and the march would become a popular concert item, performed far more often than his complete *The Damnation of Faust*. Distanced from its origins, we can hear it as a short tone poem about pride, defiance and aspiration. Fanfares using the rhythm of the Rákóczy tune lead immediately to the tune itself. There is a contrasting trio section, interrupted by assertive brass, which moves straight on to the early stages of a prolonged, vivid build-up of the kind with which Berlioz liked to end symphonic pieces. The tune returns at the height of the frenzy, and is swept away again in the rush towards the splendours of the major key.

© Robert Maycock

Overture, *Roman Carnival*, Op. 9 (1844)

This most brilliant of concert overtures owes its existence to an operatic failure. Berlioz's version of the racy memoirs left by the Renaissance sculptor and adventurer Benvenuto Cellini was accepted for production at the Paris Opéra in 1838, but survived for just three performances. After an equally unimpressive revival the next year, it disappeared from the repertoire, taking with it Berlioz's chances of having anything else performed there in his lifetime. *Benvenuto Cellini* has occasionally reached the stage since, but its dramatic problems and unrealistic demands – the climax is supposed to be the live casting of Cellini's famous bronze statue of Perseus – have prevented it from establishing itself in the mainstream.

Despite that, the score often rises to sustained heights of magnificence and excitement: its great moments include an irresistible choral carnival scene and a gentle love duet. Fortunately, Berlioz was in the habit of recycling music that he took particular pride in, if there seemed no other chance of getting it played, and he used those two sections of *Cellini* as the basis of an orchestral overture first performed in 1844 and named after the carnival itself.

Here the love duet has become one of the cor anglais player's great moments, presented early on in the overture as a passing interruption to some frenzied street life. Once the pace picks up again, the music turns into one of Berlioz's speeded-up takes on overture form, during which the material – including a growling translation of the cor anglais melody –

is reviewed as urgently as possible in an apparent bid to reach the coda at the earliest moment and then to make it build up for as long as he can. Much of this unstoppable and brilliantly orchestrated surge of energy comes straight from the opera, but Berlioz manages to extend it yet again until the newly devised close, with its gloriously unpredictable brass writing, surpasses even the thrills of the stage version.

© Robert Maycock

'Royal Hunt and Storm', from *The Trojans* (1856–8)

It would not have surprised Berlioz that many people think *The Trojans* his masterpiece. He meant it to be. But he would have been amazed at the efforts that went into getting it on to the stage in full, long after he died, because his own persistence left him jaded and cynical. As an awkward character with a dodgy operatic history, he expected a hard time from a gigantic five-acter using his own scenario and libretto drawn from Virgil's *Aeneid*. To get any kind of performance – and at the Théâtre-Lyrique rather than the more prestigious Opéra – he had to remove the first two acts. The 1863 premiere of *The Trojans at Carthage*, as this torso became known, was moderately successful and pleased his supporters. But after the first night the work was gradually shortened by the management, particularly when Berlioz went down with bronchitis caught during rehearsals. Following the run, he was rarely seen in public and for the rest of his life composed almost nothing. The first two acts (further subdivided into three) were staged in Karlsruhe in 1890 as a separate opera, *The Fall of Troy*, with *The Trojans at Carthage* the following night.

Only in the twentieth century (first at Covent Garden in 1957) was the opera given complete on a single evening, and productions remain rare. Stage practicality rather than musical quality is the cause. *The Trojans* is at once lavish and oddly static, like an old-fashioned *opera seria*; the music is thrilling but the real action is often out of sight. As even Berlioz's biographer D. Kern Holoman concedes, the work 'still lives most grandly in the mind's eye'. Tellingly the 'Royal Hunt', now widely played as a concert item, was the first scene to be cut in 1863, because the set-change took an hour.

In the complete opera, the 'Royal Hunt and Storm' forms the entr'acte which opens Act 4. The Trojan leader Aeneas and Queen Dido of Carthage are out hunting, and when a storm breaks they find shelter in a cave. The stage directions require dancers, who appear variously as hunters, naiads, fauns, satyrs and, briefly, Dido and Aeneas themselves. Towards the end, once they are in their cave, an impenetrable cloud cover descends. It is the operatic equivalent of Hollywood's train entering a tunnel. Only choral voices are used, and the orchestra carries the main weight of this ballet-cum-tone poem as it emerges from stillness and builds up momentum in vivid orchestral colours. The hunt music evolves gradually and skilfully into storm music which reaches a climax of – presumably – simultaneous thunder and lightning, and unwinds back to its beginnings.

Robert Maycock © BBC

Leonard Bernstein (1918–90)

Bernstein's gifts were so wide-ranging, and his intellect so fired by curiosity, that his life was pitted with struggle and ambiguity: as well as his work as pianist, conductor and composer, he was a passionate educator and mentor. He was born in Massachusetts to Russian émigré parents and studied at Harvard, where he first met Copland, then at Tanglewood with Serge Koussevitzky. He became an overnight success in November 1943 after taking over at short notice a concert from the conductor Bruno Walter, which was broadcast across the States. Despite the demands of his burgeoning conducting career, he found time to compose, revealing Copland, Stravinsky, jazz and his Jewish faith as major influences. He balanced his extrovert stage works *On the Town*, *Wonderful Town*, *Candide* and *West Side Story* with three symphonies – 'Jeremiah', 'The Age of Anxiety' and 'Kaddish' – which touched upon religious themes. He reached a generation of young Americans with his fifty-three televised *Young People's Concerts*, broadcast between 1958 and 1972, and in 1973 gave a probing lecture series as Charles Eliot Norton visiting professor at Harvard.

Overture, *Candide* (1956)

Though it belongs to what at that time was Bernstein's most forgotten stage piece, the overture to *Candide* had, by the 1980s, become the single most played orchestral piece by a (then) living composer.

Candide is a year older than *West Side Story* and was not surprisingly eclipsed by the latter's overwhelming fame. But it had other problems. Was it a musical, an opera, or what? It certainly got to Broadway, but it flopped. One of its problems was sticking too closely to the Voltaire original. Another, at least for the commercial theatre, was its musical language, a virtuoso evocation of eighteenth-century dances and styles alongside more contemporary and popular numbers. In an effort to gather it up from the space between the stools, Bernstein revised it twice, first changing the book and lyrics – the latter now supplied by Stephen Sondheim, who had done the same for *West Side Story* – and then making an opera-house version. Since then *Candide* has shown up from time to time in venues that range from the New York City Opera to London's West End, though its biggest success has probably been on record, where Bernstein was able to conduct a hand-picked cast just as he wished, and nobody had to worry about what kind of work it was.

If the theatre audience has meanwhile caught up with *Candide*'s musical sophistication, having experienced among other things Sondheim's own musicals, the concert public never had any trouble with the overture, which first had an independent performance in 1957. The music is a thousand miles from Broadway, it has to be said. This witty, incident-packed piece of pastiche classicism is a match for Prokofiev's 'Classical' Symphony, not least in its clever miniaturisation, and even higher-spirited. As it zips through some of the stage show's tunes, it is also whizzing past the main features of the traditional overture, complete with energetic opening theme and singable sequel. Hints of older composers culminate in Bernstein's very own take on the 'Rossini crescendo' and the quickest, most punctual end you could imagine.

© Robert Maycock

'Symphonic Dances', from *West Side Story* (1957)

Prologue – Somewhere – Scherzo – Mambo – Cha-Cha – Meeting Scene – 'Cool' Fugue – Rumble – Finale

It's sometimes hard to remember that *West Side Story* was no bolt from the blue. It has an honourable pedigree, both in its Broadway ancestry, and in its precursors in the Bernstein work-list. Musicals such as his *On the Town* (1944), *Wonderful Town* (1953) and *Candide* (1956) had all provided abundant evidence of Bernstein's extraordinary musical versatility, his boldness of style and freshness of idiom. Nor, with the Voltairean origins of *Candide* in mind, should the Shakespearean antecedents of *West Side Story* surprise us. In the line of *Kiss Me, Kate* (from *The Taming of the Shrew*) and *The Boys from Syracuse* (from *The Comedy of Errors*), Bernstein's reworking of *Romeo and Juliet* must count as one of the more successful of all reworkings of the Bard. The Jets and the Sharks, rival teenage gangs from New York's West Side, act out the doomed confrontation of the Montagues and Capulets, while Tony and Maria match Shakespeare's Veronese lovers in the intensity of their inter-tribal passion.

The stage show, and even more the film version which captured so many adolescent hearts when it first appeared in 1961, were full of a raw energy that spilled over from the narrative into a sequence of dance episodes brilliantly integrated into the original concept, but to which Bernstein nevertheless later felt able to give a separate concert-hall existence.

Such is the emotional directness of the music that it almost demands not to be analysed. We may note and enjoy the extreme rhythmic propulsion of many of the numbers, backed up by virtuoso percussion – xylophone, marimba, bongos, high-hat cymbal; the exhilarating use of syncopation; the unashamed absorption of jazz; and the clean Coplandesque sound and texture in the occasional quieter, more lyrical moments.

After the arresting Prologue, setting up the savage undercurrents appropriate to gang warfare, we hear echoes of the big number, 'Somewhere', in a dream song; a fleeting Scherzo, when the city youths dream of escaping into the pure sunlight; and then 'Mambo', accompanying the gangs as they participate in a competitive display of dancing in a school gym.

A soft 'Cha-Cha' does duty for the first encounter between the two lovers, Tony and Maria. The fugato that characterises the Jets is perfectly encapsulated in the marking 'cool'. The 'Rumble' is the fatal fight that results in two deaths, while the Finale is, after all the preceding noise, necessarily downbeat: this is, after all, a tragedy. Bernstein's brilliantly extrovert score, however, does not fade for long.

Georges Bizet (1838–75)

Bizet's early promise was fulfilled only near the end of his career. He entered the Paris Conservatoire aged nine, won prizes for piano, organ and fugue, and at just seventeen wrote his lively Symphony in C (first performed only in 1935). His fascination with the stage began with the operetta *Le docteur miracle* (1856), composed while still a teenager, and continued with *Don Procopio* (1858–9), written in Italy where he went as winner of the Prix de Rome. On returning to Paris Bizet's *Pêcheurs des Perles* (*The Pearl Fishers*, 1863) was premiered, with moderate success. A number of unsuccessful or abortive opera projects, and the Franco-Prussian War, intervened before his popular piano-duet suite *Jeux d'enfants* (1871) appeared. Bizet first won widespread acclaim for his first *L'Arlésienne* suite (1872), which was soon followed by his greatest achievement, the opera *Carmen* (1873–4), though its Spanish colours and tragic realism drew criticism.

Suite from *Carmen* (1873–5)

1 Prélude
2 Aragonaise
3 Intermezzo
4 Seguidilla
5 Les dragons de Alcala
6 Marche du toréador

The wild, passionate gypsy girl of Prosper Mérimée's novel inspired Bizet to produce a masterpiece of a score, one that overflows with brilliant set pieces and memorable tunes. One of opera's most alluring heroines, Carmen prefers independence to the ties of a conventional relationship, and is prepared to defend her right to free choice in love to the point of courting death at the hands of her cast-off lover behind the bull-ring in Seville.

Like many great operas before it – Mozart's *Marriage of Figaro*, Beethoven's *Fidelio* and Rossini's *Barber of Seville*, to name but a few – *Carmen* was at first a comparative failure. First produced on 3 March 1875 at the Opéra-Comique in Paris, it drew from the pens of the most distinguished French critics the kind of vituperative abuse reserved specially for work of originality and undeniable merit: 'vile', 'contemptible', 'obscene', 'repulsive', 'criminal'. It was also condemned out of hand as 'obscure', 'unoriginal', 'undramatic' and 'lacking in colour'! Unfortunately, the epithets heaped upon it were not quite choice enough to turn it into a *succès de scandale*, and its hostile reception broke Bizet's health and spirits. At the beginning of June 1875 the thirty-eight-year-old composer suffered two heart attacks in quick succession. He died in the early hours of 3 June, just after *Carmen* had played for the thirty-third time to a half-empty house. At the theatre, the great singer Galli-Marié, who had bravely defied all manner of personal abuse for her spirited portrayal of the title-role, collapsed off-stage after playing the scene in which Carmen foretells her own death in the cards. At that very moment, she had been seized with a terrible premonition of disaster. Had Bizet lived just a few more months, he would have seen his despised *Carmen* begin to triumph: since its Vienna production in October 1875 it has established an unshakeable pre-eminence as one of the world's best-loved and most frequently performed operas.

Two suites were extracted from the opera after Bizet's death. The first and most frequently performed of these begins with the 'fate motif' from the opening Prélude, a darkly chromatic theme played *con tutta forza* beneath sinister string tremolandos, associated with Carmen as *femme fatale*, which recurs forcefully at the end after her murder. Then comes the 'Aragonaise' which forms the entr'acte before Act 4 – a lively Spanish dance with castanet accompaniment introducing the scene at the bull-ring. The next number is the reflective Intermezzo – the Act 3 opener famous for its enchanting flute, clarinet and cor anglais solos accompanied by limpid harp arpeggios. After Carmen's 'Seguidilla' and 'Les dragons de Alcala', the marching song of Don José's regiment, the suite ends with the music from the opening of the opera associated with the Toréadors, which returns when Escamillo the bullfighter makes his triumphant entrance in Act 4.

© Wendy Thompson

Alexander Borodin (1833–87)

One of the most fervent of nationalistic nineteenth-century Russian composers, Borodin was the illegitimate son of a prince and studied medicine before becoming a distinguished chemist. Music was always a supplement to his scientific career – he joked that his musical friends wished he were sick more often, since this was when he had time to compose. In 1862 he met Balakirev who drew him into the circle of composers known as 'The Five' (along with Rimsky-Korsakov, Mussorgsky and Cui). By the time of his First Symphony (1862–7) he was a professor in organic chemistry at the Medico-Surgical Academy in St Petersburg. He worked on his opera *Prince Igor* – his principal nationalist work, along with his Second Symphony (1869–76) – until his death in 1887. Alongside the use of Russian folk song his music often carries an oriental flavour, as in his short symphonic poem *In the Steppes of Central Asia*. Borodin won posthumous popularity when themes from *Prince Igor* were adapted for the musical *Kismet*, which won three Tony awards in 1954.

'Polovtsian Dances', from *Prince Igor* (1875)

The five Russian composers who made up the group known as 'The Five' or 'The Mighty Handful' were a curious bunch. By and large they followed professions other than music: only Balakirev was a full-time composer, and a poverty-stricken one at that; Rimsky-Korsakov began his career as a naval officer; Borodin was a chemist; Cui a professor of military engineering; and Mussorgsky a civil servant. But, apart from a common taste for alcohol, they shared a passionate belief in rediscovering the roots of their national culture, and in raising Russian music, after centuries of domination by foreigners imported by the aristocracy, to the high status enjoyed by native literature in the nineteenth century. To this end they spent much of their time endlessly discussing suitable nationalist subjects for operas and other vocal and orchestral works, trying to influence composers outside their immediate circle – such as Tchaikovsky – to follow the 'approved' nationalist path rather than the bland European (i.e. Germanic) tradition, and criticising and rewriting other people's music – including each other's. Balakirev in particular was quite unable to stop handing out advice to fellow composers, and his harsh and uncompromising criticisms struck dread into sensitive souls.

Strangely enough, it was not Balakirev, but the critic Vladimir Stasov who first recommended Prince Igor to Borodin as a suitable subject for an opera. The heroic tale of Prince Igor Svyatoslavich's campaign against the Polovtsi – Turkic tribesmen from the Asiatic steppes and forerunners of the dreaded Tartars – had been discovered in 1791 in a twelfth-century manuscript. (The unfortunate manuscript itself did not long survive its temporary resurrection: it was burnt to cinders only twenty-one years later in the Moscow conflagration of 1812.) In April 1869 Stasov gave Borodin a three-act scenario based on the story, and the composer enthusiastically set to work collecting suitable materials – both musical and historical. By September he had begun composing – but in a rather desultory fashion, one number at a time, without any clear plan. This was to continue for the next eighteen years, hampered partly by the fact that Borodin's work as a professor of chemistry took up much of his time ('I'm always slightly ashamed to admit that I compose . . . For others it's a simple matter, a vocation, an end in life; but for me it's a recreation, an idle pastime which provides diversion from my real work, my work as professor and scientist'), and partly because he had omitted to take the elementary precaution of starting with a decent libretto (he wrote it himself as he went along). At his death in 1887, *Prince Igor* remained unfinished. Rimsky-Korsakov and Glazunov fell on the remains like well-meaning vultures, orchestrating, filling in some missing bits, and reconstructing others (including the overture) from their recollections of Borodin playing them on the piano. In this unsatisfactory state, the opera finally reached the stage on 16 November 1890, at St Petersburg's Maryinsky Theatre.

But although *Prince Igor* remains something of a problem opera, certain sections of it have achieved lasting popularity, particularly the brilliant 'Polovtsian Dances', which bring Act 2 to an orgiastic conclusion. 'Superfluous detail has no place in opera,' Borodin wrote. 'Everything should be drawn in bold strokes, as clearly and vividly as is practically possible for voices and orchestra.' The 'Polovtsian Dances' are a masterpiece of imagination, recreating the barbaric, colourful atmosphere of ancient Russia, tinged with the graceful melodic charm of the East.

The opera is set in 1185. The Russian steppes have been invaded by the Polovtsi tribesmen, and Prince Igor and his son Vladimir set out to defend their country. Their army is defeated and they are taken prisoner. The Polovtsi Khan, a generous and merciful ruler with whose daughter Vladimir has fallen secretly in love, orders singing and dancing to entertain his eminent 'guests' during their captivity. To one of the most lyrical and appealing melodies ever written (later immortalised as 'Stranger in Paradise' in the musical *Kismet*), a chorus of sexy young Polovtsian slave-girls sing nostalgically of their distant Oriental homeland, where the languid air moves softly over cloud-capped mountains beside the whispering sea, nightingales sing in moonlit forests and fragrant pastures bask in the brilliant sunshine. This refrain alternates with exhilaratingly rhythmic dances, and choruses in which both male and female slaves praise the valorous and mighty Khan.

Johannes Brahms (1833–97)

Often seen as a Classicist inhabiting the Romantic era, Brahms worked mainly in the established forms – concerto, sonata, symphony – rather than developing new ones, such as the tone poems of Liszt or the grandiose music dramas of Wagner. From an early age Brahms was forced to earn money for his family by playing the piano in Hamburg's seedy sailors' taverns. In 1853 a concert tour brought him famously into contact with Schumann, who publicly declared the young composer a genius. The *German Requiem* (1868) and *Hungarian Dances* (1868–80) advanced his reputation and his *Variations on the St Anthony Chorale* (1873) attracted attention ahead of his First Symphony (1876). He wrote much choral music (he conducted both the Singakademie and the Singverein in Vienna), and led a revival of interest in Renaissance and Baroque music. He also wrote over two hundred songs and much chamber and piano music, but no opera. Late in life he wrote a trio, a quintet and two sonatas inspired by the clarinettist Richard Mühlfeld, which are among his finest achievements in chamber music.

Academic Festival Overture, Op. 80 (1880)

'Gaudeamus igitur', 'Let us therefore rejoice': this hallowed German tune was virtually a student anthem in the nineteenth century. If it suggests rejoicing on graduation, then another tune that crops up in the *Academic Festival Overture*, 'Was kommt dort von der Höh?', was more associated with the start of student life, a kind of freshman's initiation song. In fact the whole overture is permeated with academic echoes – if that is a fair description of a couple of drinking songs! And isn't that the Hungarian Rákóczy March lurking near the beginning? So Brahms's description of the piece as 'a cheerful potpourri of songs à la Suppé' was spot on.

It was only half the truth, though. The *Academic Festival Overture* is also a model of discipline and restraint, with no hint of vulgarity, and plenty of hints of academic (in the best sense) ingenuity in the combination of themes and the many felicitous touches of orchestration. The award of a doctorate by the University of Breslau was, after all, an opportunity for Brahms to display his art at its most technically proficient. So in 1880, during his regular summer retreat at Bad Ischl in the Salzkammergut, Brahms took a respite from his symphonic labours to work on the overture – though it comes as no surprise to discover that he was simultaneously writing the *Tragic Overture*, satisfying the other side of his nature. And he conducted both overtures in Breslau early in 1881, when the students and professors heard 'their' piece for the first time, and rejoiced.

Variations on the St Anthony Chorale, Op. 56a (1873)

St Anthony Chorale: Andante
1 Poco più animato
2 Più vivace
3 Con moto
4 Andante con moto
5 Vivace
6 Vivace
7 Grazioso
8 Presto non troppo
Finale: Andante

By nature shy and lacking in self-confidence, Brahms was very much a late starter in the orchestral field. Although he began work on his First Symphony in 1855, when he was in his early twenties, he quickly realised that he lacked enough orchestral experience to make a success of it, and wisely laid it aside. Between 1857 and 1859 he spent two consecutive autumns in Detmold, working as pianist, chamber musician and conductor of the court choir and orchestra, and the practical knowledge of instrumental technique he acquired there was put to good effect in two early serenades for orchestra. By 1862 he had tentatively resumed work on his symphony, but once again felt unable to make much progress.

Then, in November 1870, his friend C. F. Pohl, a biographer of Haydn, showed him a score of a *Feldpartita* (a type of divertimento for wind instruments – two oboes, three bassoons, serpent and two horns) which Pohl believed to be the work of Haydn. Brahms was clearly fascinated by the theme of the second movement, which he noted down, and within three years he had written a set of orchestral variations on it, which he conducted himself in Vienna on 2 November 1873 (an alternative version also exists for two pianos). In fact, although the Variations are often described as 'Variations on a Theme of Haydn', the original *Feldpartita* which fired Brahms's imagination is now believed not to be by Haydn at all, but by his pupil Ignaz Pleyel (1757–1831), later to become the founder of the famous Parisian firm of piano-makers.

The famous theme itself (headed in the 'Haydn' manuscript 'Corale St Antonii') may be an old pilgrims' hymn from Burgenland, and in its original statement Brahms recreates the open wind sonorities of the *Feldpartita*. Then follow eight variations, each completely different in character, including one in strict triple counterpoint (no. 4), a scherzo (no. 5), a 'hunting' variation complete with horn calls (no. 6), a lyrical siciliana (no. 7), and a mysterious 'night-music' variation (no. 8).

These are followed by an extended finale constructed on the two main elements of the theme, which acts as a ground bass, anticipating by twelve years the massive passacaglia which concludes Brahms's fourth and last symphony.

Benjamin Britten (1913–76)

Born in Suffolk on 22 November 1913 (propitiously, the feast day of St Cecilia, patron saint of music) Britten began piano lessons aged five, composing songs for his mother by the age of ten. At thirteen he began composition studies with Frank Bridge before entering the Royal College of Music in 1930. His documentary scores for the GPO (General Post Office) Film Unit brought him into collaboration with W. H. Auden, a liberating force; in 1937 he not only attracted international attention with his *Variations on a Theme of Frank Bridge* at the Salzburg Festival, but also met the tenor Peter Pears, who would become his lifelong partner and an influential interpreter of his work. Britten revitalised English opera with his first stage triumph *Peter Grimes* (1945), launching the Aldeburgh Festival three years later. He performed often as a conductor and pianist, and though he wrote a significant number of chamber and choral works (among them three string quartets and the *War Requiem*, 1961) it is principally for his vocal and especially operatic output that he is remembered.

'Four Sea Interludes', from *Peter Grimes* (1945)

1 Dawn
2 Sunday Morning
3 Moonlight
4 Storm

There are two great orchestral portraits of the sea in all its aspects: Debussy's *La mer* and Britten's 'Four Sea Interludes', which he extracted from his opera *Peter Grimes* (based on George Crabbe's poem 'The Borough'). Britten lived nearly all his life beside the North Sea – his childhood in Lowestoft, his adult life in Aldeburgh, where *Peter Grimes* is set. He understood its personality as no other composer has done, and the sea in *Peter Grimes* is as important – and as inscrutable – a character as Grimes himself.

The four interludes frame the opera's story: the first, 'Dawn', forms the prelude to Act 1, after the prologue in the courtroom; 'Sunday Morning' and 'Moonlight' are the preludes to Acts 2 and 3 respectively; while 'Storm' divides the two scenes of Act 1 in the opera, but is placed last in the 'Four Sea Interludes' for obvious musical reasons.

Parallels between *La mer* and the 'Four Sea Interludes' cannot be taken very far, though both Debussy and Britten had an uncanny ability to evoke scenes and moods through orchestration, and both works begin with a depiction of dawn. Perhaps mindful of Debussy's initial low pedal note for basses and timpani, Britten begins at the opposite end of the orchestra, with a high E on flutes and violins. This is the cold grey sky of the stage directions to the opera's Act 1 scene 1. The brass chords that follow, and their later extension into a theme, suggest the latent menacing power of the sea.

'Sunday Morning', by contrast, is bright and sunny. Church bells ring out in the horns, with, later, a deep tolling bell in B flat undercutting the brilliant D major toccata. An unlikely marriage between the 'Coronation Scene' from Mussorgsky's *Boris Godunov* and the Balinese gamelan produces a wholly original orchestral sound. The brass theme of 'Dawn' appears more cheerfully on violas and cellos.

'Moonlight' is another development of this theme: the sea is calm, with a gentle swell, and flute and harp pick out the glints of moonlight on the waves.

'Storm' is self-explanatory. Towards the end there is a sudden calming and we hear, on the strings, the theme that the tormented Grimes has just sung in the opera to the words, 'What harbour shelters peace?' None for him, as the return of the storm music and the overwhelming chromatic descent to harsh E flat minor chords unmistakably inform us.

The Young Person's Guide to the Orchestra (Variations and Fugue on a Theme of Henry Purcell), Op. 34 (1945)

Theme: Allegro maestoso e largamente
Variation A: Presto
Variation B: Lento
Variation C: Moderato
Variation D: Allegro alla marcia
Variation E: Brillante: alla polacca
Variation F: Meno mosso
Variation G: –
Variation H: Cominciando lento ma poco a poco accel. al Allegro
Variation I: Maestoso
Variation J: L'istesso tempo
Variation K: Vivace
Variation L: Allegro pomposo
Variation M: Moderato
Fugue: Allegro molto

'I have a small film to write for the Board of Education,' wrote Britten to a friend late in November 1945, some six months after the triumphant premiere of *Peter Grimes*. A decade earlier, he had begun his career as a composer of film music, working for the GPO Film Unit on documentary scores such as *Night Mail* and *Coal Face*, together with propaganda films such as *Peace of Britain* (1936), which praised the concept of 'jaw-jaw' rather than 'war-war'. During the Second World War, the GPO Film Unit had become the Crown Film Unit, with Basil Wright as chief producer. He now approached Britten with the proposal of writing a score for the Ministry of Education, intended to demonstrate the instruments of the orchestra to schoolchildren. It took Britten just a couple of weeks to write the piece, which he began in mid-December 1945 and finished at midnight on New Year's Eve.

The film, *Instruments of the Orchestra*, with the London Symphony Orchestra under Malcolm Sargent as conductor/narrator, was first shown on 29 November 1946. Six weeks earlier, on 15 October, Britten's score had been given its concert premiere by Sargent and the Liverpool Philharmonic Orchestra, with a spoken commentary (usually omitted in concert performances) by Britten's librettist Eric Crozier. The work was affectionately dedicated – 'for their edification and entertainment' – to the four children of some close friends of Britten – John Maud, a civil servant, and his concert-pianist wife, Jean. Their son Humphrey played the cello, and Britten gave him a copy of the score, inscribed 'For Humphrey and his sisters with much love from Ben'.

The work is subtitled 'Variations and Fugue on a Theme of Henry Purcell', Britten's choice of theme reflecting a major preoccupation of that particular period of his life – the discovery of the music of his great precursor. For about six years, he and Peter Pears had been including music by Purcell in their recitals, with new, highly original keyboard realisations by Britten; and Purcell's exemplary handling of the English language had greatly influenced Britten's own word-setting. 'I had never realised, before I first met Purcell's music, that words could be set with such ingenuity, with such colour,' he remarked some years later. Shortly after completing *Peter Grimes*, he embarked on two works directly inspired by Purcell – the Holy Sonnets of John Donne and the Second String Quartet, both of which were premiered at the Wigmore Hall in November 1945, as part of the 250th anniversary celebrations of Purcell's death. Now he chose to base his new work on a short piece drawn directly from Purcell – a simple little hornpipe from the incidental music which Purcell supplied in the last year of his life for *Abdelazer, or The Moor's Revenge*, a gory Restoration tragedy by the celebrated female playwright Mrs Aphra Behn.

Britten's treatment of Purcell's theme – as a set of orchestral variations – is straightforward, exuberant, and reflects his extraordinary mastery of the orchestral palette. The theme is first stated by the full orchestra, after which each department – woodwind, brass, strings with harp, and percussion – takes it in turn to present its own version of it, before the theme is restated once more by the full band. Next, each instrumental family is given a short variation displaying its own particular character – flighty flutes and piccolo, plangent oboes, agile clarinets, comic bassoons; virtuosic violins (playing a brilliant variation marked 'alla polacca'), melancholic violas, warm and tender cellos, impassioned basses, shimmering harp; horn fanfares, brilliant trumpets, dignified trombones with *basso profundo* tuba; and finally a variation for percussion – timpani, bass drum and cymbals, tambourine and triangle, side drum and Chinese block, xylophone, castanets and gong, and even a whip!

Having allowed all the instruments a chance to show off individually, Britten then gradually reassembles them in a brilliant fugue, led off by the piccolo and climaxing in a majestic restatement of Purcell's theme on lower brass – at last in the major key. This is combined with the fugue material at full blast on all the other instruments, and leads to a short, triumphant coda.

The *Young Person's Guide* was received with enthusiasm, even in stuffy post-war Whitehall. 'I am glad that the Min. of Ed. chaps approve,' wrote Britten to the film's producer, Basil Wright. 'I never really worried that it was too sophisticated for kids – it is difficult to be that for the little blighters.'

Emmanuel Chabrier (1841–94)

Though he showed early promise at the piano, and composed his first pieces aged eight, Chabrier was persuaded by his father to study law in Paris, after which he took up a junior position at the Ministry of the Interior. He composed in his spare time and, being an impressive pianist, became a popular figure at the Paris salons. He embraced art and literature, counting among his friends Verlaine, Mallarmé, Renoir and Manet. Only in 1880 did he give up his job to compose full-time, after hearing Wagner's *Tristan and Isolde*. His two principal operas, *Gwendoline* (1885) and *Le roi malgré lui* (1887), fared better in Germany than in France, and he is best known for his festive orchestral pieces *España* (1883) and *Marche joyeuse* (1888). Displaying a French wit and elegance that prefigured Poulenc, his largely neglected piano pieces also foreshadowed Ravel in embracing ancient French dance forms.

España, rhapsody for orchestra (1883)

It comes as no surprise to discover that Chabrier was taught music as a child by two Spaniards who had pitched up in his native French village. When, at the age of forty, he made a protracted visit to the south of Spain, it was as if he had rediscovered a lost or suppressed part of his musical personality.

Chabrier already had an operetta or two behind him, and plenty of piano music in which local colour was of the essence; but *España*, the work that was the first to grow out of his Andalusian sojourn, was something else again. In Constant Lambert's memorable phrase, it has 'all the verve and reckless gaiety of Offenbach at his best, combined with the harmonic and orchestral subtlety of Ravel'.

España started life as a piano piece, but even in this form the hip-swinging swagger of the two main tunes, the one born of the rumbustious Northern Spanish dance known as the *jota*, the other related to the more gentle Southern Spanish *malagueña*, gives the music an increasingly infectious lilt.

When (at the insistence of the conductor Charles Lamoureux) *España* was orchestrated, Chabrier was in his element: there are magical solos, brilliant instrumental combinations, an incandescently scored accompaniment, even some deliberate wrong notes. Another Chabrier admirer, Francis Poulenc, surely got it right when he said, 'the trappings of *España* come from a large Parisian store'. It may be a Spanish picture postcard; but what a picture!

Aaron Copland (1900–90)

Very much a child of the twentieth century, Copland left the musical conservativism of his native New York in 1921 to study with Nadia Boulanger in Paris. There, influenced by the rhythmic complexity of Stravinsky, he wrote his ambitious ballet *Grohg* and returned to the USA in 1924 with a commission from Boulanger for an organ symphony (later rescored as the First Symphony). Koussevitzky premiered Copland's jazzy *Music for the Theatre* and Piano Concerto in Boston. During the 1930s Copland adopted a simpler style that led to the wide appeal of his three ballet suites on American subjects, *Billy the Kid*, *Rodeo* and *Appalachian Spring*, as well as the patriotic *Lincoln Portrait* and *Fanfare for the Common Man*. He produced three film scores for Hollywood, and in 1950 wrote a Clarinet Concerto for jazz clarinettist Benny Goodman. In the 1950s and 1960s he returned to a more progressive style, but he gave up composing in the 1970s. He was a huge influence on the formation of a distinctive American music, not only through his compositions, but also as a writer, educator, administrator and supporter of younger composers.

Appalachian Spring (Ballet for Martha), suite (1943–5)

Appalachian Spring is a key work in Aaron Copland's output, marking the point at which his desire to write music accessible to the concert-going public at large coincided most completely with his natural bent for formal clarity and cohesion, together with simplicity and directness of expression. The piece was written in 1943–4 as a ballet for the Martha Graham Company, and first performed in October 1944 at a festival presented by the Elizabeth Sprague Coolidge Foundation in the Library of Congress, Washington, DC.

The pit space there was very limited, and so Copland's original instrumentation was for an ensemble of thirteen: flute, clarinet, bassoon, piano and nine strings. In the spring of 1945, however, he arranged the score – or a continuous suite derived from it – for symphony orchestra, and in this form it soon became one of his most popular works. Later, in 1958, he published this same suite in the original, luminous chamber scoring.

The suite is what Copland called 'a condensed version of the ballet, retaining all essential features but omitting those sections in which the interest is primarily choreographic'. The latter part of this statement is perhaps over-modest, as revivals of the ballet by the Graham company, together with radio and CD recordings of a more nearly complete version of the original score, have revealed eight minutes or so of entirely self-sufficient vintage Copland which he suppressed in the concert version. But even those of us who welcome occasional performances of the extra eight minutes must reluctantly admit that without them the suite is formally much tauter.

The title of the ballet was taken – by Graham rather than Copland – from a poem by Hart Crane. The action is based on 'a pioneer celebration in spring around a newly-built farmhouse in the Pennsylvania hills in the early part of the last century'. In the slow opening section the characters enter in turn: a Revivalist Preacher, a Pioneer Woman experienced in the ways of the wilderness, a young Husbandman, his Bride, and a group of four women followers of the Preacher. All take part in a general dance, in Copland's most energetic vein. This is followed by a short episode in which the Followers pray together, a hesitant solo dance by the Husbandman, and a 'love duet' between the Husbandman and the Bride. The Revivalist then leads an extended dance, with decidedly secular echoes of square-dance rhythms, and culminating in some apparently equally secular advances by the Revivalist to the Followers. A broad chordal section accompanies a dance by the Pioneer Woman, who embodies 'the rocky confidence of experience'; then at a much faster tempo there is a dance for the young Bride, in which her husband is briefly persuaded to join. The theme earlier associated with prayer returns in an episode in which the Revivalist gives a blessing to the couple.

At this point Copland introduces the traditional Shaker melody 'The gift to be simple' as the theme for a set of variations, danced mostly by the Husbandman and the Bride. (In the ballet these are in a slightly different order, and interrupted by a long episode, the eight minutes not in the suite, in which the Revivalist reminds the new householders of 'the strange and terrible aspects of human fate'.) The variations culminate in a broad restatement of the melody, to which the Revivalist leads the dancing. But then the Bride begins to pray, and – as the 'prayer theme' returns once more – is joined by the others. The Pioneer Woman leads the Followers quietly away; the Revivalist tries to break in on the Husbandman and the Bride but is ignored, and also departs; at the end (in the memorable words of the synopsis) 'the couple are left quiet and strong in their new house'.

© Anthony Burton

Billy the Kid, ballet (1938)

Introduction: The open prairie – Street in a frontier town – Mexican dance and Finale – Prairie night (Card game at night) – Gun battle – Celebration (after Billy's capture) – Billy in prison – His escape – Billy in the desert – Billy's death – The open prairie again

Much of Copland's music in the late 1930s and early 1940s was written to be immediately useful. He wrote later about the 'heady wine' of feeling needed:

> Previously our works had been largely self-engendered: no-one asked for them; we simply wrote them out of our

own need. Now, suddenly, functional music was in demand as never before, certainly as never before in the experience of our serious composers. Motion-picture and ballet companies, radio stations and schools, film and theatre producers discovered us. The music appropriate for the different kinds of cooperative venture had to be simpler and more direct. There was a 'market' especially for music evocative of the American scene – industrial backgrounds, landscapes of the Far West, and so forth . . . No wonder we were so pleased to find ourselves sought after and were ready to compose in a manner that would satisfy both our collaborators and ourselves.

Prominent in this category of functional music were Copland's three great ballet scores on American subjects, all drawing – in the democratic spirit of the time – on traditional folk tunes. And in the first of these, *Billy the Kid*, Copland also created the distinctive sound-world representing the Far West on which many subsequent composers have drawn. At the same time, though, the work also demonstrates the continuity of Copland's musical language throughout his career: it includes many episodes of changing metres and sharp dissonances which could not have come from any other pen.

The subject of *Billy the Kid* is the short life and violent death of the notorious outlaw William Bonney. The idea of basing a ballet on this apparently un-balletic subject was proposed to Copland early in 1938 by Lincoln Kirstein, on behalf of his pioneering Ballet Caravan company (which at the time had Elliott Carter as its musical director). The detailed scenario was by the choreographer Eugene Loring, who also danced the role of Billy. Copland composed the score during a visit to Europe in the summer of 1938, beginning it in a studio on the rue de Rennes in Paris. He took the traditional tunes from printed collections of songs sent to him by Kirstein, finding himself unexpectedly attracted by the possibilities they offered. 'Perhaps', he later commented, 'there is something different about a cowboy song in Paris.'

The ballet was first performed in Chicago in October 1938, with a two-piano accompaniment; it was only the following May that it was presented in New York in its full orchestral dress.

The complete score of *Billy the Kid* lasts about half as long again as the familiar concert suite: in assembling the suite, Copland cut some of the sections slightly, and removed two extended sequences altogether. The ballet begins with a spacious Introduction evoking the open prairie. The busy scene of a street in a frontier town is conjured up with quotations and fragments of cowboy songs, including 'Great grand-dad', 'The old Chisholm Trail' and 'Git along little dogies'; there is a dance for a group of Mexican women, in 5/8 time; the song 'Old Paint' is introduced and built to a sonorous climax. The twelve-year-old Billy appears for the first time. A fight erupts in which his mother is accidentally killed, and he immediately stabs the men responsible – thus beginning his career as an outlaw.

The next scene depicts a card game played by Billy and his outlaw friends under the stars; this quiet, brooding nocturne is based on the song 'Bury me not on the lone prairie'. There is a percussive gun battle, in which Billy is captured; this is followed by the townspeople's raucous celebrations, including an imitation of an out-of-tune saloon piano. Billy is imprisoned, but escapes into the desert, where he rests quietly with his girlfriend: the slow waltz here is adapted from the cowboy song 'Come wrangle yer bronco'. The posse catches up with him and he is killed; there is a solemn funeral. The final section of the ballet, to quote Copland's own description, 'makes use of materials from the introduction, but with different coloration to convey the idea of a new dawn breaking over the prairie'.

Anthony Burton © BBC

~ *Fanfare for the Common Man* (1942)

Later acclaimed as the 'Dean of American music', Aaron Copland first made his name in the 1920s as an *enfant terrible* of the avant-garde. After the premiere performance of his Organ Symphony in 1925, its conductor, the rather conservative Walter Damrosch, observed: 'If he can write like that at twenty-five, in a few years he'll be ready to commit murder.'

For musicians like Damrosch the prediction came true; the uncompromisingly harsh and dissonant Piano Variations of 1930 must have seemed like musical homicide. But the politics of the 1930s affected Copland deeply: the Great Depression and the threat of war in Europe had a democratising influence on the arts, and Copland sought a more socially useful role in music for theatre and film, and for children. He made a conscious effort to achieve what he called 'an imposed simplicity'.

This quest for accessibility quickly became evident in a series of ballet and film scores on all-American themes such as *Rodeo* and *Billy the Kid*, but also in shorter pieces such as *Fanfare for the Common Man*, one of a series of patriotic fanfares by different composers commissioned by Eugene Goossens for the Cincinnati Symphony Orchestra's 1942–3 concert season. While the majority of fanfares have traditionally celebrated royal or ceremonial events, this one is truly democratic, celebrating the achievements of the broad mass of humanity. Copland later reused it in the fourth movement of his Third Symphony, also written during the Second World War.

~ *El salón México* (1932–6)

Copland made the first of his many visits to Mexico in 1932, for the first ever concert devoted entirely to his music, arranged by the composer and conductor Carlos Chávez. During his stay, Copland was taken by Chávez to a popular dance hall in Mexico City where the music was, he recalled, 'harsh, flavoursome, screechy and potentially violent'. He immediately conceived the idea of a piece to be named, after the dance hall, *El salón México*. The project took several years to reach fruition, but the work was eventually completed and orchestrated in 1936, and, appropriately, first performed in Mexico City under Chávez in August 1937. The European premiere followed at a concert in the 1938 festival of the International Society for Contemporary Music in London (conducted by Adrian Boult); Serge Koussevitzky conducted the work in Boston, and made the first recording; and, with the help of a piano arrangement made by the young Leonard Bernstein, the piece was launched on the international scene. As Copland said later, 'It started the ball rolling toward the popular success and wide audience I had only just begun to think about.'

El salón México was thus the starting-point of Copland's 'populist' phase of the 1930s and 1940s, in which he consciously reached out beyond the specialist audience of new music concerts to 'the music-loving public' in general. It is significant that, aware of the success of different national schools of composition in the previous half-century or so, he chose to do so using traditional music, albeit not yet that of his own country: that was to come with the triptych of 'American' ballets, beginning with *Billy the Kid* (1938). But it is also significant that he treated his folk materials – not in fact the numbers he heard in the dance hall, but taken from printed collections – with great freedom and in his personal idiom, to create, rather than a picture-postcard impression of Mexico, a more rounded portrait of the country and its inhabitants. He later described how, in *El salón México*, he had felt that he suddenly knew the essence of the Mexican people: 'their humanity, their shyness, their dignity and unique charm'.

The piece is scored for a large orchestra, with 'local colour' in the shape of wood blocks and güiro in the percussion, and solos for trumpet, clarinet and the little E flat clarinet (which

Copland wanted played 'with the flavour of a native Mexican instrument'). Latin-American rhythms predominate: syncopated groupings within 4/4 bars, alternating bars of 3/4 and 6/8, and superimposed triplets and duplets. But Copland overlays these with his own changing metres and cross-rhythms, as part of the process of adapting and transforming the original Mexican tunes.

There are five continuous sections: an extended introduction presenting much of the material in its simplest form, a main quick section, a more relaxed interlude, a scherzo-like episode, and a varied reprise of the main quick section, at an even higher level of energy than before.

Claude Debussy (1862–1918)

Though his music sometimes seems to blur conventional detail and emphasises colour and atmosphere more than the supposedly Germanic characteristics of thematic development and structure, Debussy disliked being labelled an 'impressionist' composer. Born above his parents' china shop close to Paris, Debussy entered the Paris Conservatoire aged ten and left twelve years later as winner of the Prix de Rome. He wrote a number of songs during the 1880s before falling under the dual influences of Wagner (he visited the Bayreuth Festival in 1888 and 1889) and Javanese gamelan music (heard at the Great Exposition of 1889). His distaste of academic formality meant he was capable of drawing on the popular ragtime in his 'Golliwogg's Cake Walk' (which also included a sardonic quotation from Wagner's *Tristan and Isolde*) and spinning an austere web of symbolism in the operatic masterpiece *Pelléas et Mélisande* and in the ballet *Le martyre de Saint Sébastien*. Aside from his epoch-making *Prélude à 'L'après-midi d'un faune'* and his seascape *La mer*, other principal orchestral works include the *Images* (incorporating the Spanish-influenced 'Ibéria') and *Nocturnes* (featuring another evocation of the seas in its third movement, 'Sirènes'). His two books each of *Préludes*, *Études* and *Images* are major contributions to the piano repertoire.

La mer, three symphonic sketches (1902–5)

1 De l'aube à midi sur la mer
2 Jeux de vagues
3 Dialogue du vent et de la mer

How are we meant to listen to *La mer*? Do we follow it with our brain, or do we just let it wash over us? Debussy was precise about the matter. He wanted his art to sound free, in a particular way, with 'a freedom derived not from a more or less literal reproduction of Nature, but from the mysterious correspondences between nature and the imagination'.

This intricately detailed and powerful work is summed up by its apparently offhand subtitle: 'Three symphonic sketches' (*Trois esquisses symphoniques*). They are sketches in the visual artist's sense – nothing to do with sketchiness – and they are as organised as a symphony. Their meaning is to be experienced as directly as a painting, but it depends on a manipulation of sound and time in ways we are not meant to notice. In many Austro-German Romantic works, the musical processes seem to correspond to the inner workings of the human heart and mind. In *La mer*, the processes match the way our imagination feeds on what we see happen in the world outside.

Mysterious indeed; except that Debussy understood the mysteries. In our time, musicians have begun to discover how he did it. To take one facet, explored in Roy Howat's book *Debussy in Proportion*, he often derived the proportions in time of his musical forms – how long successive sections of the music last – from the proportions in space of aesthetically pleasing visual forms. The 'mysterious correspondences' are mathematically exact. If we feel that listening to the ebb and flow of *La mer* is somehow like watching the sea itself, that is because Debussy calculated the effect.

He took three years to complete *La mer*, starting after the premiere of his opera *Pelléas et Mélisande* (1902) and interrupted by the upheavals of leaving his wife Lilly for the worldly Emma Bardac (dedicatee of several of Fauré's works and mother of the Dolly enshrined in his 'Dolly' Suite). Some of Debussy's final adjustments to the score were made while staying at the Grand Hotel, Eastbourne, in 1905, though his feelings for the sea had been formed during childhood stays by the Mediterranean and visits to Normandy. Like Roussel, he had sometimes dreamed of becoming a sailor, though in Debussy's case the dreams remained idle.

At its first performance, conducted by Camille Chevillard in the Concerts Lamoureux series on 15 October 1905, *La mer* did not go down especially well with the Paris audience who, conditioned by *Pelléas*, apparently expected something even more atmospheric.

Debussy had by now moved on from his symbolist phase, and in some aspects *La mer* does come close to French symphonies of the time. That is not so surprising when you consider his musically formative years: he may not have attended the Schola Cantorum – Parisian home of all things symphonic and the power-base of César Franck's self-anointed successor Vincent d'Indy – but he nevertheless fell under its influence. From one angle, *La mer* falls right into the line of the great French *symphonie* that runs from Franck to Roussel. Themes from the first sketch, 'From dawn to midday at sea', are recycled in the last, 'Dialogues of the wind and the sea', and other ideas bear a family resemblance. Its chief vessel of creative energy is the melody that floats in at first light on muted trumpet and cor anglais, and reappears at significant moments – as do the quiet, rhythmically distinctive wind chords that precede the blaze of the full midday sun (perhaps this is the 'bit at a quarter to twelve' that Erik Satie said he liked). After a kind of scherzo, 'Play of the waves', the finale steers through stormy developments towards a resplendent assembly of its main themes.

All these points locate *La mer* in its period: d'Indy himself would have been proud of its final burst of counterpoint. But they are not what make it unique. Symphonically, the first sketch has the role of a prelude. While it is happening, though, that is not what it feels like: the music grows in unpredictable ways, like the marine weather, seemingly arbitrary but secretly determined. 'Jeux de vagues' is even freer from conventional sorts of development and variation. Visions recur as part of a perpetual evolution in transparent, fleeting orchestration that gives listeners the same pleasure as a sequence of perfectly placed brushstrokes.

Robert Maycock © BBC

Prélude à 'L'après-midi d'un faune' (1892–4)

In 1865, bizarre though it may now seem, Stéphane Mallarmé first conceived his poem 'L'après-midi d'un faune' as a monologue for the theatre, complete with stage directions. Persuaded, however, by his friends that the two versions he wrote were unsuited to the stage, he spent the next ten years or so making painstaking revisions until he had recast the poem completely. The result, an 'eclogue' as he called it, was published in 1876 with illustrations by Manet. Debussy much admired the poem and envisaged writing incidental music for it. This became the *Prélude à 'L'après-midi d'un faune'*, a musical interpretation of the atmosphere in which an indolent faun lusts after two nymphs whom he espies one sultry afternoon.

Music cannot convey the undertones of lesbianism implied in the poem, nor can it investigate the dream world poised between sleeping and wakefulness that Mallarmé explored. Yet the poem contains clues which hint at music – the phrase 'A vain, sonorous and monotonous line' which may have inspired the flute solo that plays such an important part in the score, the words 'a credulous song', and the reference to Syrinx (the nymph turned into reeds from which Pan made his flute). At first somewhat perplexed by Debussy's intention, Mallarmé contended that his poem was already 'musical' in that he had taken the greatest care to choose words of musical quality. When, though, Debussy played him the score at the piano, he exclaimed after a long pause: 'I wasn't expecting anything like that! This music prolongs the emotion of my poem and gives it a warmer background than colour.'

Mallarmé was present at the first performance on 22 December 1894, and, like the rest of the audience, acclaimed the work, saying that it was perfectly at one with his text and went even further in depicting a nostalgia treated with delicacy and richness. The *Prélude à 'L'après-midi d'un faune'* quickly became Debussy's most popular work, yet its technique was revolutionary. Instead of themes that were developed in a conventional way it featured motifs that materialised and almost immediately dissolved or evaporated, or were transmuted into others. The heat haze that envelops the faun as he drifts in and out of sleep with his lascivious thoughts is evoked by ceaseless fluidity and ambiguous tonal shifts handled with innate subtlety. The famous flute solo emerges on ten occasions, each time dressed in different harmonies.

Having spent long and arduous hours in rehearsal helping the orchestral players to grapple with the novel layout of the score, Debussy sometimes grew tired of explaining his work further. To a conductor anxious for advice on how the flute solo should be played, he riposted: 'It's a shepherd playing the flute, his ass in the grass.' More helpfully, he remarked that the *Prélude* was 'a general impression of the poem, since by following it more closely the music would only get out of breath, like a cart-horse competing for the Grand Prix with a thoroughbred.'

James Harding © BBC

Frederick Delius (1862–1934)

Born in Bradford, Delius rejected a role in his father's wool-trade business, and ran an orange plantation in Florida before studying at the Leipzig Conservatory (1886-8). He moved first to Paris, then, in 1897, to nearby Fontainebleau – after which he wrote his fourth and most successful opera, *A Village Romeo and Juliet* (1900–1), the Walt Whitman setting *Sea Drift* (1903–4) and his Nietzsche-inspired *A Mass of Life* (1904–5). He also wrote a series of evocative tone poems – including *Brigg Fair* (1907), *Summer Night on the River* (1911) and *On Hearing the First Cuckoo in Spring* (1912). His pantheism fuelled an impressionistic flair for orchestration, and he drew regular inspiration from black American music (heard on his plantation) and from Scandinavia (he had befriended Grieg in Leipzig, and he spent many holidays in Norway). In 1907 Thomas Beecham began an unswerving championship of Delius's works (he regarded the composer as 'the last great apostle in our time of romance, beauty and emotion in music'). By 1925 syphilis had blinded Delius, and his last works were dictated to his amanuensis, the composer Eric Fenby.

Brigg Fair, an English rhapsody (1907)

Delius is best known for orchestral pieces in a pastoral mood, expressing both rapture and nostalgia with exquisitely subtle harmony and delicate instrumental colour. *Brigg Fair* is the first of these. He based it on a folk song which Percy Grainger collected in 1905 from a Lincolnshire bailiff with a particularly rich store of songs, Joseph Taylor. (Brigg is a market town in the north of the county.) With typical enthusiasm, Grainger wasted no time in making his own setting for tenor and chorus, and showed it to Delius, who composed his orchestral rhapsody the following year, dedicating it to Grainger. Soon after Hermann Suter conducted the premiere in Basle in 1907, *Brigg Fair* was performed a good deal, with various conductors (including Beecham), both in this country and abroad, and one of its earliest admirers was Bartók, who heard it in Zurich in 1910.

When Joseph Taylor recorded the folk song for the Gramophone Company in 1908, he was seventy-five and could only remember the first two verses:

> It was on the fifth of August,
> The weather fine and fair;
> Unto Brigg Fair I did repair –
> For love I was inclined.
>
> I rose up with the lark in the morning,
> With my heart so full of glee,
> Of thinking there to meet my dear,
> Long time I wished to see.

The remaining four verses describe meeting the loved one and end with a vow of constancy. There is nothing inherently regretful about the song, but Delius sometimes gives it an irresistibly wistful character by veiling it in harmonies that slide downwards, one of the most recognisable features of his music in general.

Brigg Fair is often described as a set of variations; but each variation is only as long as the tune – it's varied eighteen times altogether – which is why Percy Grainger called Delius's piece, rather forbiddingly, a passacaglia (strictly speaking, a work built on a continuously repeated bass line). To offset this potentially stiff format, Delius begins with a blissful, relaxed evocation of nature, a particular joy for the flutes, and this mood of reverie returns twice, after the sixth and twelfth variations. The first of these interludes is particularly poignant, as a simple rising triplet yearns again and again to the voluptuous accompaniment of lulling woodwind, and finally dies away on an echoing horn. After this idyll, the next series of variations works up optimistically to a climax, then the mood turns solemn, with trumpet and trombone intoning the tune against a tolling bell, before a majestic transformation for full orchestra, shifted up a semitone. Following the brief second interlude, the tune's original lilt is restored, light-hearted, and the music sweeps towards its final climax. To end, the tune returns, quietly, in its original form on the oboe, which had introduced it.

'The Walk to the Paradise Garden', from *A Village Romeo and Juliet* (1900–1)

Shakespeare's famous tragedy of young love thwarted and doomed by family enmity has inspired many musical variations on similar themes, ranging from Tchaikovsky to Prokofiev and Bernstein. One of the less well known is Delius's opera *A Village Romeo and Juliet*, written at the turn of the twentieth century. Based on a short story by the Swiss writer Gottfried Keller, the opera was first performed in a German version prepared by Delius's wife Jelka at the Berlin Komische Oper in 1907. Three years later, Sir Thomas Beecham conducted the English premiere at Covent Garden, and while the opera itself is rarely staged today, the famous orchestral interlude 'The Walk to the Paradise Garden', written originally to cover an extended scene-change, quickly became one of Beecham's best-loved 'lollipops' and has remained a firm favourite with audiences.

The story of *A Village Romeo and Juliet* concerns the feud between two farmers in mid-nineteenth-century Switzerland, and its devastating effect on the lives of their innocent children. A row develops over the ownership of a plot of land that separates the farmers' estates – a plot whose rightful owner is the sinister Dark Fiddler – and they forbid their respective children, a boy named Sali and a girl named Vrenchen, to play with each other. But as the children grow up, they fall in love. They meet secretly on the disputed plot of waste ground, but their tryst is interrupted by the Dark Fiddler, who reminds them that their parents' greed has brought nothing but ruin and unhappiness through costly lawsuits. As the lovers kiss, Vrenchen's father appears and drags her away. Sali hits him on the head, causing irreparable brain damage, and he is committed to an asylum.

Sali and Vrenchen visit the fair at Berghald, where they are recognised, and their arrival is greeted by nudges and whispers. Sali suggests that they should walk to another spot nearby – the Paradise Garden, where they can 'dance the night away'. 'The Paradise Garden – how lovely that sounds,' says Vrenchen, and, hand in hand, the two lovers make their way – during the famous atmospheric interlude – to the garden, a wild, overgrown spot where a dilapidated house overlooking the river has been converted into a tavern, frequented by peasants and strolling players. As Sali and Vrenchen enter at sunset, the Dark Fiddler comes forward to meet them. The peasants and vagabonds drink the lovers' health, and for a moment they consider throwing in their lot and joining the travelling company. But one girl advises them to marry – 'Our sort of life would never do for you'. A bargeman is heard approaching, and his song – 'Passing strangers drifting by' – strangely affects the young couple. Sali gently asks Vrenchen if they, too, should 'drift away down the river'. Without hesitation, the lovers board a moored barge full of hay. Sali casts off, and at the same time pulls the bung from the bottom of the boat. To the wild strains of the Dark Fiddler's violin, the barge slowly moves out into midstream and begins to sink. As the Dark Fiddler watches, the haunting song of the bargeman is heard in the distance.

Paul Dukas (1865–1935)

A friend of Debussy at the Paris Conservatoire, Dukas is known principally for his colourful symphonic scherzo *The Sorcerer's Apprentice* (*L'apprenti sorcier*, 1897), popularised by the Disney film *Fantasia*. He produced few other works, owing to his severe self-criticism, which led him to destroy a number of works before his death. His Symphony in C appeared in 1896, though more significant are the opera *Ariane et Barbe-bleu* (1899–1906) on Maeterlinck's play (a scenario Bartók would tackle over ten years later), and the exotic ballet *La péri* (1911–12). Dukas's two major piano works, the Sonata and the *Variations, interlude et final sur un thème de Rameau*, are sadly overlooked. From 1928 until his death he taught composition at the Paris Conservatoire, where his pupils included Duruflé and Messiaen. He wrote much criticism, and edited volumes of works by Rameau, Couperin, Domenico Scarlatti and Beethoven.

The Sorcerer's Apprentice (1897)

A sorcerer instructs his apprentice to fill a tub with water in preparation for his evening's work. Once the sorcerer is out of the way, the boy decides to test his knowledge by casting a spell on a broom, which does the fetching and carrying for him. Unfortunately, the apprentice doesn't know how to stop the broom bringing more and more water, so in desperation he cleaves it in two with an axe. This simply doubles the problem, because two brooms now fetch even more water than before, until the sorcerer returns and puts things to rights.

Myth and legend inspired several of Dukas's works. In the only one of them to have become a regular concert item, he took a ballad by Goethe – a sort of cautionary tale in folkloristic vein – as the pretext for an orchestral showpiece.

Dukas has always been admired for his orchestral writing, and it has a lot in common with the music of another orchestral wizard, Rimsky-Korsakov. But equally striking is the way in which Dukas creates tension and builds up excitement by means of symphonic development, reworking motifs in different rhythmic and harmonic contexts with a sense of long-term progression.

In the slow introduction, flutter-tongued flutes and muted violins slithering downwards in a mix of chromatic and whole-tone harmonies create an atmosphere of the supernatural, in which anything might happen; this passage, incidentally, anticipates the opening of Debussy's ballet *Jeux* by some fourteen years. The scherzo's main theme is adumbrated, in slow motion, on a solo clarinet, then, at a much brisker tempo, on a muted trumpet; once the tempo has settled down for the scherzo itself, the theme is first heard in its full form on the bassoon, an instrument which evokes the broom in the ballad not only because of its woody tone quality but also by its very appearance.

A second theme is introduced by a chorus of the higher woodwind and highlighted by a tinkling glockenspiel. With its carefree swishing movement, it has a distinctly Mediterranean or Spanish flavour and works ever higher as the broom gets to work, until trumpets and horns signal alarm (in 'augmented', or whole-tone, triads ascending chromatically to symbolise a situation which is getting out of control) and the deliriously swirling violins suggest the rising flood.

Four violent chops from the entire orchestra come at the moment when the apprentice takes an axe and hacks the broom in two, prompting a new start, again on bassoon, though five notes lower than originally. This leads to a second build-up and an acceleration bringing back the slithering motif from the introduction and joining it with the main theme, before the sorcerer himself restores order with a minatory fanfare. The mysterious stillness of the opening returns, and the tale is ended.

Adrian Jack © BBC

Antonín Dvořák (1841–1904)

It was Brahms who recognised Dvořák's talent when, around 1875, he recommended the Czech composer to his own publisher, Simrock. Born in a village north of Prague in 1841, Dvořák worked as a viola player at the Provisional Theatre, then as an organist. The success of tours in the 1880s led to wider recognition as a composer, and his appointment in 1891 as director of the newly founded National Conservatory of Music in New York. During his three years in America he was influenced by Negro and indigenous Indian music, composing the 'New World' Symphony and the 'American' Quartet, Op. 96. But the pull of his homeland, whose folk music and pastoral beauty was reflected strongly in his music, was great. He returned to a post at the Prague National Conservatory, later becoming director. He never achieved the success of his older compatriot Smetana in the field of opera, but wrote three concertos (for violin, cello and piano), some fine string quartets, and established the Czech oratorio with his *Stabat mater* in 1883. He is best known for his symphonies and his sets of *Slavonic Dances*, originally written for piano duet, then arranged for orchestra.

Overture, *Carnival*, Op. 92 (1891)

By the age of fifty Dvořák had achieved international eminence. His works – which by then included eight of his nine symphonies – were being played all over Europe, especially in Britain, and in March 1891 Prague University conferred an honorary doctorate on him. Three months later he received an invitation from Mrs Jeannette Thurber to become Director of the newly founded National Conservatory of New York, at a very attractive salary. Dvořák was tempted by the prestigious offer, but negotiations took a further six months before the contract was signed. While he was considering the implications of moving to America, Dvořák worked on a linked series of three concert overtures, on the themes of 'Nature, Life and Love'. These were later given individual titles – *In Nature's Realm*, *Carnival* and *Othello* – and Dvořák conducted all three as a cycle at a special farewell concert at the National Theatre in Prague on 28 April 1892, shortly before he sailed for America.

All three overtures are linked by a single 'Nature' theme and exemplify Dvořák's belief in Nature as God's creation, and also as the giver – and taker – of life. *In Nature's Realm* is a peaceful pastoral idyll, while *Othello* was clearly inspired by Shakespeare's powerful study of the destructive effects of human passion. The central overture of the cycle, *Carnival* (dedicated to the university in Prague which had honoured him), depicts a rumbustious peasant fair (with strong echoes of Wagner's 'Venusberg Music' from *Tannhäuser*): the lively fair scene encloses a contrasting central episode filled with the cool tranquillity of the Bohemian woods.

Symphonic Variations, Op. 78 (1877)

For Dvořák, 1877 was a year of professional achievement and personal tragedy. He enjoyed the support of Brahms, who recommended him once more for an Austrian State Stipendium; and he relinquished his organist's post at St Adalbert's Church in Prague in order to concentrate on composition and private teaching. But that year his domestic life suffered a series of savage blows: both his surviving children – three-year-old Otakar and a baby daughter of ten months, Rozarka – died within the space of a few weeks. Shortly afterwards, Dvořák's first great love, his vivacious and attractive sister-in-law Josefína Čermáková (whose death eighteen years later would inspire the elegiac coda of his Cello Concerto), finally married the titled admirer who had supplanted the young composer in her affections.

Like Mozart, he seemed to be able to bury his private grief in work which bore no trace of the circumstances of its composition. In the late summer of 1877 he began work on a set of twenty-seven Symphonic Variations for orchestra, based on the theme of his patriotically inspired male-voice part song 'Já jsem huslar' ('I am a fiddler'). The new work received its first performance on 2 December in Prague, with Ludevít Procházka conducting the orchestra of the Czech Provisional Theatre. It does not seem to have made much of an impression. Dvořák's publishers, who had only just begun to take an interest in his music, at first only wanted smaller-scale pieces, and after its première the Symphonic Variations lay neglected for a decade.

In 1887, by which time Dvořák was considerably better known in Europe as the composer of seven symphonies and the immensely popular Slavonic Dances, he dug out the Variations for a concert in Prague, at which he himself conducted. They were now enthusiastically received. Then Dvořák wrote to the conductor Hans Richter, offering the Symphonic Variations for a series of concerts in London. Richter accepted – 'a splendid embellishment for my programme' – and on 13 May 1887, after the first rehearsal, wrote:

> It is a magnificent work! I am happy to be the first to perform it in London, but why did you hold it back for so long? These Variations can take their place among your finest compositions.

On 4 December 1887 Richter introduced the work to Viennese audiences at a Vienna Philharmonic concert. 'Never has there been so great a hit,' reported the composer. 'The performance went splendidly, and the public applauded loudly . . . Brahms has made me a present of a lovely cigar-holder for the Variations.'

Dvořák offsets the restrictions of writing in variation form by producing a theme that has so many instantly recognisable fingerprints that he need only hint at one of them, while varying every other musical parameter, to ensure a truly 'symphonic' sense of continuity. The theme is harmonically simple – like the theme of Beethoven's Diabelli Variations – so it can underpin the furthest-flung melodic invention.

The phrase structure of the theme is unusual: seven plus six plus seven bars, instantly recognisable, yet wide open to development. And the melody itself mixes commonplace elements, effective in their simplicity, with rather exotic Bohemian inflections, either of which can focus the ear on the theme, or else provide the basic fodder for variation. And, unlike many of his predecessors, Dvořák really does write *symphonic* variations: the music gradually evolves until a particular aspect of musical argument has been thoroughly explored, when the focus moves elsewhere.

So the first three variations could not be simpler; in fact, the theme itself is present and complete in each of them, simply decorated with counter-melodies. Variation 4 makes the first significant change, smoothing out the final seven-bar phrase into a more regular eight bars. Variations 5 and 6 run continuously: in the sixth the phrase lengths are entirely altered, although the theme itself retains its ternary structure. The divide between Variations 7 and 8 is further blurred, with a melodic motif being carried across the end of one into the other; and Variation 8 is no longer ternary. Nor, indeed, are Variations 9, 10 and 11; instead they form a little independent ternary movement on their own.

Variation 12, with its violin solo, acts as a stabiliser, reminding the listener of the original theme. Then follows a series of five brilliantly contrasted character variations: first a virile dance; then a delicate, almost chorale-like variation with gentle solos for the flute and horn; Variation 15 is grand and pompous; 16 is very fast and furious; and 17 is actually marked 'scherzo'. More importantly, it is the first in 3/4 time, rather than 2/4.

Having escaped from his metrical straitjacket, Dvořák finally turns his attention to tonality. So far, everything has been in C major. Now, in Variation 18, the music moves into D major. Then come five variations all in B flat minor.

The twenty-sixth, penultimate variation returns to D major, leading back to C for the last variation and finale, which is – in time-honoured fashion – a fugue. Or rather it starts off like a fugue: like all good red-blooded nationalists, Dvořák cannot stay academic for long, and the whole thing soon turns into a whirling Czech dance.

© Wendy Thompson

Edward Elgar (1857–1934)

Elgar rose from humble beginnings (his father was a piano tuner and organist) to become Britain's leading composer: he was knighted in 1904, awarded the Order of Merit in 1911 and became Master of the King's Musick in 1924. Born in Worcester, he failed in his early attempt to establish himself in London, though his reputation grew steadily during the 1890s. The 'Enigma' Variations of 1899 first brought him to national attention, followed closely by his darkly imaginative *Dream of Gerontius* (1900). He was over fifty when he produced his First Symphony, the first of his large-scale orchestral works, which was followed by the Violin Concerto, the Second Symphony and the Cello Concerto. After the death of his wife in 1920 he lost the will to compose, though in 1932 the BBC commissioned his Third Symphony. Elgar left 130 pages of sketches for the symphony at his death, which were elaborated by the British composer Anthony Payne. Fittingly, the completed work was finally premiered by the BBC Symphony Orchestra in 1998.

Overture, *Cockaigne* ('In London Town'), Op. 40 (1900–1)

The year 1900 should have been one of Elgar's most triumphant. The 'Enigma' Variations – the finest orchestral work yet written by a British composer – had brought him fame and success the previous year, and after the eventually acclaimed premiere of his *Sea Pictures* at the 1899 Norwich Festival, Elgar set to work confidently on a large-scale choral commission for the Birmingham Triennial Festival of 1900. The work was *The Dream of Gerontius* – long recognised as one of the undisputed masterpieces of British choral music. But its premiere on 3 October 1900 was a shattering experience for Elgar. He had been late sorting out his proofs; the choir and conductor (Hans Richter, then with the Hallé Orchestra) were under-rehearsed, and the soloists simply not up to the job. After attending a particularly uninspiring rehearsal, Elgar wrote to his close friend August Jaeger, 'I feel very much ashamed of myself as author of *Gerontius* – a sort of criminal – and wonder if I shall ever get up sufficient courage to go to Birmingham at all.' His worst fears were confirmed at the performance: with one or two perceptive exceptions, public and critics were blinded to the work's outstanding qualities by the inadequacies of the performers. 'As far as I'm concerned, music in England is dead,' Elgar wrote bitterly to Jaeger.

To add to his woes, Elgar was chronically short of money and his wife had just undergone a throat operation. Nevertheless, on returning home to Malvern after the failure of *Gerontius*, he immediately set to work on a new commission from the Philharmonic Society – the overture *Cockaigne*, subtitled 'In London Town'. At the end of the manuscript, Elgar added the words 'Meteless and moneless on Malverne hills' (a quotation from *Piers Plowman*). 'The P. [Philharmonic Society] won't pay anything,' he wrote to Jaeger, complaining of his financial losses over *Gerontius*. 'I must earn money somehow – I will not go back to teaching & I think I must try some trade – coal agency or houses – I really wish I were dead over & over again but I dare not, for the sake of my relatives, do the job myself.'

It seems all the more remarkable that, in this trough of despair, Elgar could produce one of his freshest, most genial works. 'It's cheerful and Londony, "stout and steaky",' he told Jaeger. Completed on 24 March 1901, *Cockaigne* was first played at a Philharmonic Society concert in the Queen's Hall in London on 20 June. Jaeger evidently had misgivings about the piece, but Elgar was confident of its success: 'Never mind about *Cockaigne* – I think you'll find it all right some day.' He sent the score to Richter in August, saying, 'Here is nothing deep or melancholy – it is intended to be honest, healthy, humorous and strong, but not vulgar.' The Hallé first played it on 24 October, to Elgar's great delight. '*Cockaigne* was glorious last night under Richter,' he wrote. 'I don't think any of you London Johnnies know what orchestral playing is until you hear the Manchester orchestra.' However, he told Richter that 'it has taught me that I am not satisfied with my music and must do, or rather try to do, something better and nobler'. These lofty ideals were subsequently realised in the First Symphony, which Elgar was contemplating at this time.

According to Michael Kennedy, the French word '*Cockaigne*' means 'an imaginary country, a land of luxury and idleness', but for some reason it was adopted into English in 1824, meaning 'London, the land of Cockneys'. (When Elgar's piece was first played in Latin America, the programme-note writer, unable to glean any information about composer or work, used his own imagination and stated confidently that the piece 'portrayed the terrible ravages of the drug [cocaine] in the East End of London'!) In fact, Elgar said that the idea for this tone poem came to him one gloomy day in the Guildhall: 'Looking at the memorials of the city's great past and knowing well the history of its unending charity, I seemed to hear far away in the dim roof a theme, an echo of some noble melody.'

Variations on an Original Theme ('Enigma'), Op. 36 (1899)

Theme (Enigma)
1 C. A. E.
2 H. D. S.-P.
3 R. B. T.
4 W. M. B.
5 R. P. A.
6 Ysobel
7 Troyte
8 W. N.
9 Nimrod

10 Dorabella
11 G. R. S.
12 B. G. N.
13 * * * (Romanza)
14 E. D. U.

The first performance of the 'Enigma' Variations under Hans Richter at the Queen's Hall on 19 June 1899 transformed Elgar from only a moderately successful provincial composer to a national figure, the recognised standard-bearer of British music in his generation. His reputation had been rising, with a series of impressive choral works performed at various provincial festivals. But the London premiere of an out-and-out orchestral masterpiece, dazzling in its ingenuity, technical skill, and range of expression, marked the coming of age of the 'English Musical Renaissance' begun by Hubert Parry in 1880.

The immediate popular success of Elgar's work far outshone Parry's own fine Symphonic Variations, premiered two years before. With typical generosity, Parry had recommended Elgar's Variations to Richter's agent, and afterwards described it to the conductor Landon Ronald as 'the finest work I have listened to for years. Look out for this man's music; he has something new to say and knows how to say it.'

Elgar's work is larger and more elaborate than most previous essays in the form, such as Brahms's 'Haydn' Variations and the Symphonic Variations of Franck, Dvořák and Parry. He may well, however, have been influenced by the very contemporary precedent of Richard Strauss's 'Fantastic Variations on a Theme of Knightly Character', *Don Quixote*, premiered in 1898. Elgar's is a set of 'character variations' in all senses, dedicated 'to my friends pictured within'; and also features (though much less extensively than Strauss) solo viola and cello. He seems to have attached the title 'Enigma' after the score was complete. Supplying information to the programme-note writer for the first performance, Elgar wrapped it up in a conundrum:

> The *Enigma* I will not explain – its 'dark saying' must be left unguessed . . . further, through and over the whole set another and larger theme 'goes', but is not played . . . So the principal Theme never appears, even as in some late dramas . . . the chief character is never on the stage.

There are two 'enigmas', then: the 'dark saying' of the original theme, and the 'larger theme' which 'is not played'. This latter may not even be a musical theme at all, but an idea or ideal, though most writers have assumed it to be a pre-existing theme to which Elgar's forms a counterpoint. Many tunes have been canvassed over the years. 'Auld Lang Syne' (a theme of friendship) is a perennial contender; 'Twinkle, Twinkle, Little Star' was a recent candidate. There is better circumstantial evidence that it could be 'Britons never will be slaves' from that Last Night of the Proms regular, Thomas Arne's 'Rule, Britannia!' – if so, Elgar indulged in subtle (and typical) word-play about his 'chief character', and he was celebrating his native country, with his friends as representative Britons. But no one knows for sure.

As for the 'dark saying', the 'Enigma' theme is a remarkable invention in its own right, its constituent phrases structured as rhythmic palindromes (two quavers – two crotchets / two crotchets – two quavers) and its two halves juxtaposing G minor and G major, shadow and light, pensive and lyrical. Commentators are generally agreed that it stands for Elgar himself (two quavers plus two crotchets says, darkly, 'Edward Elgar'), as a private person. Thus the ensuing variations portray their subjects – fourteen people, one dog – through his perception of them. At the early performances they were only identified by initials, and it's worth stressing that we don't really need to know anything about them: the Variations are superbly effective as 'pure' music (whatever that is), as a great essay in the art of thematic development. However, a bit of anecdotal background certainly adds to the fun, and Elgar gave fairly full identification of his friends in notes he supplied for pianola rolls of the Variations issued in 1929 by the Aeolian Company. I quote some phrases below:

1. 'C. A. E.': a loving portrait of the composer's wife, (Caroline) Alice – 'a prolongation of the Theme with what I wished to be romantic and delicate additions'.
2. 'H. D. S.-P.': the pianist Hew David Steuart-Powell, who often played piano to Elgar's violin.
3. 'R. B. T.': the eccentric Richard Baxter Townsend rode about Oxford on a tricycle, continually sounding his bell. In amateur theatricals Elgar had enjoyed his caricature of an old man, 'the low voice flying off occasionally into "soprano" timbre'. His variation is followed by that of his brother-in-law . . .
4. 'W. M. B.': William Meath Baker, a hospitable country squire, caught announcing the arrangement of carriages to his guests and inadvertently banging the door as he leaves.
5. 'R. P. A.': Richard Arnold, a sensitive pianist, the son of the poet Matthew Arnold. 'His serious conversation was continually broken up by whimsical and witty remarks.'
6. 'Ysobel': the solo viola incarnates Isabel Fitton, an amateur violist, 'pensive and for a moment romantic', and unusually tall: thus the wide intervals in the solo part.
7. 'Troyte': one of Elgar's closest friends, the Malvern architect Arthur Troyte Griffith, a pianist of only modest abilities: his struggles with cross-rhythms are suggested here, along with his argumentative nature.
8. 'W. N.': Winifred Norbury's infectious laugh, and the pastoral tranquillity of her eighteenth-century house, where she lived with her sister, are 'sedately shown'.
9. 'Nimrod': Elgar's nickname for his great friend, champion and publisher A. J. Jaeger (a typical Elgarian pun transforming Jaeger, German for 'hunter', into 'Nimrod the mighty hunter' from the Book of Genesis). This noble, resplendently affectionate Adagio is the generous heart of the whole work, and one of the most famous passages in British music. Beginning with a reminiscence of Beethoven's 'Pathétique'

Sonata, it is 'the record of a long summer evening talk, when my friend discoursed eloquently on the slow movements of Beethoven'.

10. 'Dorabella': Elgar's name (out of Mozart's *Così fan tutte*) for his friend Dora Penny, niece of 'W. M. B.' The woodwind imitate her slight stammer. Elgar once told her that 'she of all people' should recognise the 'larger theme' of the Variations. (All pennies carried the image of Britannia.)

11. 'G. R. S.': George Sinclair was organist at Hereford Cathedral. But the real subject here is his great bulldog, Dan, who made a too-enthusiastic leap at a cat on the bridge at Hereford, fell into the River Wye, paddled furiously upstream to find a landing place and emerged with a triumphant bark. 'G. R. S. said, "Set that to music." I did; here it is.'

12. 'B. G. N.': Basil Nevinson, an amateur cellist, made up a piano trio with Elgar and Steuart-Powell (the H. D. S.-P. of Variation 2). He receives one of Elgar's most notable cello solos, in an elegiac movement scarcely less deeply felt than 'Nimrod'.

13. '* * * (Romanza)': 'a lady who was, at the time of composition, on a sea voyage . . . the drums suggest the distant throb of the engines of a liner over which the clarinet quotes a phrase from Mendelssohn's *Calm Sea and Prosperous Voyage*.' In the manuscript of his notes Elgar identified her as Lady Mary Lygon, who sailed to Australia with her brother, who had been appointed Governor of New South Wales – but that was in April 1899, well after the variation was written. Elgar's wish to hide the dedicatee behind asterisks has suggested that there may be more to this hauntingly nostalgic music than meets the eye. It's possible he was concealing (from Alice?) a reference to Helen Weaver, whom he had loved and been briefly engaged to in 1883–4. In 1885 she had emigrated to New Zealand, in search of a cure for her lungs.

14. 'E. D. U.': Now in public mode, Elgar (or 'Edoo', as Alice called him) reclaims his theme for a Self-portrait of the Artist

as a Devilish Fine Fellow. He gives himself the longest variation, makes the biggest noise, wraps everything up with enormous ebullience. He sounds like a man who knows he's on his way to the top, and by this stage in the Variations he probably had a good idea of how soon he was going to get there. This is both a grand finale and one in the eye for every discouraging acquaintance, supercilious academic and carping critic. The dashing composer sweeps on to his destiny, flanked by Alice and Jaeger (note the recall of 'C. A. E.' and the magniloquent apotheosis of 'Nimrod'), truest representatives of all those who believed in him.

Falstaff, symphonic study in C minor, Op. 68 (1912–13)

Elgar particularly enjoyed writing *Falstaff*, and thought it one of his best works. He called it a symphonic 'study' because it was a portrait – not just of Falstaff, but of Shakespeare and all human life. It is not programme music providing a series of incidents with connecting links such as Richard Strauss's *Ein Heldenleben*, Elgar said, though that did not stop him publishing an article just one month before the first performance in the autumn of 1913, outlining characters and events in such detail that he almost disproved the point.

Falstaff is one of Shakespeare's most discussed characters. Opera composers have treated him, in the main, as a buffoon, drawing on *The Merry Wives of Windsor*, although Verdi added a philosophical dimension by dipping into *Henry IV Part 1*. Elgar concentrated entirely on both parts of *Henry IV*, and quoted commentaries describing Falstaff as a character as complex as Hamlet:

> made up wholly of incongruities; a man at once young and old, enterprising and fat, a dupe and a wit, harmless and wicked, weak in principle and resolute by constitution, cowardly in appearance and brave in reality; a knave

> without malice, a liar without deceit; and a knight, a gentleman and a soldier, without either dignity, decency, or honour.

Falstaff is not only witty himself, but the cause of wit in others. And who wouldn't prefer him to Hamlet as a drinking companion?

He was, in fact, modelled on a historical character, Sir John Oldcastle, who was a friend of Henry V and became High Sheriff of Herefordshire, but was banished and convicted of heresy, for which he was hanged in 1417. But while Shakespeare's *Henry* plays trace real incidents in England's history, Falstaff is essentially his own invention, down to his surname ('False-staff', perhaps) – a thoroughly bad, if sometimes lovable, influence on the future Henry V, who disowns his ancient friend when he succeeds to the throne.

Elgar once said he had musical daydreams in the same way that other people had daydreams of heroism and adventure, and that he could express almost any thought that came into his head in terms of music. Larger than life, Falstaff gave him the pretext for some of his most daring and capricious invention, beginning with the swaggering opening theme, depicting Sir John 'in a green old age, mellow, frank, gay, easy, corpulent, loose, unprincipled, and luxurious'. The next big theme, straight and noble, is Prince Hal's (Henry V to be), which Elgar could well have marked 'grandioso', as he does when it returns near the end of the work. These two characters fire the impetuous first section, which is quite brief.

After a pause, Falstaff's exploits begin with a switch to a faster tempo and a light, skittish mood. This is a much longer section, which Elgar said 'should chatter, blaze, glitter and coruscate'. It introduces a crowd of Falstaff's female acquaintance, and includes, in atmospheric detail, his ludicrous midnight exploit (a botched bullion robbery) at Gadshill, ending with his return to the Boar's Head tavern where he holds court, and drinks himself to sleep, to the unmistakable sound of snoring.

A gentle pastoral episode follows – 'somewhat antiquated in mood,' Elgar said – representing Falstaff dreaming of his youth. A fanfare on muted brass calls Falstaff and his ramshackle regiment to battle against the King's enemies at Shrewsbury, in which the fat knight does not cut a heroic figure. Then, on his way back through Gloucestershire, he rests in Shallow's orchard. This second rustic interlude, with its evocative 'sadly-merry pipe and tabor music', is rudely curtailed by the announcement that Falstaff's 'tender lambkin', Prince Hal, is now King. When Henry V appears 'gorgeous as the sun at midsummer', Falstaff greets him, but is disowned; the music disintegrates in a few disjointed recollections, and after a brief, affecting phrase on clarinet, Falstaff dies, insignificantly, with a quiet chord of C major on muted brass instruments.

Adrian Jack © BBC

Overture, *In the South* ('Alassio'), Op. 50 (1903–4)

Elgar and his wife spent the winter of 1903–4 in Italy, mainly at Alassio on the Italian Riviera. His health was bad and he was depressed by the recent deaths of friends. He had promised a symphony to Hans Richter, who had hoped to include it in a three-day Elgar Festival he was due to conduct at Covent Garden in March 1904, but could make virtually no progress on it. In fact, the symphony would not be completed until 1907; but in the Italian ambience Elgar recovered his spirits. One afternoon in the Vale of Andora, 'basking in the sun on the old Roman road', with the Alps and the Mediterranean both in view, he saw a shepherd standing by an ancient ruin, 'and in a flash it all came to me – the conflict of armies in that very spot long ago . . . the contrast of the ruin and the shepherd'. What came to him was the inspiration for *In the South*, begun at once, finished in Malvern on 21 February 1904 and duly premiered at the Elgar Festival with the composer conducting.

The result is as much symphonic poem as overture. Elgar wrote lines from Byron's *Childe Harold's Pilgrimage* on the manuscript:

> . . . a land
> Which was the mightiest in its old command
> And is the loveliest . . .
> Wherein were cast . . .
> . . . the men of Rome!
> Thou art the garden of the world.

More than most of Elgar's works, *In the South* shows direct links to Richard Strauss, whose own first symphonic poem, *Aus Italien*, had been inspired by an Italian holiday. Elgar's overture displays thematic affinities to Strauss's *Don Juan* and *Ein Heldenleben* (whose key it also shares), and its flamboyant orchestral panache seems calculated to outdo even his great contemporary.

The work begins in an imperial E flat major, with a vaunting, leaping theme. Originally sketched several years before as a portrait of Dan, the bulldog of 'Enigma' Variation no. 11, 'triumphant after a fight', its optimistic élan makes a perfect starting-point for Elgar's Italian adventures.

The first-subject group reaches a sonorous climax with a broad nobilmente theme descending in great waves, after which gentler, more pastoral ideas form a transition. One of these has a sighing, repeated three-note figure which, according to Elgar, speaks the name of a village near his holiday retreat: 'Moglio, Moglio'. The expressive second subject proper is pensively lyrical and slightly florid in a perhaps rather 'Italianate' way.

The transition themes initiate the development, which soon works up some military excitement but is brought short by an awesome vision. A heavy upward-tramping music, like the inexorable progress of an army in slow march time, is combined with an extraordinary set of sustained, dissonant, overlapping entries descending from the heights, like the piers of some immense structure dropping plumb and parallel across a steep valley. One of the most original passages in all Elgar, this music was inspired by the ruined viaduct at Turbia and clearly evokes the might of ancient Rome in manpower and architecture.

As this fades into history (to be distantly recalled a little later), a second piece of development in military vein sets in, only to subside to a languorous romantic nocturne in which (perhaps as a nod to Berlioz's *Harold in Italy*) a solo viola takes the lead in the style of an Italian popular song. At the end of this virtually self-contained episode – Elgar was able to publish it separately for small orchestra as *In Moonlight* (Canto popolare) – the recapitulation steals in, quietly at first, with the nobilmente theme crowning all with glory and a last bark of the 'Dan' theme for an exultant close.

Introduction and Allegro for Strings, Op. 47 (1904–5)

As a young man Elgar played the violin, and indeed earned part of his living from teaching it (a photograph exists of him holding his violin, his other hand restraining a large dog). Though a competent pianist, he was first and foremost a string player; and a love and feeling for stringed instruments informs all his music, from the subtle beauty of the solo writing in his violin and cello concertos to the affectionate care he always lavished on even the humblest passages in his orchestral works. ('Come along, seconds, I wrote this specially for you,' he is alleged to have exhorted his violins in rehearsal.)

The Introduction and Allegro is rooted in this deep understanding of the string orchestra; and so completely does it express the essence of string writing, both in solo and ensemble, that subsequent works for string orchestra have had to measure themselves against its example. In turn, its example is taken from the Baroque concerto grosso, in which a solo group is pitted against a larger ensemble.

Immediate impulses came from a Welsh tune Elgar claimed to have heard in the distance when holidaying at Llangranog (or 'Llangringoggywoggypygwgssill', as he jestingly called it) in 1901 – its falling interval of a third haunts the opening and the coda – and from A. J. Jaeger ('Nimrod' of the 'Enigma' Variations), who suggested that Elgar should compose something brilliant, such as a scherzo or a fugue, for the strings of the newly formed London Symphony Orchestra. Elgar did indeed write into the music what he called 'the devil of a fugue', and he was to describe the work proudly to his friend Frank Schuster as 'the string thing most brilliant with a real tune in it however'.

Audiences were slower to agree. The first performance, in an all-Elgar programme at Queen's Hall in 1905, was somewhat coolly received; and when it was given at a Hallé concert that December, the applause was (according to Ernest Newman's account) 'moderate' – which did not prevent the conductor Hans Richter from promptly playing the piece through again.

Few would now dissent from the view that it is one of the finest works for concerted strings ever composed. The opening is characteristic in its bold statements answered by a gentler, more hesitant and melancholy figure; and this ambivalence marks the work, as it does so much of Elgar's music. For all the lyricism of the Welsh tune and the brilliance of the fugue, not to mention the mastery of dramatic effect whereby the Allegro is regained after the tensions of the central section, there is a certain wryness in the emotion. Over the gentle, almost vulnerable answer to the initial grand gestures, Elgar wrote in the manuscript the phrase 'smiling with a sigh'. The full sentence (from Shakespeare's *Cymbeline*) is more appropriate: 'Nobly he links a smiling with a sigh.'

Pomp and Circumstance March no. 1 in D major ('Land of Hope and Glory') (1901)

In the thesaurus of musical clichés, 'pomp and circumstance' (a phrase borrowed from Shakespeare's *Othello*) has come to stand for what is thought to be the more stridently jingoistic, imperialist side of Elgar's nature. But Elgar's intentions in the marches to which he gave the title were far from militaristic. He told an interviewer in May 1904: 'I do not see why the ordinary quick march should not be treated on a large scale in the way that the waltz, the old-fashioned slow march and even the polka have been treated by the great composers.' In other words, he wanted to bring the quick march off the parade ground and into the concert hall.

In the same interview, he said that *Pomp and Circumstance* was 'merely the generic name for what is a set of six marches', of which 'two have already appeared, and the others will come later'. In fact, there were only ever five, and the last saw the light of day as late as 1930. But the first two came with relative ease between January and August 1901. And no. 1 in particular was an immediate hit from the time of its first performance, in Liverpool in October 1901. When Henry Wood introduced it to London at a Promenade Concert the same month (the Proms were later in the year in those days), the audience, Wood recalled, 'simply rose and yelled', and insisted not just on an encore but on an unprecedented third hearing.

The March is notable for the fizzing energy of its outer sections (marked 'Allegro, con molto fuoco' – 'Fast, with great fire'), and its characteristically detailed and sonorous scoring. But its outstanding feature is the noble melody of the central G major trio section, which returns in full orchestral splendour in the coda.

Elgar himself recognised this as 'a tune that comes once in a lifetime', and for a while thought of reserving it for a symphony. Early in 1902, a few months after the first performances of the March, he reused the melody in the finale of his *Coronation Ode for King Edward VII*, with words fitted to it by the author of the Ode, Arthur Christopher Benson. And later the same year, at the behest of the publisher Boosey's, Benson and Elgar adapted it again as a solo song for the contralto Clara Butt, and for the lucrative sheet-music market. Benson retained (more or less) the first two lines from the Ode, but replaced his former invocation to 'Truth and Right and Freedom' by a new couplet expressing imperial ambition with a confidence typical of the age. A century later, in very different times, these remain the words to which by long-standing custom audiences join in with Elgar's great melody.

Serenade for Strings, Op. 20 (1892)

1 Allegro piacevole
2 Larghetto
3 Allegretto

Composed in 1892, six years before the 'Enigma' Variations, this little serenade (Op. 20) is the earliest of Elgar's works in the repertory today. It is in fact the only work before the 'Enigma' Variations that is frequently played. Ambitious scores like *The Black Knight* and *Caractacus* are virtually forgotten, yet these three slight movements for strings alone remain alive – a souvenir of Elgar's struggle for recognition beyond the Midland counties.

So far as scale is concerned, the survival of the Serenade may seem a trick of fate, but the substance of the music leaves a very different impression. Quite apart from the excellent understanding of stringed instruments, which is evident throughout, the work is full of a typically Elgarian lyric poetry. The personal 'fingerprints' abound – the confidently arching themes, the melodic interval of a seventh, a certain formal waywardness in the outer movements – and the music is mature in the sense that its ideas are fully realised.

The first movement is the most extended and is held together by the rhythmic figure from the opening bars (violas). The main theme of the Larghetto anticipates the broad eloquence of the Adagio from the First Symphony (1908); equally characteristic is the 'smiling with a sigh' type of motive which forms the introduction and coda. The finale begins in a rhythmically active 12/8, but after a working out of its single thematic idea a return is made to material from the opening movement.

Manuel de Falla (1876–1946)

With Albéniz and Granados, Falla cultivated the heritage of Spanish music to create a new nationalist idiom which produced, in his case, a small number of gem-like works of the highest quality and individuality. Falla was born in Cádiz and studied in Madrid with Felipe Pedrell from 1902. He composed a number of *zarzuelas* (traditional Spanish operettas) without great success, and left for Paris with the score of his opera *La vida breve* (*A Brief Life*). In Paris he met Dukas, Debussy, Ravel and Stravinsky, and *La vida breve* was staged at the Opéra-Comique. He returned to Madrid in 1914 completing his *Noches en los jardines de España* (*Nights in the Gardens of Spain*, 1914) and his two popular ballets: *El amor brujo* (*Love, the Magician*, 1914–15), and *El sombrero de tres picos* (*The Three-Cornered Hat*, 1916–19 for Diaghilev's Ballets Russes). In 1920 he settled in Granada, where he wrote his puppet opera *El retablo de maese Pedro* (*Master Peter's Puppet Show*, 1919–22) and Harpsichord Concerto for Wanda Landowska (1923–6). Falla spent his last years in Argentina, leaving his 'scenic cantata' *Atlántida* incomplete (it was later completed by a pupil and first staged in 1962).

'Ritual Fire Dance', from *Love, the Magician* (1915)

The 'Ritual Fire Dance' from *El amor brujo* (usually translated as *Love, the Magician*) is one of Falla's most popular works. However, its subtitle is rather less well known, and can only be appreciated in the context of the ballet as a whole; it reads 'Para ahuyentar los malos espiritus' or 'To keep evil spirits away'.

Falla began work on what was originally conceived as a 'gitaneria' in the form of a collection of songs, dances and spoken verse on the gypsy theme (the text was by the poet Martínez Sierra) shortly after he returned to Spain from

Paris. His own cultural roots drank deeply from the Andalusian well of inspiration, and this had already resulted in the one-act opera *La vida breve*, which established him as Spain's leading composer. He may well have heard the tale of the gypsy girl Candelas from the mother of Pastora Imperio, whose dance troupe was to give the first performance of *El amor brujo* in Madrid in 1915.

The story, as in the case of *La vida breve*, tells of the power of love to dominate life – and death. Candelas is haunted by the memory of her former lover, whose ghost, with inconsiderate insistence, disrupts her new relationship with Carmelo. She tries various means of exorcising the ghost, and eventually persuades another girl, Lucía, to distract the jealous but ever unfaithful spirit so that she and Carmelo can seal their love with a kiss and banish its malign presence for good. As the subtitle to the 'Ritual Fire Dance' suggests, the dance represents Candelas's earlier, unsuccessful attempt at exorcism; she draws a magic circle on the ground, crosses herself and, as midnight strikes, the dancing begins. Falla's fascination with the musical tradition of the Andalusian *cante jondo* (the so-called 'deep song' of the gypsies) is the key to *El amor brujo*, and his ability to distil its essence is nowhere more clearly heard than in this dance, so evocative of a smouldering passion that is not to be easily ignored – or dismissed.

The Three-Cornered Hat, Suites nos 1 and 2 (1916–19)

Scenes and Dances from Part 1:

1 Introduction – Afternoon
2 Dance of the Miller's Wife (Fandango)
3 The Corregidor – The Miller's Wife – The Grapes

Three Dances from Part 2:

1 The Neighbour's Dance (Seguidillas)
2 The Miller's Dance
3 Final Dance

Along with *Noces en los jardines de España* (*Nights in the Gardens of Spain*) and his ballet *El amor brujo* (*Love, the Magician*), Manuel de Falla's *El sombrero de tres picos* (*The Three-Cornered Hat*) marks the first stage of his obsession with the Spanish psyche. He had, for instance, already rediscovered for himself the *cante jondo*, the primitive Arab-influenced song of Andalusia, and though he quotes folk material only rarely, its spirit pervades the whole ballet, which is based on a celebrated story by Pedro de Alarcón. In 1916 Diaghilev saw a preliminary version of the piece in Madrid, where it took the form of a pantomime; he persuaded Falla to turn it into a ballet proper, and produced it at the Alhambra Theatre in London in July 1919. Ernest Ansermet conducted, the dancers included Léonide Massine and Tamara Karsavina, and Picasso designed the sets, costumes and curtain.

The plot revolves around a story of jealousy and intrigue: a miller is jealous of his beautiful and wholly faithful wife. She has, however, caught the eye of the local corregidor, or resident magistrate (the three-cornered hat is a symbol of his office), and when he attempts to win her favour, the couple teach him a lesson.

That same evening, seeking revenge, the corregidor has the miller frogmarched off to jail, and during his absence again attempts to seduce his wife. Escaped miller and corregidor somehow exchange costumes, policemen chase the wrong man, mistaken identities are revealed, and the corregidor's effigy is tossed in a blanket.

Falla's music contains some magnificent set pieces, which he later separated into these two suites. He was soon to go beyond the magnificent catalogue of transfigured national dances that makes up *The Three-Cornered Hat*, but for brilliance of colour and sheer physical excitement, he never surpassed this spectacular ballet that followed his return to his homeland from Paris in 1914.

Gabriel Fauré (1845–1924)

Fauré received his early training at the École Niedermeyer, where he was given a thorough grounding in counterpoint and church music. He worked at a number of churches, assisting both Widor and Saint-Saëns, before becoming assistant organist and choirmaster at the Madeleine in 1877. Though his earlier music, such as the *Cantique de Jean Racine* (1865) and the *Requiem* (1887–94), was written in a conservative Romantic style, his works of later years – including the lyric drama *Prométhée* (1900), the Piano Trio (1923) and the String Quartet (1924) – were of bolder expression. Notable in his output of over fifty songs are the cycle of Verlaine settings, *La bonne chanson* (1892–4). In 1896 he became a professor at the Paris Conservatoire, where he taught Ravel, Koechlin and Nadia Boulanger, and acted as director from 1905 to 1920, when a hearing impediment forced him to retire. Aside from his body of song repertoire he had a fondness for the piano, writing thirteen each of Nocturnes and Barcarolles, five Impromptus and a Ballade.

Pavane, Op. 50 (1887)

During the hard-working early years of his marriage, Fauré continued to pursue musically advantageous social connections. News of the *Pavane* slipped out in letters of September 1887. At first for orchestra only, by then it had acquired verses by the fashionable aesthete Robert de Montesquiou, model for the central character in Joris-Karl Huysmans's decadent novel *À rebours*, published three years earlier. The words were full of stylised, Verlaine-like artifice. Fauré claimed to admire them and they were included at the work's public premiere in April 1888 at the Société Nationale, but the choral parts are rarely performed nowadays – they are only a light overlay.

The work's main melody, heard on the solo flute, is one of Fauré's simplest and most effective uses of orchestral colour. Subtle changes and shifts of harmony amplify its character and extend it persuasively towards a final cadence that, typically, avoids the obvious. The personal mixture of modal and tonal qualities also colours the more assertive middle section, built on a dramatically descending bass line.

© Robert Maycock

Pelléas and Mélisande, Suite, Op. 80 (1898; orch. 1901)

1 Prélude
2 Fileuse
3 Sicilienne
4 La mort de Mélisande

Maurice Maeterlinck's play recounting the tragic encounter between a mysteriously reluctant pair of lovers became a rallying point for the symbolist movement as soon as it appeared in 1892. In the long run its greatest achievement was to inspire Claude Debussy immediately to start an operatic version, which set nearly all of the text and has kept Maeterlinck's name more current than any of his other work – not that he appreciated the point to start with (he refused to see the opera for nearly twenty years). From its première in 1902, Debussy's opera became the definitive statement of symbolism in the performing arts. Some idea of the play's wider impact can be gathered from the number of musical treatments it attracted from composers of quite different aesthetic persuasions.

The nearest match, perhaps, was the pre-atonal Arnold Schoenberg, the composer of *Verklärte Nacht*, who wrote his hour-long symphonic poem *Pelleas und Melisande* in 1902–3. Jean Sibelius wrote his incidental music, rather more pictorial, for a Helsinki production of the play in 1905. Seven years later came a concert overture by Cyril Scott. But the first theatre score was commissioned for London in 1898, from the unlikely source of Gabriel Fauré.

In the preceding years the French composer had been attempting to establish a presence in London, with more social than musical success, and the spur to this collaboration was the actress Mrs Patrick Campbell, who played Mélisande in the short run of staged performances at the Prince of Wales Theatre that resulted. They met in the spring of 1898, when she read to him in French 'those parts of the play . . . which to me most called for music'. It was to be a substantial score of nineteen numbers. Fauré had only May in which to write it, and passed the numbers on to his pupil Charles Koechlin to orchestrate, a task completed by 5 June. Performances began a fortnight later, with Fauré conducting and Koechlin in attendance. Local reviews were unfavourable, though Maeterlinck apparently liked the production better than he would Debussy's opera. Most of Fauré's score is for instruments alone, except for a 'Chanson de Mélisande' (set in English, and presumably sung by Mrs Campbell). There is a fair amount of repetition and cross-reference, focused on four main movements: the prelude and three interludes. Fauré later made these into a concert suite, in two stages: a three-movement version, for which he reorchestrated Koechlin's score for larger instrumental forces, was published and performed in 1901; the 'Sicilienne' was then added unaltered in 1909.

In their concert form, these four pieces have the weight, if not the working-out, of a short symphony, with two powerful slow movements framing a pair of scherzos. The Prélude sets out to characterise the essence of the drama, specifically through an opening theme that represents the character of Mélisande and a second theme of tragic import; a horn call near the end sets up the arrival of Mélisande's future husband Golaud and the start of the play.

The 'Fileuse', originally played before Act 3, is a portrait of Mélisande spinning (in a scene that Debussy omitted). The 'Sicilienne', introducing Act 2 and popular as a flautists' recital item, was actually transcribed straight from Fauré's Op. 78 for cello and piano – the one self-borrowing in the score. The 'Death of Mélisande' is the prelude to the final act, an intense lament all the more devastating for its brevity. In the original theatre score, the closing eight-bar phrase, a thing of rare and epigrammatic beauty, returned on its own at the end of the play.

Robert Maycock © BBC

George Gershwin (1898–1937)

Having left school at fifteen to accompany a Tin Pan Alley song-plugger, Gershwin was set for a career in musicals; his first Broadway show, *La La Lucille*, opened in 1919 when he was still aged twenty. The influence that the jazz idiom could have on the classical world became clear with the success of his *Rhapsody in Blue* in 1924, after which Gershwin turned more and more to so-called classical forms. His Piano Concerto in F followed a year later and in 1928 came his brilliantly colourful tone poem *An American in Paris*. Meanwhile he had struck up a partnership with his gifted lyricist brother Ira resulting in a sequence of songs and shows. Not wanting to stifle Gershwin's highly developed talents, both Ravel and Nadia Boulanger declined to give him lessons (Ravel famously commented that given the amount the young American was earning, it was he who should be giving the lessons). Musicals and songs for films continued to flow, but Gershwin's most ambitious and influential project was the 'folk opera' *Porgy and Bess* (1935). He died suddenly, before he was forty, of a brain tumour.

An American in Paris (1928)

Writing about Gershwin's *Rhapsody in Blue*, Leonard Bernstein suggested that it might not be 'a real composition in the sense that whatever happens in it must seem inevitable, or even pretty inevitable. You can cut out parts of it without affecting the whole in any way except to make it shorter. You can remove any of these stuck-together sections and the piece still goes on bravely as before.' Some of these comments apply equally to *An American in Paris* – and yet the symphonic poem is arguably the most successful and coherent of Gershwin's concert pieces. There are several novel touches in the orchestration, not least the French taxi horns, but it matters more that Gershwin's idiom has advanced towards the foothills of modernism, adding Stravinskyan polychords to his usual array of excellent tunes.

Still best known as a Broadway songwriter, Gershwin was determined to achieve more in the classical field when, in the spring of 1928, he travelled to Europe, encountering such luminaries as Prokofiev, Ravel, Milhaud and Poulenc, and buying up all of Debussy's sheet music. Fittingly enough, it was in the French capital that he worked on the long-planned concert work. He wrote of the piece:

> My purpose here is to portray the impressions of an American visitor in Paris as he strolls about the city, listens to the various street noises and absorbs the French atmosphere. The opening gay section is followed by a rich 'blues' with a strong rhythmic undercurrent. Our American friend, perhaps after strolling into a café and having a few drinks, has suddenly succumbed to a spasm of homesickness. The harmony here is both more intense and simple than in the preceding pages. This 'blues' moves to a climax, followed by a coda in which the spirit of the music returns to the vivacity and bubbling exuberance of the opening part with its impressions of Paris. Apparently the homesick American, having left the café and reached the open air, has downed his spell of blues and once again is an alert spectator of Parisian life. At the conclusion the street noises and French atmosphere are triumphant.

The first performance was given in Carnegie Hall on 13 December 1928 by the Philharmonic-Symphony Orchestra of New York conducted by Walter Damrosch, an ardent enthusiast for the more conservative brands of American music. Technical facility was not his strongest suit, but the less-than-perfect performance probably did little to influence those commentators predisposed to criticise 'Jasbo in Montparnasse'. Paul Rosenfeld was a good example of the kind of music critic who liked to give Gershwin's concert pieces a hard time. In *An Hour with American Music* (published in 1929), his disdain is biblical:

> *An American in Paris* is poorer in themes than either of its predecessors; and when, after losing its way, the music turns into the lively, somewhat meaningless sort of flourish usually supplied in the finales of musical comedy first acts, we seem to hear Gershwin's instrument, like Balaam's ass, reproving the false prophet; directing him to the sphere congenial to his gift.

And today? The fact that *An American in Paris* has outlived so many pieces whose compositional credentials were never queried by the critics raises some basic aesthetic questions: if a musical work continues to be played for three generations, just how flawed can it be?

Mikhail Glinka (1804–57)

Regarded as the father of Russian musical nationalism, Glinka set the stage for the activities of the group of composers known as 'The Five'. He was slow to arrive at this: his early songs and chamber music were in the distinctly European mould which had come to dominate the concert hall. Ironically it was his three years in Italy, where he met Bellini and Donizetti, plus a period in Berlin, which helped crystallise Glinka's resolve to celebrate his homeland in music after his return in 1834. The result was *A Life for the Tsar*, the first of his two major operas, premiered in 1836. *Ruslan and Lyudmila*, a magical tale after a poem by Pushkin, followed six years later, though was less enthusiastically received. His creative inspiration fell away in the last fourteen years of his life, during which he travelled widely in Europe; however, his orchestral fantasy *Kamarinskaya* (1848), which skilfully combines two folk tunes, was a strong influence on future Russian composers.

Overture, *Ruslan and Lyudmila* (1842)

Ruslan and Lyudmila was Glinka's second opera, written after the unexpected success of *A Life for the Tsar*, premiered in St Petersburg in December 1836, had turned him overnight into a national cultural hero.

He immediately looked for a follow-up, hitting on Pushkin's poem *Ruslan and Lyudmila*. During its composition, which took five years, Glinka's concentration was distracted by personal problems, particularly his separation from his wife (whom he had married in 1835) and his scandalous affair with the singer Ekaterina Kern. *Ruslan* was finally completed and first performed in 1842, but was coolly received, to Glinka's distress. Part of the reason for its apparent failure lay in its essentially undramatic nature: Glinka had originally wanted Pushkin himself to devise the scenario, but the great poet died in a duel in February 1837, and the story-line was hastily thrown together 'in a drunken quarter of an hour' by a friend of the composer. The opera also lacks cohesion: Glinka had written 'set pieces' over a five-year period and then patched them together at the end. But despite its faults, *Ruslan* contains music of striking originality, tinged both by the characteristic inflections of Russian folk music, and by a strong vein of oriental fantasy.

The story is complex: Lyudmila is courted by three suitors: the knight Ruslan, the poet prince Ratmir and the cowardly warrior Farlaf. She is abducted from a feast in their honour by the dwarf Chernomor, whom Ruslan eventually defeats with the aid of a magic sword obtained after overcoming the gigantic head of a sleeping monster on a battlefield. Eventually Ruslan and Lyudmila are united.

Although the opera is rarely performed outside Russia nowadays, the brilliant and colourful overture has remained a popular orchestral showpiece. The triumphant opening is taken from the scene of jubilation at the end of the opera; while the lyrical second theme is taken from Ruslan's great Act 2 aria, in which he reaffirms his resolve before confronting the gigantic head.

George Frideric Handel (1685–1759)

Even before he had left his Saxon home town of Halle, Handel began to absorb musical influences from France and Italy, while exploring the library of music at St Michael's Church. He became organist at Halle Cathedral and worked at the Hamburg Opera House, composing his first opera, *Almira*, in 1705. He then spent more than three years in Italy, during which time he set Latin religious texts, including his *Dixit Dominus* and, it is believed, the *Gloria in excelsis Deo*, rediscovered only in 2001. The oratorio *La resurrezione* was performed in Rome on Easter Day 1708 and the opera *Agrippina* in Venice in 1709. The next year he was appointed Kapellmeister to the court of Hanover, but promptly took leave to visit England, where he essentially remained until his death. Among the first of his productions in London was *Rinaldo*, prompting a string of over thirty Italian-style operas, though the success of *Messiah* in 1742 persuaded him to concentrate on oratorios. Among his instrumental works are the *Water Music* and *Music for the Royal Fireworks*, as well as sets of *concerti grossi* and organ concertos.

Music for the Royal Fireworks (1749)

1 Ouverture: Adagio – Allegro
2 Bourrée
3 La paix: Largo alla siciliana
4 La réjouissance: Allegro
5 Menuets 1 and 2

By 1748 the long-protracted War of the Austrian Succession had stagnated, with neither side (Austria, England and the Netherlands ranged against France, Prussia and Spain) able to claim a decisive advantage over the other. To the relief of all parties, an armistice was agreed in May and a peace treaty officially concluded at Aix-la-Chapelle (present-day Aachen) in October. Never one to miss a trick in promoting his own interests, King George II, who had pursued the war to preserve his German territories, was now eager to portray himself as the architect of European peace.

To this end a lavish celebration with fireworks was planned in London's Green Park for 27 April 1749. The King and his masters of ceremonies spared no expense, enlisting the services of the famous Florentine theatrical designer Giovanni Servandoni, who concocted a spectacular firework 'Machine' in the form of a Doric temple, 'adorned with Frets, Gilding, Lustres, Artificial Flowers, Inscriptions, Statues, Allegorical Pictures &c'. During the display the fireworks were designed to create dazzling, multicoloured pictures and conjure up allegorical scenes, culminating in the image of the King bringing peace to Britannia, Neptune and Mars.

As by far the country's most celebrated composer, Handel was the automatic choice to provide music for this Baroque extravaganza. The King, who at first had been reluctant to have any music at all, relented on condition that only 'warlike instruments' – woodwind, brass and percussion – were involved. True to form, though, Handel proved even more intransigent, insisting on strings as well – no doubt to mitigate the problems of intonation and ensemble created by a huge band of wind and brass instruments. On 28 March the Duke of Montague, Master General of the Ordnance, wrote to Charles Frederick, 'Comptroller of His Majesty's Fireworks as well as for War as for Triumph', in semi-literate English:

> Now Hendel proposes to lessen the nomber of trumpets, &c. and to have violeens. I dont at all doubt but when the King hears it he will be very much displeased. If the thing war to be in such a manner as certainly to please the King, it ought to consist of no kind of instruments but martial instruments. Any other I am sure will put the King out of humour, therefore I am shure it behoves Handel to have as many trumpets, and other martial instruments, as

possible, tho he dont retrench the violins, which I think he shoud, tho I beleeve he will never be persuaded to do it.

Whether Handel did indeed 'retrench' the violins, in accordance with the King's wishes, is not known. But it is likely that, as usual, he got his own way. His score calls for twenty-four oboes, nine horns, nine trumpets, three sets of timpani, twelve bassoons, a contrabassoon and a serpent (curved wooden wind instrument, the bass of the cornett family); and since two separate sources mention a 'band of 100 musicians' at the first performance, it would seem that the wind and brass were doubled by strings, as invariably happened at later, indoor, performances in Handel's lifetime. Handel was, however, forced to drop his initial objection to a public rehearsal in Vauxhall Gardens. This took place on 21 April, and attracted an audience of more than twelve thousand (at 2s. 6d. a ticket), causing a three-hour jam on London Bridge (the only one open to wheeled traffic at the time). Handel's music duly launched the fireworks celebrations on 27 April, and seems to have gone down well, though the display itself was marred by rain, while part of the specially built pavilion accidentally caught fire.

The Fireworks Music is a French-style suite in the Versailles tradition, consisting of an overture and a succession of contrasted dances. In the Ouverture, Handel creates music of rolling grandeur from the simplest diatonic material: note, for instance, how he conceals the inevitable limitations imposed by the natural brass instruments of the day by subtly varying the harmonisation of the main theme on each of its three appearances; or how, in the Allegro section, with its antiphonal exchanges between various instrumental combinations, Handel expands and develops the conventional opening fanfares with a thrilling sweep and sense of colour.

In calculated contrast, the first of the dances, a tripping Bourrée, is lightly scored for two upper parts and bass, without brass; the rising chromatic scale in the second part, first in the middle, then in the top voice, is a piquant touch amid the overwhelmingly diatonic surroundings.

Next comes a siciliana entitled 'La paix' (Peace), with surprisingly full, rich orchestral textures for a gentle pastoral movement, followed by 'La réjouissance' (Rejoicing), a rollicking Allegro, based, again, on fanfare-like motifs and marked to be played three times by different instrumental groupings.

To conclude his celebratory *pièce d'occasion* Handel writes a pair of minuets. The first is a delicate, rather wistful piece in D minor (the only sustained use of the minor key in the suite), while the second, in the work's home key of D major, recalls Purcell's great trumpet tunes in its mixture of nobility and easy memorability.

Richard Wigmore © BBC

Water Music, Suite no. 2 in D major (*c*.1717)

1 [Allegro]
2 Alla Hornpipe
3 Trumpet Minuet
4 Lentement
5 Air

Though his greatness was readily acknowledged by his contemporaries, Handel was always aware of the need to cultivate the right contacts. When he first arrived in England in 1710, not long after taking up a post back in Germany as Kapellmeister to the Elector of Hanover, he quickly moved to establish himself not only in operatic circles, but also at court. By the time of Queen Anne's death in 1714, he had composed music for a number of royal and state occasions and won himself a royal pension. Furthermore his failure to return to Hanover and consequent dismissal from the Elector's service the previous year was not as reckless a move as it might at first have appeared. Everyone knew that, when the ailing Anne died, the Elector would succeed to the British throne, and there is evidence to suggest that the Hanoverian court was quite happy for Handel to remain in London as a useful source of inside information.

The story that Handel won back the Elector's favour after the latter's accession as George I by secretly providing music for a royal river party on the Thames must therefore be taken with a pinch of salt. Nor is it clear when this event took place, since there were royal river parties every summer between 1715 and 1717, and Handel's music is known to have been heard only at the last of them. It is not unlikely that Handel composed for all of them, however, and that the so-called Water Music is thus a compilation.

A newspaper account of the 1717 party, which went at night in open barges from Whitehall to Chelsea and back, tells us that the King liked Handel's music 'so well, that he caus'd it to be plaid three times on going and returning'. He had good reason to, for this is an extraordinarily rich collection of pieces, covering a wide range of styles and employing an orchestra whose diverse colourings must have been a revelation to English ears. The nineteen pieces fall into three groups, each characterised by a different instrumental sonority: those with trumpets and horns (the latter quite a novelty in the orchestras of the time) are clearly suited to bold outdoor performance; while in the movements with flute we perhaps hear the more intimate sounds destined to accompany the royal repast onshore at Chelsea. The five movements of this suite all feature a pair of trumpets, rendering them fit, one can imagine, to provide a grand ending to the night's festivities.

Lindsay Kemp © BBC

Paul Hindemith (1895–1963)

A gifted violinist from an early age, Hindemith studied violin and composition at Frankfurt's Hoch Conservatory. After serving in the German army and while leader of the Frankfurt Opera Orchestra (1915–23) he produced three controversial one-act operas. Throughout the 1920s he was a prominent member of Europe's modern-music scene, playing viola in the Amar Quartet, which he founded in 1921 to promote new music. Alongside his often expressionistic, parodying scores of the 1920s he wrote much instrumental music for amateurs and children (*Gebrauchsmusik*), believing in the importance of music's role in everyday life. His opera *Mathis der Maler* (1934–5), based on the life of the painter Matthias Grünewald, was banned by the Nazi regime, and in 1935 Hindemith left Germany. He counselled on Turkey's music education programme and in 1940 he moved to the USA, becoming professor at Yale where he taught and founded the Yale Collegium Musicum as a workshop for the revival of early music. Though he took US citizenship in 1946 he returned to Europe in 1953 to a post at Zurich University. Despite his early experimentalism, Hindemith's polyphonic skill represented a distinctly German trait that could be traced back to Bach.

Symphonic Metamorphoses on Themes of Weber (1943)

1. Allegro
2. *Turandot* Scherzo: Moderato
3. Andantino
4. March

In 1939, shortly after Hindemith finally left Nazi Germany for good and went into exile in Switzerland, he began discussions with the choreographer Léonide Massine about possible new ballet collaborations. One of these was to be a ballet based on the music of Weber. Early in 1940 Hindemith moved across the Atlantic to become visiting professor at Cornell University; in April that year Massine brought his troupe to Cornell, but they quarrelled over the proposed music and decor for the ballet, and the scheme was shelved. Hindemith decided to use his drafts for the Weber ballet as the basis of a four-movement orchestral piece, and the result was the Symphonic Metamorphoses on Themes of Carl Maria von Weber, completed in August 1943. Premiered in January 1944 by the New York Philharmonic under Arthur Rodzinski, it went on to become, and remains to this day, one of Hindemith's best-loved and most-performed compositions; so his work for Massine was hardly wasted.

The first and last of the four movements are based on nos 4 and 7 respectively of Weber's *Huit pièces pour le pianoforte à 4 mains*, Op. 60, published in 1818. Hindemith's third movement is also based on a piano-duet work, no. 2 of Weber's Six Pieces, Op. 10, from 1809. The second movement, though, is based on a tune from the overture that Weber composed that same year for a production of Schiller's *Turandot*. As well as transposing some of Weber's themes to new keys, Hindemith treats them entirely in his own mature manner, reshaping their contours, putting them through modulations and tricking them out with species of counterpoint unheard of in Weber's time, to produce a largely good-humoured orchestral showpiece.

The '*Turandot* Scherzo' goes further, in fantasy and stylistic mixing, than the other three movements. In fact, it is a rare glance back to the sins of Hindemith's youth: perhaps the oriental court of *Turandot* reminded him of the Burmese setting of *Das Nusch-Nuschi*, his scandalous one-act opera of 1920. In the opening section he surrounds the little pentatonic 'Chinese' tune with a veritable thesaurus of oriental-sounding percussion (note its first few notes in vast-spaced augmentation on tubular bells), while the central episode, based on a naughtily syncopated variant, is a rollicking fugue in jazz style for winds and percussion, recalling his own essays in swing and ragtime from the early 1920s. Practically every instrument appears, however briefly, as a soloist in this orchestral tour de force.

The '*Turandot* Scherzo' casts its shadow forward into the first movement. There is an indefinably Eastern flavour to the rather truculently assertive A minor subject with which the work begins (though this is perhaps sufficiently accounted for by the fact that the original Weber piano piece is headed 'All'ongarese' – 'In the Hungarian style').

The brief slow movement (Andantino) consists of a tender minor-key melody, introduced by woodwind, and two variations on it: the first shared between strings and woodwind, and the second featuring a cool, elaborate flute counterpoint to the principal theme.

Peremptory fanfares set the finale in motion. This is a spirited march, sometimes playful, sometimes passionate. While the first theme is still a little truculent, the second, starting in a mood of comic excitement, grows increasingly triumphant as the movement proceeds and, together with the fanfares, brings the proceedings to an end in decisive and swaggering style.

Gustav Holst (1874–1934)

Holst was born in Cheltenham and studied under Stanford at the Royal College of Music, where he befriended his contemporary Vaughan Williams. He began his professional career as a trombonist, but later became a committed teacher, his principal positions being at St Paul's Girls' School (1905–34) and at Morley College (1907–24) in London. His keen encouragement of community and non-professional music-making is evidenced by his numerous military and children's songs, as well as his *St Paul's Suite* for strings. Like Vaughan Williams he was inspired by folk music, which he used to great effect in his *Somerset Rhapsody* (1907); but an interest in Eastern mysticism also fed into many of his works, among them the early opera *Savitri* (1908), the four groups of *Choral Hymns from the Rig Veda* (1908–12) and the large-scale cantata *The Hymn of Jesus* (1917). An interest in astrology bore fruit in his orchestral suite *The Planets* (1914–17), a work whose unique and fascinating sound-world has been widely aped by film-music composers. Ten years later he wrote his own favourite among his works, the tone poem *Egdon Heath* (1927).

***The Planets*, Op. 32** (1914–17)

1 Mars, the Bringer of War
2 Venus, the Bringer of Peace
3 Mercury, the Winged Messenger
4 Jupiter, the Bringer of Jollity
5 Saturn, the Bringer of Old Age
6 Uranus, the Magician
7 Neptune, the Mystic

Gustav Holst began composing his symphonic suite *The Planets* in mid-1914, starting with 'Mars', which he completed just before the outbreak of the First World War in August.

'Venus' and 'Jupiter' were written in the same year, and 'Saturn', 'Uranus' and 'Neptune' in 1915; 'Mercury' came last, and Holst did not complete the instrumentation until 1917, even though some of his friends and pupils acted as amanuenses in preparing the very large full score for the biggest orchestra he had ever used. In 1918 he was appointed Musical Organiser for the YMCA in the Near East, based at Salonika in Northern Greece – and as a farewell present his friend and fellow-composer Balfour Gardiner paid for a private performance of *The Planets* to be given at the Queen's Hall before an invited audience, by the Queen's Hall Orchestra conducted by the young Adrian Boult. Albert Coates gave the suite its first complete public performance in 1920. The piece has never looked back.

More than eighty years after that memorable private performance, *The Planets* remains by far Holst's most popular work. Indeed, its popularity came to distress him during his lifetime. Doubtless in his later years, in works such as *The Hymn of Jesus*, *Egdon Heath* and the *Choral Fantasia*, he achieved things that were more profound, more perfectly realised in structure, and even more deeply personal in their expression. But *The Planets* is the first fully effective statement of his maturity; its conception has a boldness, excitement and epic sweep that remain immediately impressive after a hundred hearings; and, however uneven it may be, it enshrines some of Holst's most characteristic musical utterances in highly memorable forms.

The unevenness has, in any case, been overstressed by critics (following the lead of Holst's daughter Imogen, the severest of them all). Viewed simply as a display of orchestral mastery on the largest scale, the work would have been a tour de force for any English composer working in 1914. It is one of the twentieth century's great colouristic showpieces (though far more than just that); and it is easy to forget, through over-familiarity, what an original contribution Holst was making to the orchestral literature. Though a Russian and French heritage is generally apparent in the handling of the instruments, and though there are hints too of Stravinsky and of Schoenberg's Op. 16 Five Orchestral Pieces (which Holst had recently heard), the cumulative sound is like that of no other work, as the material is like that of no other composer. And both sound and material are made wonderfully appropriate to their subject-matter.

In her biography of her father, Imogen Holst quotes him as writing to a friend:

> As a rule I only study things that suggest music to me. That's why I worried at Sanskrit. Then recently the character of each planet suggested lots to me, and I have been studying astrology fairly closely. It's a pity we make such a fuss about these things. On one side there is nothing but abuse and ridicule, with the natural result that when one is brought face to face with overwhelming proofs there is a danger of going to the other extreme. Whereas, of course, everything in this world – writing a letter for instance – is just one big miracle. Or rather, the universe itself is one.

Despite this clear indication of his interest, most commentators on Holst have tended to minimise the importance of astrology and the esoteric both for his own thinking and for *The Planets* in particular. However, recent research by Raymond Head has revealed the extent of Holst's involvement with these subjects, and his significant connection with the noted astrologer Alan Leo (1860–1917), whose book *The Art of Synthesis* (1912), discussing the character of each of the seven then-known planets in a separate chapter, may well have coloured Holst's conception of his orchestral suite. Leo's chapter headings are similar to the titles Holst gives his movements, and they actually coincide with 'Neptune, the Mystic', while 'Mercury, the Winged Messenger' is to be found in Leo's earlier volume, *How to Judge a Nativity*, which Holst also possessed.

Raymond Head points out that the order in which Holst introduces the seven planets is neither heliocentric nor according to their relative distance from the Earth, but in a clear astrological pattern 'symbolising the unfolding experience of life from youth to old age'. The suite is thus inspired by the prime astrological concept of planetary influences, by which each planet possesses its own distinct elemental character, disseminated through the heavens by its rays (and thus influencing the natal horoscope of every human being). Holst essentially offers a series of character portraits of the planets (and also to some extent of the classical gods from which they take their names), an idea that gives clear focus and function to every movement of his vast symphonic suite.

'Mars', the astonishing opening movement, is a kind of heavy toccata that seems like an apocalyptic pre-vision of the European conflict that was brewing throughout the summer of 1914. With its merciless rhythmic ostinato for timpani, harps and strings played col legno (with the wood of the bow), howling chromatic melodic spans for trombones and tubas, and rampant tenor tuba and trumpet fanfares, it remains the classic musical statement of the horrors of mechanised warfare – before that term was ever coined. It's an astonishing demonstration of the orchestral mastery towards which Holst had been groping for many years – but which here bursts out in full panoply.

'Venus', by contrast, is cool emotional assuagement, with an uncharacteristic tinge of romance entrusted to solo violin. Flutes, celesta, harps and strings – whose vibrant sonorities bring the movement to an end – also supply the most characteristic timbres of 'Mercury'. This is the archetypal example of Holst's protean, quicksilver scherzos, quick as an arrow, insubstantial as air, bracingly bitonal.

Perhaps more conventional in effect but always stirring in performance, the galumphing cross-rhythms, carnival merriment and great big tune of 'Jupiter' make it a scherzo of another sort, with a different world's worldliness, and a broader humour entirely.

To pass from its triumphal coda to the aching coldness of 'Saturn', one of Holst's most personal, slow, haunted processions of mortality, is a salutary shock, comfort giving way to the comfortless in its insistent brazen bells.

'Uranus' – third, last and most sheerly fantastic of the work's scherzos – is a brilliant, sardonic evocation of 'the God of Bewildering Untruth' (in Malcolm Sargent's phrase). Beginning with a peremptory brass invocation on the notes G, E flat, A, B (all good magicians need a personal sigil or magical mark – turn these notes into German nomenclature, and you get the only 'musical' letters in the name GuStAv H.), the movement develops into a wild dance of alchemical athleticism that ends with a glimpse of real, dumbfounding marvels out in the cosmic beyond.

It is to these purely metaphysical regions that 'Neptune' finally beckons us, in the suite's most rarefied music. Marked pianissimo throughout, and scored with exquisite refinement, its soft, disembodied harmonies and distant, wordless women's chorus evoke a release from the confines of space and time. In the 'endless', and certainly cadence-less, alternations of the final two chords, we seem to be contemplating the mysteries of eternity.

Colin Matthews (b. 1946)

Along with his brother David, also a composer, Colin Matthews worked with Deryck Cooke on his performing version of Mahler's uncompleted Tenth Symphony. He later acted as musical assistant to Benjamin Britten and has edited for publication some of Britten's early pieces – including the Double Concerto, first performed in 1997. As founder and executive producer of the NMC recording label he has been a notable champion of British contemporary music. His own scores include chamber music (three string quartets, two oboe quartets) and extended works for voice and ensemble (*The Great Journey*, 1988, and *Continuum*, 2000). His orchestral output has grown since 1992 through associations with the London Symphony Orchestra (1992–9) and the Hallé

Orchestra, and from a number of BBC commissions, including the large-scale choral-orchestral 'Renewal', which was commissioned for the 50th anniversary of Radio 3 in 1996, and won a Royal Philharmonic Society Prize.

'Pluto, the Renewer' (1999–2000)

When I was asked to add 'Pluto' to *The Planets*, I had mixed feelings. To begin with, *The Planets* is a very satisfying whole, and one which makes perfect musical sense. 'Neptune' ends the work in a way wholly appropriate for Holst – an enigmatic composer, always likely to avoid the grand gesture if he could do something unpredictable instead. How could I begin again, after the music has completely faded away as if into outer space? And, even though Pluto was discovered four years before Holst's death in 1934, I am certain that he never once thought to write an additional movement (he was in any case decidedly ambivalent about the work's huge popularity). In addition, the matter of Pluto's status as a planet has for some time been in doubt – it may well be reclassified as no more than an asteroid, thrown way out of the main asteroid belt between Mars and Jupiter. (Another intriguing fact about Pluto is that its elliptical orbit means that for the past twenty years it has been nearer to us than Neptune.)

Yet the challenge of trying to write a new movement for *The Planets* without attempting to impersonate Holst eventually proved irresistible. It quickly became clear that it would be pointless to write a movement that was even more remote than 'Neptune' unless the whole orchestra were to join the chorus off-stage. Nor did I feel that I should rely on the astrological significance of Pluto, which is more than a little ambiguous (not that astrologers seem to have problems with a minute planet of which they have only just become aware). In any case I am a thoroughgoing sceptic as far as astrology is concerned and, apart from choosing the title 'Pluto, the Renewer', left that aspect to one side.

The only possible way to carry on from where 'Neptune'

leaves off is not to make a break at all, and so 'Pluto' begins before 'Neptune' has quite faded. And it is very fast – faster even than 'Mercury': solar winds were my starting-point. The movement soon took on an identity of its own, following a path which I seemed to be simply allowing to proceed as it would: in the process I came closer to Holst than I had expected, although at no point did I think to write pastiche. At the end the music disappears, almost as if 'Neptune' had been quietly continuing in the background.

Pluto is dedicated to the memory of Holst's daughter Imogen, with whom I worked for many years until her death in 1984, and who I suspect would have been both amused and dismayed by this venture.

Arthur Honegger (1892–1955)

Honegger composed in almost every medium: opera, symphony, oratorio, ballet and chamber music, as well as for the new mediums of radio and film. He was born in northern France to Swiss-German parents and studied at the Paris Conservatoire, alongside Milhaud and Ibert. By 1918, the year of his graduation, he had completed a string quartet, a violin sonata, a piano trio and around twenty songs. Along with Poulenc, Milhaud and others he became a member of the group known as Les Six, from whose flippant rhetoric he dissociated himself early on. He continued to embrace modernism, however, in the 'symphonic movements' *Pacific 231* (depicting a steam train in motion) and *Rugby* (1928, reflecting the fashionable glamour of sport), and in the ballet *Skating Rink* (1921). His greatest achievements stem from his more serious compositions: the oratorio *Le roi David* (1921), and *Jeanne d'Arc au bûcher* (1934–5, in collaboration with Claudel); and his five symphonies – of which the third, 'Liturgique' (1945–6), represented the composer's musings on mankind's search for peace following the German occupation of France.

Pacific 231 (1923)

All true trainspotters know that Honegger's title is a tautology. Far from being the locomotive number, '231' is the Continental code for the arrangement of its wheels, translating into English as 4-6-2, which is alternatively known as 'Pacific'. Not that such details need bother listeners to this fusion of a machine-age tone poem and a study in rhythm – any more than they bothered the composer, who took a somewhat anthropomorphic attitude to the subject. 'I have always had a passion for locomotives,' he said. 'To me, they are living beings whom I love as others love women or horses.' Stoking the fires of desire indeed.

Even so, *Pacific 231* is hardly an obsessive's piece. Honegger had a broad, humanistic view of life, and this crossing of the tracks belongs among the brave-new-world artistic evocations of technical and industrial progress that sprang up internationally after the Great War. Other musical instances include Antheil's *Ballet mécanique*, Mosolov's *Iron Foundry* and Varèse's *Amériques.*

It begins and ends with organised rhythmic compressions and extensions – not much like steam-train noises if you're thinking literally again, but a clever way to poeticise the effect or, as Honegger put it, 'to express in terms of music a visual impression and physical enjoyment'. Once the train has built up momentum, it moves inexorably towards a state of functional ecstasy, great weight achieving high speed, as the brass sing out over the full orchestra.

Leoš Janáček (1854–1928)

Born in the northern Moravian village of Hukvaldy, Janáček trained as a teacher and organist, and was choirmaster at an Augustinian monastery before becoming choirmaster of the Brno Philharmonic Society. He achieved recognition late in life with the first Prague performance of his opera *Jenůfa* (1894–1903) in 1916, when he was sixty-two. His new-found success, and his intense infatuation with Kamila Stösslová, a married woman thirty-eight years his junior, resulted in a highly productive dozen years before his death, during which he wrote his operas *Katya Kabanova* (1919–21), *The Cunning Little Vixen* (1921–3) and *The Makropulos Case* (1923–5), two string quartets (1923 and 1928), and the blazing Sinfonietta and *Glagolitic Mass* (both 1926). He was a passionate Czech nationalist and collected Moravian folk songs earlier in his career, but worked in a more modern idiom than his compatriots Smetana and Dvořák. He was intrigued by everyday sounds and by nature, and made a particular study of Czech speech-rhythms, which characterised his vocal and non-vocal writing.

Sinfonietta (1926)

1 Allegretto
2 Andante
3 Moderato
4 Allegretto
5 Allegro

As perspectives shift regarding early twentieth-century music, the name of Janáček comes sharply into focus. If the higher priests of modernism, as far as audiences are concerned, still seem to sit atop the ivory tower, Janáček now speaks more and more vividly to new generations of listeners. From being the wild and woolly provincial that Prague ideologues in the first decades of the twentieth century perceived him to be, his position is now secure as one of the finest opera composers of the modern age and the principal operatic representative of his native land. Several years before Janáček's operas joined the international repertoire, he was known largely as the composer of a Sinfonietta incorporating large numbers of brass instruments: the irresistible urgency of its opening was the stuff of which television signature tunes were made, but more than this, the Sinfonietta communicated its composer's all-consuming enthusiasm for life.

As with many of Janáček's works, for instance the operas *Katya Kabanova* and *The Cunning Little Vixen* or the two string quartets, the existence of the Sinfonietta had nothing to do with abstract concerns – the interface between life, experience and creativity was crucial to its composition. The second decade of the twentieth century was a difficult time for Janáček. Although he was a central figure in the musical life of Brno, the Moravian capital, his impact on the musical establishment of Prague was still minimal. Most worryingly of all, his third opera *Jenůfa*, his most significant work to date, had still not been accepted for performance in the Prague National Theatre, despite a succession of premieres from the more conventional mediocrities of the native tradition. The acceptance of *Jenůfa* in 1916, albeit 'improved' by the chief conductor Karel Kovařovic, was the crucial event in a remarkable change in fortune and led to an extraordinary personal renaissance. Janáček came in from the cold of provincial exclusion to be taken up by the intellectual great and good, though notably not by the wing that persisted in seeing the true line of development in Czech music as passing from Smetana to Fibich, Kovařovic and Ostrčil – for them, Janáček and his friend Dvořák remained unfactorable features in the landscape, large but largely to be ignored.

Public success initiated an extraordinary run of luck for Janáček. He fell in love with a much younger woman, and his nation, for nearly three hundred years a political backwater of the Austrian Empire, at last had the prospect of independence. The latter years of the First World War made it clear that Austrian dominance over its empire was at an end, and even before 1918 Janáček was turning his hand to writing music of a 'new era'. A string of masterpieces, initiated by the second part of the opera *The Excursions of Mr Brouček* – set in late medieval Prague and, not surprisingly, celebrating the virtuous side of the Czech character – advanced and secured a reputation that had languished for too long.

The seed of what Janáček disarmingly described as a 'nice little Sinfonietta' was a fanfare composed for a gymnastics festival in 1926; it rapidly grew into the Sinfonietta that exists today – dedicated to the Czechoslovak Armed Forces. Janáček's aim, as he enthusiastically described, was to celebrate 'contemporary free man, his spiritual beauty and joy, his courage, strength and determination to fight for victory'. He also added a further gloss on his intentions for the pictorial content of the work with titles for each of the movements: 'Fanfares', 'The Castle', 'The Queen's Monastery', 'The Street' and 'The Town Hall'. With a certain justifiable chauvinism, Janáček added that the Sinfonietta also drew its inspiration from a vision of the growing greatness of the Moravian capital, Brno, in the early days of Czechoslovak independence.

The tremendous fanfares which open the Sinfonietta, and also bring it to its blazing conclusion, were prompted by a military band concert heard in the southern Bohemian town of Písek. After this prelude the succeeding four movements are a characteristically Janáčekian re-creation of a traditional sinfonia in four movements. But nothing from this period in his life is conventional, and at the climax of the second movement an exhilarating and breezy Maestoso introduces a new theme, though it bears a distant relationship to the fanfares of the introduction. The reflective mood which begins the third movement is dispersed by threatening gestures from the trombones which cause the temperature to rise towards a wild Prestissimo before the calm of the opening returns. A chattering, insistent Scherzo, once again with a main melody that nods towards the trumpet fanfare of the opening, leads to the finale. Starting quietly it swells to a triumphant climax crowned by the return of the opening fanfares.

Jan Smaczny © BBC

Taras Bulba, rhapsody for orchestra (1915–18)

1 The Death of Andriy
2 The Death of Ostap
3 The Prophecy and Death of Taras Bulba

As early as 1905 Janáček, with his lifelong enthusiasm for Russian literature, had thought of basing an orchestral work on Gogol's account of the Cossack hero Taras Bulba, who in 1628 spearheaded the campaign against the Poles. It was not, however until 1915, with the future independence of his own homeland under threat, that he began to write his 'musical testament' to the courage of the Russians, traditionally the saviours of the Slav peoples. Janáček originally subtitled the work (which he completed in 1918) 'Slav Rhapsody', and it is clearly Taras Bulba's words at the stake to which he was finally condemned – 'there is no fire nor suffering in the whole world which could break the strength of the Russian people' – that lie at its core.

By the time Janáček had completed *Taras Bulba*, the Prague premiere of *Jenůfa* (26 May 1916) had at last earned him international recognition. Already in his sixties, he was about to enter the tremendous creative upsurge that lasted for a further decade and resulted in four operas as well as the Sinfonietta and the *Glagolitic Mass*. *Taras Bulba* bears witness to his ability to harness the elemental expressive strength integral to his highly original compositional style as an outlet for his fervently-held belief in the future of Slavonic culture.

In this symphonic rhapsody, Janáček followed closely the three major episodes of the story of Taras Bulba: the death at his own hands of his deserter son Andriy; that of his second son Ostap, tortured and killed by the Poles; and his own confrontation with death when, with the flames leaping around him he is granted a vision of the indomitable courage of the Russians. The first part brings into focus the conflict between love and war: Andriy discovers that the girl he loves, the daughter of a Polish nobleman, is among the starving inhabitants of the besieged town of Dubno. He determines to find her, and, under cover of night, enters the town by a secret underground passage. The ardour of his quest is evoked by a haunting melody on the cor anglais over a throbbing string accompaniment; this alternates with the distant sound of the organ and the more immediate and threatening bells that the composer apparently intended to represent the anguished prayers of the besieged. This swells into a passionate love scene punctuated by gunshot-like cymbal clashes and a menacing motif on the trombones that constantly alludes to the approach of the Cossacks. Andriy is drawn into the battle, fighting on the enemy's side, but when Taras Bulba appears, he hangs his head in shame and accepts death at his father's hands. In his last moments he recalls his great love as Taras gallops back into battle.

In the second part a harsh string ostinato pitted against a sustained background of woodwinds and harp seems to impel the second son, Ostap, overcome by grief at his brother's defection and death, towards his own fate. Captured and tortured by the Poles, his screams of pain (on the E flat clarinet) pierce through the wild Mazurka which the enemy dance to celebrate their victory, and are heard by his father, whose brief appearance amid the throng is made known by the blast of trumpets. The Poles stamp out another victory dance – a krakowiak – in the fast section as Taras, nailed to a tree, awaits his own death. He is granted the final satisfaction of witnessing his faithful warriors escape their captors by a daring feat of horsemanship, and, left alone with his pain, his spirit finds liberation through his insight into the true essence of the Russian people. The whole piece has progressed inexorably to this magnificent climax in which the organ and brass combine in a chord progression of transcendental power.

Felix Mendelssohn (1809–47)

The grandson of a philosopher, Mendelssohn combined musical precociousness of a Mozartian order with a lifetime of learning and travelling. He gave his first performance as a pianist aged nine, and composed thirteen early string symphonies between 1821 and 1823. By the time of his first visit to London, aged twenty, he had already spent time in Paris. After returning to Berlin, where he had studied philosophy with Hegel, he undertook a major tour of Europe, which inspired the 'Scottish' and 'Italian' Symphonies as well as the *Hebrides* overture. He became conductor of the Lower Rhine Music Festival, Music Director of the Leipzig Gewandhaus Orchestra (1835), and founded the Leipzig Conservatory (1843). He showed vivid scene-painting ability in his overtures (especially *A Midsummer Night's Dream* and *Calm Sea and Prosperous Voyage*), but he produced some of his best work in the standard classical forms: an enduringly popular Violin Concerto, seven string quartets and two piano concertos. Of his three oratorios, *Elijah* was especially favoured by the English choral societies of the Victorian era.

Overture, *The Hebrides* ('Fingal's Cave'), Op. 26 (1830; rev. 1832)

In 1829 Mendelssohn paid a visit to England and, like Dr Johnson and Keats before him and Queen Victoria after him, felt the lure of the Highlands. In July he set off with his Berlin friend Karl Klingemann, poet and diplomat, recently appointed to London. On 7 August they were in Tobermory, on Mull. At five o'clock next morning they took the steamer to the Isle of Staffa, 'with its strange basalt pillars and caverns'. Klingemann tells also that the barometer sank and the sea rose, and his travelling companion found himself 'on better terms with the sea as a musician than as an individual or as a stomach'. (Mendelssohn had already cursed his overture *Calm Sea and Prosperous Voyage* during the rough Hamburg–London crossing.) Klingemann goes on: 'We were put out in boats and lifted by the hissing sea up the pillar stumps to the celebrated Fingal's Cave. A greener roar of waves surely never rushed into a stranger cavern.' Fingal was the hero of an epic poem, said to have been translated in 1762 from the Gaelic Ossian, but largely the work of the translator, Macpherson, himself.

Mendelssohn wrote to his family: 'In order to make you understand how extraordinarily the Hebrides affected me, the following came into my mind there,' and enclosed the opening ten bars of this overture (twenty bars as he first laid them out, on two staves but with scoring and dynamics indicated). But the letter enclosing the music is dated 7 August, the day before the trip to Staffa; and it doesn't sound as though Mendelssohn was in any condition to jot down the first bar 'while actually standing in Fingal's cave', as Donald Tovey had him do!

In fact, it was over a year (December 1830, in Rome) before Mendelssohn had time to complete his work, calling it *Die einsame Insel* (the solitary isle). Almost at once he reworked it, then calling it *Die Hebriden*. In 1832 he revised it again, writing to his sister Fanny that the 'would-be working-out of the movement tastes more of counterpoint than of train oil, sea gulls, and salted cod – it should be just the other way round'. According to Larry Todd, all the revisions reflect this process of compromise between the poetic images and the demands of formal unity. The score was finally printed as *Fingalshöhle*.

If its conception was less romantic than one would like to think, the overture as we finally have it is not one whit less so. It provokes speculation about illustrative music, the changing of natural sights and sounds into crotchets and quavers. There is no direct imitation, but how easy it is to hear waves, wind, gulls, and to feel the lift and surge of the sea! It has much to do with the scoring – timpani rolls, sustained high notes, billowings in between. The main motif is brief enough to keep its identity when smooth or ruffled, and when channelled along new keys. A storm blows up in the development. In the recapitulation, the beautiful second subject is becalmed. It is fascinating that such a spontaneous-sounding piece should have been the product of so much thoughtful and hard-working revision.

© Diana McVeagh

A Midsummer Night's Dream, Overture, Op. 21 and Incidental Music, Op. 61 (1826, 1843)

Overture
Nocturne
Scherzo
Wedding March

Mendelssohn's music for Shakespeare's magical comedy *A Midsummer Night's Dream* embodies two small miracles: first, that as a seventeen-year-old boy he was capable of writing a concert overture not only of such accomplishment but also in such perfect sympathy with the play; second, that at twice that age he was able to recapture the atmosphere of the Overture so completely in his incidental music for a stage production.

The Overture was composed at the Mendelssohn family home in Berlin – much of it, apparently, in a summer house in its garden – in July and August 1826. A well-educated and widely read young man, Mendelssohn was inspired to write it by Schlegel's German translation of the play. According to the memoirs of his older friend Adolf Bernhard Marx (backed up by a surviving draft manuscript), Marx encouraged Mendelssohn to carry out the project, but then criticised his first attempt: after the opening, which was as it is in the final version, he found the continuation 'perfectly praiseworthy' but with 'no *Midsummer Night's Dream* in it'. When

Mendelssohn had got over his initial sulky reaction, Marx explained that he felt the Overture should include not only the fairies and the lovers, but also 'the ruffians and even Bottom's lovesick ass's braying'. Mendelssohn fell in with Marx's ideas, and the completed Overture was first performed in the family house later in 1826. A public performance followed in Stettin (now Szczecin) early the following year, and the piece soon became widely popular: it was a staple item in Mendelssohn's concert programmes on his visits to England. However, he did not publish it until 1832, and then only in orchestral parts and a piano-duet reduction. The full score appeared in 1835, in a volume of 'Three Concert Overtures' – the others were *The Hebrides* (*Fingal's Cave*) and *Calm Sea and Prosperous Voyage* – dedicated to the Crown Prince of Prussia.

Five years later, the Crown Prince ascended the Prussian throne as King Friedrich Wilhelm IV, and set out to re-establish Berlin as a major cultural centre. One of his coups was to persuade Mendelssohn to accept the post of director of the music section of the city's Academy of Arts. In 1842, the King commissioned Mendelssohn to write incidental music for productions of three plays, including *A Midsummer Night's Dream*. Mendelssohn added to his Overture another twelve numbers: entr'actes, songs for women's (or children's) voices, shorter cues for entrances and exits, and melodramas to underscore key speeches. In some of the numbers he quoted ideas from the Overture; and in all of them he re-entered the magical world he had created seventeen years earlier. The production took place at the New Palace in Potsdam in October 1843, with the music under the composer's direction (and after no fewer than twelve orchestral rehearsals); the first concert performance was given in one of Mendelssohn's London concerts the following May. While full performances of the score remain rare treats, especially in the theatre, the more substantial entr'actes are familiar in the concert hall and on disc; and the main section of the last entr'acte is known everywhere simply as 'the Wedding March'.

The Overture, in E major, is scored for a modest orchestra including no more than pairs of woodwinds, horns and trumpets, but with a part for the ophicleide, a now-obsolete bass keyed bugle (it is usually played on a tuba). The piece begins with a sequence of four quiet chords which transport the listener immediately to the enchanted wood of Shakespeare's play; they usher in a minor-key dance for divided violins, in the fairy vein of which Mendelssohn was such a master. Further ideas evoke in turn the ceremony of Duke Theseus's court, the two pairs of young lovers lost in the wood, and the 'rude mechanicals' who meet there to rehearse their play (complete with the 'hee-haw' of Bottom when he is magically disguised with an ass's head). The central development section is dominated by the fairies; but it ends with a disjointed version of part of the lovers' theme, suggesting a heartbreak which is healed by the return of the magical chords. The chords make a last reappearance in the coda, after a reflective reminiscence of what has earlier been a jubilant idea. In its final transformation, this is a virtually exact quotation from a chorus of sea-nymphs in Weber's last opera, *Oberon*, a piece distantly related to Shakespeare's *A Midsummer Night's Dream* and similarly an exploration of fairyland; Mendelssohn must surely have intended the reference as a memorial tribute to Weber, who had died in London in June 1826.

The Nocturne, also in E major, comes after the end of Act 3, when the lovers have all fallen asleep, and the fairy Puck has put right the havoc he has previously wreaked among them by a second application of his magic potion. Although the middle section hints at past agitation, the serene main melody, for solo horn with bassoons, clarinet and double basses, reflects Puck's closing words, 'all shall be well'.

The Scherzo precedes Act 2, in which the play first moves to the 'wood near Athens' and enters the domain of the fairies. It is in G minor, which is also the key of the quicksilver scherzo of Mendelssohn's string Octet of 1825 (subsequently orchestrated); and, like that movement, it is in a through-composed sonata form. There is a second subject for strings in octaves, quiet yet firm, and a development section including some sudden, menacing crescendos to fortissimo. The piece audibly belongs to the same world as the fairy dance of the Overture, though there is no direct quotation, and the emphasis this time is as much on the woodwind as on the strings – especially, in the closing stages, on the first flute.

The Wedding March introduces the scene of the marriage of Theseus and Hippolyta in Act 5. It is in the key of C major, though the harmony of the main theme initially feints towards the 'fairy' E minor; there is a strenuous first trio section in G major, and a soaring second trio in F major which leads back to the last return of the march. The scoring adds to the orchestra of the Overture a third trumpet, essential for the triadic build-up of the opening; a pair of cymbals, tactfully employed; and three trombones, which come into their own in the coda.

Anthony Burton © BBC

Darius Milhaud (1892–1974)

Milhaud was one of the twentieth century's most prolific composers, producing more than 440 works, including twelve symphonies, fifteen operas and eighteen string quartets (of which nos 14 and 15 can be performed either separately, or together as an octet). He entered the Paris Conservatoire initially as a violinist, and whilst there wrote his first opera, *La brebis égarée* (1910–15). The music of Brazil had an impact on his music after he spent a two-year period there (1917–18) as secretary to the poet and French ambassador Paul Claudel. After the war, he discovered jazz in London and the USA, writing his ballets *Le boeuf sur le toit* (1920) and *La création du monde* (1923), the latter combining Latin and jazz music with avant-gardist tendencies. Milhaud travelled widely and following the Second World War taught in California and at the Paris Conservatoire. His quirky humour is seen in his choice of texts, which include Daudet's poems inspired by a florist's catalogue (*Catalogue de fleurs*, 1920) and descriptions from a brochure of farming equipment (*Les machines agricoles*, 1919).

~ ***Le boeuf sur le toit*, Op. 58** (1920)

The Ox on the Roof or The Nothing-Doing Bar, a fictional American nightspot, was the stage setting of a 1920 scenario by Jean Cocteau, friend and mentor to the group of composers known briefly as Les Six. Having collaborated the previous year with Picasso and Satie – another Six mentor – on the ballet *Parade*, Cocteau now turned to Raoul Dufy for design and the up-and-coming Six-ist Darius Milhaud for music, and presented the city's fashionable audiences with a kind of high-art vaudeville. The score has long outlived the milieu, and was soon claimed for concert hall and dance stage. As time has gone by, the presence of Paris, in the music at least, has also seemed to fade in the face of two other locations: Provence and Brazil.

The first is more a matter of colour than abstract technique. Most of Milhaud's large output sounds as firmly rooted in the bright and ominous shades of his native Provence as a painting by Cézanne: featuring prominent and diverse wind tone, the lines interact energetically and build up by vivid contrast rather than blend. But the mark of Latin America is unmistakable. At the end of the Great War, Milhaud worked for the French diplomatic service, which sent him to Brazil from 1917 to 1919 as assistant attaché to Paul Claudel, the writer. It must have been an unusually cultured and adventurous mission, at least off-duty. The mix of Latin and black music in Rio de Janeiro made a huge impact on Milhaud. *Le boeuf* is one of several works he wrote in immediate response, and the effect was lasting, reinforced by the Brazilian bands that went to play in Paris.

For *Le boeuf*, Milhaud made his own extended version of the Brazilian *choro* form, in which varied melodic forays are held together by a recurring refrain. He was prodigal with his material – apart from the refrain, there is little repetition – and he uses his Western composer's privilege not only in varying the refrain itself but in stealing or inventing tunes from several Latin styles. The first episode, for instance, is more like a tango. Right through, the energy and inventiveness never flag, and somehow at the end that refrain still sounds fresh and ready for the rest of the night's dancing.

Robert Maycock © BBC

La création du monde, Op. 81 (1923)

Ten years after the celebrated opening night of *The Rite of Spring*, the Théâtre des Champs-Élysées in Paris was the scene of another controversial premiere: the first performance of *La création du monde* ('The Creation of the World'), given by Rolf de Maré's Ballets Suédois on 25 October 1923. Its inspiration was the art of Africa. This was reflected in the decor and costumes by Fernand Léger, and in the scenario, based on African mythology, by Blaise Cendrars (and presumably also – though he seems to be the forgotten man of the whole enterprise – in the choreography of Jean Börlin). But what provoked the indignation of the Parisian public was that in his score Darius Milhaud matched these African elements with what he felt to be their musical equivalent, the idiom of jazz.

Milhaud had discovered jazz in 1920 at the Hammersmith Palais, in the commercialised form played by the white American Billy Arnold and his band; later, his enthusiasm had been encouraged by his friend and compatriot Jean Wiéner, an accomplished jazz pianist. But his most significant encounter with jazz had come on a visit to New York in 1922, when he had made many visits to Harlem – some years before such excursions became fashionable – to listen to bands playing in the New Orleans tradition in theatres and dance halls. The orchestra of *La création du monde* is a slightly enlarged version of some of the groups he had heard there: six woodwind, four brass, piano, percussion, and what would be a solo string quintet except that the place of the viola is taken by an alto saxophone. There are many other touches of jazz colouring in the scoring, not least in the array of percussion instruments; and the influence of jazz is also perceptible in some of Milhaud's inflections of the melodic line, harmonic progressions and syncopated rhythms. But the great achievement of *La création du monde* is that it goes beyond this kind of mimicry of elements of the jazz idiom to recreate, in several extended passages, the frenzied exuberance and the free-for-all precision of an improvised jam session.

The ballet consists of an overture and five short scenes, played without a break, and linked by repetitions of some of the main themes. After the quiet ending of the overture, the curtain rises on a darkened stage, on which three giant deities pronounce magic spells around the formless mass of pre-creation matter, to the accompaniment of a jazz fugue. In the gentler second scene, as the stage gradually lightens, the giants bring forth trees, and then a succession of animals. The third scene, in a more animated tempo, sees the emergence of a man and a woman. The fourth scene, even more lively in tempo at the beginning and end, but with a broader middle section, is their dance of desire, accompanied by witch-doctors and soothsayers. In the short final scene, the man and woman are left alone, united in an embrace which presages the beginning of the human race.

Wolfgang Amadeus Mozart (1756–91)

More than two hundred years after his death, Mozart stands as a focal figure of Western classical music, not only for his astonishing precocity and inventiveness, but for the staggering range and quality of his music. His father Leopold, a violinist, paraded his son's talents around the European capital cities when he was as young as six. By sixteen, Mozart had absorbed a variety of musical fashions, having travelled to England, Germany, France, Holland and Italy. He worked for the Prince-Archbishop in Salzburg during his teens, producing symphonies, concertos and masses as well as operas. In 1780 he went to Munich to compose *Idomeneo*, his first great opera, and the following year he moved to Vienna, where in the four years beginning in 1782 he wrote fifteen of his twenty-seven piano concertos, which he played himself in concerts. *The Marriage of Figaro*, the first of his three operatic collaborations with the court poet da Ponte, appeared in 1786, followed by *Don Giovanni*. In his last three years he set his last da Ponte text, *Così fan tutte*, and wrote two highly contrasted operas, *Die Zauberflöte* and *La Clemenza di Tito* (1791), as well as the three final symphonies (Nos 39–41) and the gem-like Clarinet Concerto. He left his Requiem incomplete at his death.

Serenade in D major, K250, 'Haffner' (1776)

1 Allegro maestoso – Allegro molto
2 Andante
3 Menuetto and Trio
4 Rondeau: Allegro
5 Menuetto galante and Trio
6 Andante
7 Menuetto and Two Trios
8 Adagio – Allegro assai

On 22 July 1776 Marie Elisabeth Haffner, daughter of a wealthy Salzburg merchant and former mayor who had died four years earlier, married Franz Xaver Späth. The bride's brother, Sigmund, asked his friend Mozart to write a serenade for performance in the garden of the Haffner family home on the evening before the wedding. Such pieces were customarily performed in Austrian and southern German towns to celebrate important social and domestic occasions: university graduation ceremonies, civic functions, weddings, birthdays, name-days and other landmarks in the lives of prominent citizens – such as Sigmund Haffner's own ennoblement in 1782, for which Mozart provided another serenade (subsequently shortened and revised as the so-called 'Haffner' Symphony, K385). Indeed, by the summer of 1776, Mozart already had around twenty divertimentos and serenades to his credit: some light and unpretentious, scored for small wind band; others more weighty, such as the first of two six-movement divertimentos scored for a pair of horns and solo strings, written for the Countess Lodron; the Serenata notturna, which exploits echo effects between two contrasting instrumental groups; and the septet divertimento, K251, for oboe, two horns and solo strings, said to have been written for Nannerl Mozart's name-day. The 'Haffner' Serenade, however, represents both a beginning and an ending: it is the first substantial orchestral work of Mozart's maturity, and the last of a group of four large-scale serenades written between 1773 and 1776, which each contain a mini-violin concerto – a traditional feature of the Salzburg serenade.

The 'Haffner' Serenade also marks the end of Mozart's preoccupation with the violin as a solo-concerto instrument; from this time onwards he was to favour the piano. Taught by his father, he was a highly competent violinist, and his five violin concertos – all youthful works but still mainstays of the repertory – date from the same period as the four concertante serenades. Indeed, the scale and virtuosity of the 'Haffner' Serenade's concerto suggest that this may well have been the '*Finalmusik* with the Rondo' that Mozart played in Munich in

September 1777 at the house of one Count Salern. And in December, Leopold wrote to ask his son (by then in Mannheim) if he could not have his 'Haffner music', his Concertone or one of his Lodron serenades performed there to impress the Elector. This may also have been the 'Nachtmusik' which the violinist Kolb played, together with an unspecified Mozart concerto, in front of Herr von Mayer's house in Salzburg on 9 July 1778, while Mozart and his mother were in Paris: Leopold and Nannerl listened to it across the water, and thought it sounded charming.

The Serenade has eight movements, originally preceded by a separate March (K249) which opened and closed the festivities. The key – D major – is the customary one for works of a ceremonial nature, favoured by both Wolfgang and his father. The outer movements are both straightforward, tonic-key sonata structures in bright, festive style, scored for strings with pairs of oboes, bassoons, horns and trumpets (but no drums). Both are prefaced by slow introductions. The main musical interest of the work is centred in the second, third and fourth movements, which together constitute a G major violin concerto. A lightly scored Andante, in which the solo line is supported by strings with pairs of flutes, bassoons and horns, precedes a disturbingly angular G minor Menuetto with a brighter Trio, in which the soloist holds centre stage, accompanied by winds alone. Then comes the *pièce de résistance* – the sparkling, elegantly feminine Rondeau with its plangent E minor central episode – formerly known to aspiring violinists in Fritz Kreïsler's rather heavy-handed 'arrangement'.

These three movements are balanced in the Serenade's second half by a graceful A major Andante in free rondo form scored for strings with pairs of oboes and horns, framed by two Minuets. The first is a 'Menuetto galante' with a Trio scored for solo strings; while the second is a more forthright affair with a pair of Trios, the first featuring solo flute and bassoon, the second more fully scored with pairs of flutes, bassoons, horns and trumpets.

However her marriage turned out, Elisabeth Späth was a lucky bride. Mozart's 'first great orchestral work – an amalgam of the highest technical ability and musical genius' (H. C. Robbins Landon) was a wedding gift which would outlast all the dinner services and silver teaspoons in the world.

Serenade in D major, K320, 'Posthorn' (1779)

1 Adagio maestoso – Allegro con spirito
2 Menuetto and Trio: Allegretto
3 Concertante: Andante grazioso
4 Rondeau: Allegro ma non troppo
5 Andantino
6 Menuetto and Two Trios
7 Finale: Presto

Mozart's orchestral serenades and divertimentos are not heard in live performance very often, but then, unlike his piano concertos and symphonies, they were never intended for the concert hall. Instead, they were composed to adorn the superior functions and celebrations of Salzburg town life – a grand wedding perhaps, or more commonly the festivities surrounding the end of the university academic year – and would have been performed outdoors amid the balmy air of an Austrian summer evening, to an audience who one imagines was paying less than full attention.

The 'Posthorn' Serenade was composed for one of those end-of-year student celebrations in August 1779, the seventh time Mozart provided the *Finalmusik* (as he would have called it), and its layout of movements reflects the course such festivities took. The hired musicians would meet in the town in mid-evening, march to the Prince-Archbishop's summer residence at Mirabell, perform their Serenade there, then return to the Universitätsplatz to perform it again in front of the professors and students. A *Finalmusik* would thus consist of marches for the musicians framing a leisurely spread of as many as seven or eight movements of differing types.

Although this may appear at first a rather casual collection, it tends to fall into three distinct categories, namely symphonic, concerto and dance: in K320 the dances are movements 2 and 6, while movements 1, 5 and 7 are the symphonic, and 3 and 4 the concerto movements. Mozart himself evidently saw it this way, because he later disassembled this 'one-off' Serenade to give all three groups of movements independent existence: nos 3 and 4 as a 'Concertant-Simphonie' performed in Vienna in 1783; nos 1, 5 and 7 as a 'symphony' published in 1791; and nos 2 and 6 inserted into a set actually used to accompany dancing. Presumably he had another use for the marches too, since they are not part of the Serenade manuscript, and subsequently acquired a separate number (335) in Köchel's catalogue of Mozart's works.

K320, then, is not a dashed-off occasional piece, but one whose constituent parts Mozart was happy to recycle in front of more discerning audiences – and justifiably, too, since it demonstrates much of the orchestral experience and expertise he had gained at the time he wrote it. At the beginning of 1779 he had returned from a sixteen-month tour which had included visits to Mannheim and Paris, where the *sinfonia concertante* (a lightweight concerto for several instruments) was a popular form, and no doubt he was remembering this, together with some of the fine wind playing he had heard on his travels, when he conceived the third and fourth movements of the Serenade. A violin would usually be the soloist here, but Mozart substitutes lovingly intricate cameos for pairs of flutes, oboes and bassoons.

The three symphonic movements, too, are in their dynamism every bit the equal of the 'real' symphonies (nos 32–4) which Mozart was composing at this time. The first movement mixes the vigour and excitement of an operatic overture with the compositional resource of a symphonic allegro, and even goes a step further in novelty by opening with a slow introduction (a device he would not use in a symphony for another four years) and then reintroducing it later on in the movement. The minor-key Andantino is a movement of uniquely Mozartian depth and sadness, the sort which pops up from time to time to surprise us even in such public entertainment pieces as this; and the Finale bustles with energy and momentum.

The two Menuetto movements provide the Serenade's most relaxed and unbuttoned music, opportunities for Mozart to indulge in some humour. The first features a poky little duet for solo flute and bassoon, while the second brings a piccolo into the limelight, followed by the instrument which has given the Serenade its name, the posthorn. The fanfares of this rather basic trumpet – normally used by coachmen to signal their arrival and departure – were perhaps a reminder to the students that they would soon be on their way. Within two years Mozart himself would have left Salzburg behind, and the genre of the orchestral serenade with it.

Eine kleine Nachtmusik, K525 (1787)

1 Allegro
2 Romance: Andante
3 Menuetto and Trio: Allegretto
4 Rondo: Allegro

From February 1784 until his death Mozart kept a catalogue of newly completed works. As well as the date and a brief description, he entered the musical beginning of each composition (the latter necessary to identify pieces, such as dances, that had similar titles and were in the same key, as well as providing a useful aide-mémoire to the content of individual works). On 10 August 1787 the composer recorded the following: 'A small Night Music (Eine kleine Nacht Musik), consisting of an Allegro, Menuett [*sic*] and Trio, Romance, Menuett and Trio, and Finale – 2 violins, viola and bass instruments'.

The title 'Nachtmusik' was a reasonably common one, the German equivalent of the Italian *notturno*, and had been used by Mozart previously to describe his Serenade in E flat (K375). It signalled a work that was to be played not in a formal concert but at some social event like a birthday or a name-day. In the closely packed streets and courtyards of Vienna, where in poor weather wily pedestrians could cross the inner city without getting wet, it was possible to book ensembles of players to serenade an unsuspecting recipient; the biographies of both Haydn and Mozart give charming and humorous accounts of such occasions. This particular 'Nachtmusik' was 'kleine' because its movements were fewer and on a smaller scale than most works of this type, and were less ambitious than movements in contemporary quartets, concertos and symphonies by the composer; also the performing resources consisted of strings only. Mozart, therefore, was giving a routinely precise description of a work that had probably been quickly composed. In later generations the description became a title, a symbol of Mozart's greatness, if not an embodiment of the values of the whole of Western classical music.

It is not known why Mozart composed the work and its rise to popularity in the second half of the nineteenth century luckily postdates the period when legends and anecdotes about the composer were at their most fertile. During the summer of 1787 the Mozart family lived outside the city walls of Vienna, to the east, in the Landstrasser Hauptstrasse, where the composer was fully occupied with the opera *Don Giovanni*. The *Nachtmusik* could have been intended for a neighbour or somebody in the city.

Mozart's catalogue clearly indicates that the work had five movements, but only four have survived. The missing movement, the first minuet, was carefully cut out of the autograph early in the nineteenth century by an unknown person anxious to own something by the then venerated Mozart; it has never been rediscovered.

Although Mozart undoubtedly conceived the work for an

ensemble of one player per part, orchestral performances are now the norm – understandably, since original music for string orchestra from this era is very scarce. The title of the slow movement, Romance, is again a generic one, indicating a movement with a simple, highly memorable melody interrupted by a contrasting section.

Modest Petrovich Mussorgsky (1839–81)

For most of his lifetime, and for some time afterwards, Mussorgsky was considered something of a dilettante. In 1856 he entered a regiment of the Guards in St Petersburg and in the same year, with no training in composition, made an abortive attempt at an opera. Conscious of his inexperience he took lessons from Balakirev, through whom he became part of the group of composers known as 'The Five', and as early as 1859 determined on his path as a nationalist composer. Beset by a series of misfortunes – chronic alcoholism, financial problems and his need to take on work as a civil servant – his output suffered. His vivid orchestral tone poem *Night on a Bare Mountain* (1867) and his virtuosic piano suite *Pictures at an Exhibition* (1874, later orchestrated by Ravel, among others) are regularly performed, but his greatest achievement was in opera, despite the fact that he only managed to complete *Boris Godunov* (1868–9, based on Pushkin). His other major opera *Khovanshchina*, as well as other works, first appeared posthumously, heavily edited by Rimsky-Korsakov.

Night on the Bare Mountain (1867), arr. (1881–6) by Nikolay Rimsky-Korsakov (1844–1908)

Mussorgsky had his first serious thoughts of a musical depiction of evil goings-on in 1860, when he told Balakirev he had been commissioned to write a stage work, 'a whole act to take place on the Bare Mountain (from Mengden's drama *The Witch*)'. Nothing seems to have come of this project, but by 1866 he was thinking about an orchestral tone poem on a similar theme, evidently influenced by Liszt's *Totentanz*, which he had heard in March that year. In July 1867 he wrote to the historian Vladimir Nikolsky:

> If my memory serves me right, the witches used to gather on [the Bare Mountain] . . . gossip, play tricks and wait for their boss – Satan. When he arrived they, i.e. the witches, would form a circle around the throne on which the boss was sitting, in the form of a kid, and sing his praises. When Satan had become sufficiently frenzied with the witches' praise, he would give them the order for the Sabbath, selecting for himself those witches that took his fancy.

These are the scenes that Mussorgsky depicts in his vivid score, known in full as *St John's Night on the Bare Mountain*. He completed it, appropriately enough, on the eve of St John's (Midsummer) Day 1867, but its audacious harmonies and acerbic orchestral effects were criticised by Balakirev and the piece was never performed in Mussorgsky's lifetime.

However, Mussorgsky found a further use for this 'Bare Mountain' music in 1872, when he collaborated with Rimsky-Korsakov, Borodin and Cui on the opera-ballet *Mlada*. It fell to Mussorgsky to compose (in Act 3) a scene on Mount Triglav, in which mystic, obscene rites were to be performed by the mythological Chernobog (the Black God) and other diabolical beings. For this Mussorgsky recast the Bare Mountain music, adding text for solo voice and chorus. But this version, too, was destined for oblivion, for the impresario who had commissioned the opera-ballet became nervous about the expense, and the project was abandoned.

Later still, in 1880, while he was composing his comic opera *Sorochintsy Fair*, Mussorgsky decided to include an interlude in which Cherevik, a young peasant, sleeps and dreams of evil happenings on Bare Mountain. So the Mount Triglav scene from the abortive *Mlada* was duly inserted, complete with the choral and solo vocal parts, and with the music modified where necessary.

When Rimsky-Korsakov came to put Mussorgsky's manuscripts in order after his death in 1881, he found the *Sorochintsy Fair* version of the 'Bare Mountain' music the most satisfactory of the three, though even this he thought unsuitable for performance or publication. He therefore composed a new version, 'preserving in it all that was best and coherent in the Mussorgsky and adding as little of mine as possible', but characteristically altering details of harmony, orchestration and structure where he felt them to be ill-judged. It took him about two years to organise the score to his satisfaction, and he conducted it in St Petersburg in October 1886.

Mussorgsky's original scores are now fairly familiar: the first (1867) version, stark, austere and strikingly individual, has now been recorded and is frequently performed. But it is Rimsky's version that has become widely known in the West, and, if lacking the elemental force of Mussorgsky's own writing, it nevertheless impresses through its brilliant, full-blooded orchestration.

Pictures at an Exhibition (1874), orch. (1922) by Maurice Ravel (1875–1937)

Promenade
1 Gnomus
Promenade
2 Il vecchio castello
Promenade
3 Tuileries (Dispute d'enfants après jeux)
4 Bydło
Promenade
5 Ballet of the Unhatched Chicks
6 'Samuel' Goldenberg and 'Schmuyle'
7 Limoges: Le marché (La grande nouvelle) –
8 Catacombae (Sepulchrum romanum) – Cum mortuis in lingua morta
9 The Hut on Hen's Legs (Baba Yaga) –
10 The Great Gate of Kiev

Victor Hartmann's promising career as an architect, painter, illustrator and designer was cut short by his death at the age of thirty-nine in 1873. In February 1874 there was a memorial exhibition of his work in St Petersburg, and this was the stimulus for Mussorgsky to compose his piano suite *Pictures at an Exhibition* to the memory of his dead friend.

The Hartmann exhibition contained four hundred items. Only a quarter of them have survived, and of these only six relate directly to Mussorgsky's music. Among the lost works are the inspirations behind 'Gnomus', 'Bydlo', 'Tuileries', 'Il vecchio castello' and 'Limoges'. This hardly matters, though, because Mussorgsky's imagination goes far beyond the immediate visual stimulus. It tells us little about the music to learn that the half-sinister, half-poignant 'Gnomus' was inspired by a design for a nutcracker (you put the nuts in the gnome's mouth), or that 'Baba Yaga' was a harmless and fussy design for a clock, hard to connect with Mussorgsky's powerful witch music.

Mussorgsky, a song composer of genius, could sum up a character, mood or scene in brief, striking musical images, and this is what he does in *Pictures*. The human voice is never far away: 'Bydlo', a picture of a lumbering ox-cart, and 'Il vecchio castello' ('The Old Castle') could well be songs; some of the Promenades and 'The Great Gate of Kiev' suggest the choral tableaux in his operas; in 'Tuileries' we hear the cries of children playing and in 'Limoges' the squabbling of market-women. 'Goldenberg' is a particular case: do the blustering of wealthy Samuel and the whimpering of poor Schmuyle represent two different characters? Or is there something more sinister here, a reflection of the anti-Semitism endemic in Russian society? The combination of the two types of music suggests that this is perhaps a single person bearing two forms of the same name; and that however smart and prosperous he becomes, deep down 'Samuel' will always remain 'Schumuyle' from the ghetto.

Pictures might have been just a loose collection of pieces, but Mussorgsky in fact devised something far more complex and interesting. The 'Promenade' that links the pictures is on one level a framing device, representing the composer (or perhaps the listener) walking around the exhibition. Sometimes he passes directly from one picture to another, without reflection. Sometimes he is lost in thought. On one occasion, he seems to be distracted by seeing something out of the corner of his eye (the false start to the 'Ballet of the Unhatched Chicks'), and turns to look more closely. 'Cum mortuis' is not itself a picture, but represents the composer's reflections on mortality after seeing the drawing of Hartmann and two other figures surrounded by piles of skulls in the Paris catacombs. The composer is also drawn personally into the final picture as the Promenade emerges grandly from the texture of 'The Great Gate of Kiev'.

Although Mussorgsky must have played *Pictures* to his friends, there is no record of any public performance until well into the twentieth century. It was indeed only after the success of Ravel's orchestration that performances of the piano version became at all common. The piano writing of *Pictures* is often said to be unidiomatic, and Mussorgsky certainly never cared for conventional beauty of sound or pianistic virtuosity for its own sake. There are aspects of the texture that are hard to bring off successfully, such as the heavy chordal style of some Promenades, 'Bydlo' and 'The Great Gate of Kiev'; the tricky repeated notes in 'Goldenberg' and 'Limoges'; and the sustained tremolos in 'Cum mortuis' and 'Baba Yaga'. But these are all part of Mussorgsky's desired effect.

Pictures at an Exhibition has been subjected to many arrangements (including one by Sir Henry Wood, founder-conductor of the Proms), but none so brilliant as Ravel's, which was commissioned by the Russian conductor Serge Koussevitzky, and first performed by him in Paris on 19 October 1922. Ravel was already a great enthusiast for the music of Mussorgsky. He had collaborated with Stravinsky on orchestrating parts of his opera *Khovanshchina* for Diaghilev's Paris performances in 1913, and far preferred Mussorgsky's barer original score of *Boris Godunov* to the more colourful edition by Rimsky-Korsakov. With *Pictures* there are only three major differences between Ravel's orchestration and the piano original, which he knew only from Rimsky's 1886 edition: the omission of a Promenade between 'Goldenberg' and 'Limoges'; the addition of some extra bars in the finale; and the dynamics of 'Bydlo', which Mussorgsky marked to begin loudly, not with a slow crescendo.

Ravel's orchestral colours and techniques are far more elaborate than anything that Mussorgsky might ever have conceived, so his work must be considered more a free interpretation than a simple transcription. Some of his choices of instrumentation for solo passages are unforgettable: the opening trumpet, for example, or the alto saxophone in 'Il vecchio castello' and the tuba in 'Bydlo'. Even more remarkable is the range of colour that Ravel achieves, and the way in which the essence of the music is faithfully reproduced while the original piano textures are presented in an altogether different sound medium. Ravel and Mussorgsky could hardly have been more different as men and as composers, but *Pictures at an Exhibition* has justly become famous as a collaboration between two great creative minds.

Andrew Huth © BBC

Francis Poulenc (1899–1963)

Poulenc's first published work, the vocal/ensemble piece *Rapsodie nègre* (1917), established his place in chic avant-garde Parisian circles: there he had met Satie and was drawn into the group that became known as Les Six. After three years' study (1921–4) with Charles Koechlin he scored further success with his Diaghilev ballet *Les biches* (1924). Poulenc's urbane wit triumphed in the *Concert champêtre* (1927–8; a harpsichord concerto written for Wanda Landowska), and the Concerto for Two Pianos (1932). Later in the 1930s, the death of a friend and a visit to the shrine of Notre Dame de Rocamadour inspired a return to Catholicism; the *Litanies à la vierge noire* (1936), Mass (1937) and *Quatre motets pour un temps de pénitence* (1938) followed in close succession. For the rest of Poulenc's life devoutness and ironic wit formed characteristic strands in his work, exemplified by his two full-scale operas, the surreal comedy *Les mamelles de Tirésias* (1939–44) and the religious tragedy *Dialogues des Carmélites* (1953–6). His songs were largely written for the baritone Pierre Bernac, with whom Poulenc collaborated as pianist until the end of his life.

***Les biches*, suite** (1923)

1 Rondeau
2 Adagietto
3 Rag-Mazurka
4 Andantino
5 Final

Much of Poulenc's music from his twenties and early thirties is a helter-skelter of tragic pose and genuine emotion, high camp and sheer glee. Sophisticates and ordinary listeners have always loved it, though until recently the sober-minded types in between tended to look down on it, much as they belittled the 'self-pity' in Tchaikovsky. Such half-aware homophobia is hardly the frame of mind in which to approach the milieu of the Ballets Russes and Serge Diaghilev, begetters of *Les biches*, the work that hustled Poulenc into the fashionable public eye when he was twenty-four. 'Dear Diaghilev, irreplaceable Diaghilev, you were the wonderment of my twenties,' he said later. 'I owe you my most violent aesthetic shocks.'

The couturier Germain Bongard seems to have had the idea of this ballet with songs, originally to be called *Les demoiselles* ('the girls') before the composer seized on a word that means both 'doe' and 'darling' and was once a term for a kept woman. For its Monte Carlo premiere on 6 January 1924, with choreography by Bronislava Nijinska and designs by Marie Laurencin, there were seventy-two rehearsals and the performance received eight curtain-calls. By May it had been seen in Paris, and the Ballets Russes brought it to London in 1925 and 1926.

Poulenc always valued the music's 'cynical freshness'. Later he rescored it so that the vocal parts – in three numbers that borrow seventeenth-century songs – became optional. But an inconsequential scenario has still restricted its scope for revivals, and the music's popularity stems from the concert suite, which simply leaves out the overture and the sung movements. Its most famous two numbers come first.

Introduced by three expectant bars for the lifting of the stage curtain, the Rondeau rips the drapery aside with an in-your-face tune: here I am, says Poulenc, and there's nobody quite like me, one-quarter Stravinsky and one-quarter Mozart and the rest all my own. Just as personally, the mood switches without warning into a desolation so abject you can hardly believe it, like Tchaikovsky with curdled harmonies, and straight back again. Then in the Adagietto comes another Poulenc prototype, the melody that in anybody else's hands would be corny but in his holds a fine balance between poise and pathos. Rag and Mazurka get thoroughly confused before the spirit of a latter-day Mozart at his cheekiest takes over for the rest of the suite.

Robert Maycock © BBC

Sergey Prokofiev (1891–1953)

An *enfant terrible* in his earlier years, Prokofiev entered the St Petersburg Conservatory aged thirteen, creating a stir with his early taste for rhythmic energy and grating dissonance. A rich period around the time of the Revolution brought the lyrical First Violin Concerto and the 'Classical' Symphony, before a spell in the USA, where his opera *The Love for Three Oranges* and the Third Piano Concerto were unfavourably received. He went on to Paris, drawn to the epicentre of the avant-garde, before moving his family to the USSR in 1936. Adopting a more direct, lyrical style in line with prevailing socialist-realist ideals, he produced the ballet *Romeo and Juliet* and the children's tale *Peter and the Wolf* (both 1936), the film music for Eisenstein's *Alexander Nevsky* (1938) and *Ivan the Terrible* (1945), and the epic opera based on Tolstoy's *War and Peace* (1943). Despite his compliant efforts, Prokofiev was denounced by Communist officials in 1948 ('the unfeeling essence of his music is alien to our reality'), though he had managed to placate them by 1951, when he won the Stalin Prize.

~ ***Romeo and Juliet*, Op. 64, Suites nos 1, 2 and 3** (1935–6; arr. 1936/1946)

Romeo and Juliet was Prokofiev's greatest achievement in the field of ballet music. In it, after his earlier one-act works, he produced a full-length score worthy to stand alongside the masterpieces of Tchaikovsky. Its strength of narrative and characterisation, its coherent use of thematic material, its richness of invention, and its sheer danceability have all made it irresistibly attractive to ballet companies and choreographers. In Britain we are most familiar with Kenneth MacMillan's version for the Royal Ballet, first seen in 1965; but the international repertoire also contains versions by, among others, Leonid Lavrovsky, Frederick Ashton and John Cranko.

It was in 1934 that Prokofiev conceived the idea of a ballet based on Shakespeare's tragedy *Romeo and Juliet*. It was first intended for the Kirov Theatre in Leningrad but, after a political purge, the company cancelled the project. Prokofiev then signed a new contract for the work with the Bolshoi Theatre in Moscow. He worked out a scenario with the Leningrad theatre director Sergey Radlov, keeping close to the outline of Shakespeare's plot – except that at the end they originally planned a happy ending, until this was vetoed by the Bolshoi. Prokofiev drafted the score, at high speed, between May and September 1935, and then went on to orchestrate it. The ballet was put into rehearsal at the Bolshoi that autumn, but after several months it was dropped, because the music was thought impossible to dance to. In the end, the first production was mounted by a Yugoslav company in Brno, Czechoslovakia, in December 1938. The work was eventually presented in the USSR by the Kirov, in January 1940; for this production (choreographed by Leonid Lavrovsky) Prokofiev made some additions and changes to the score. It reached the Bolshoi only in 1946.

Even before *Romeo and Juliet* was seen on stage, however, some at least of its music was heard in the concert hall, in the form of two 'symphonic suites' which Prokofiev compiled in 1936. He added a third suite some ten years later. These suites are very much concert pieces: the movements are arranged into well-balanced sequences, without any attempt at a résumé of the story; some are heavily cut, omitting subsidiary episodes, passages of narrative, or reminiscences of themes associated with particular characters; some are even conflations of two or three different sections of the full ballet score, with newly composed transitions. However, where the orchestration of the suites diverges from that of the ballet, the suites may well preserve Prokofiev's original scoring; he is known to have thickened some of his writing during rehearsals for the Kirov production, after the dancers complained that they could not hear the orchestra from the stage.

Scythian Suite, Op. 20 (1915)

1 The Worship of Veles and Ala
2 Chuzhbog and the Dance of the Evil Spirits
3 Night
4 March of Lolly and Procession of the Sun

Given a famously riotous premiere by the Ballets Russes in Paris in 1913, Stravinsky's *Rite of Spring* offered a revolutionary response to the musical potential inherent in the 'primitive' material of Russian folk song. Though an admirer of Stravinsky's masterpiece, the young Sergey Prokofiev had by then already successfully established his own iconoclastic style in which barbaric elements played havoc with the premises and expectations of late-Romantic musical language. And no doubt the legendary impresario Diaghilev had already marked out the author of the scabrous *Suggestion diabolique* and *Toccata* as another possible composer for his Ballets Russes. Even so, their collaboration, when it came, was not without problems. Having rejected plans for a dance piece derived from Prokofiev's Second Piano Concerto and for an opera based upon Dostoyevsky's *The Gambler* (which Prokofiev nevertheless later completed), Diaghilev encouraged the composer to write a 'primeval' ballet, 'Ala and Lolly', on the subject of the ancient Scythians, whose nomadic empire (on what later became Russian soil) was said to have reached its zenith around 400 BC. Prokofiev did so, only to find that Diaghilev had lost interest and scrapped the project.

Undaunted, and an inveterate recycler of unused material, the composer reworked the aborted ballet score into the *Scythian Suite* (first performed to great and satisfactory scandal in Petrograd in January 1916). In it he condensed the original, flimsy scenario by the poet Gorodetsky into four concise movements relating the mortal hero Lolly's rescue of Ala, daughter of the sun god Veles, from the clutches of the evil god Chuzhbog.

If the latter bears something of a resemblance to Khaschei in Stravinsky's *Firebird* of 1910, then that is all part of the confection which, though it failed to dent Stravinsky's reputation as high priest of modern music, is inventive, incisive and utterly characteristic of Prokofiev. A case in point is the memorably strident theme that follows the frantic introduction. And if the quieter music that ensues, evoking a sacrifice to Ala, sounds akin to the 'pagan night' of *The Rite of Spring*, then the highly balletic second movement, depicting the wiles of the enemy god, is entirely typical of its composer in its powerful use of charged, propulsive rhythms and extremes of dynamic contrast. The orientalisms of the third movement ('Night') are merely theatrical compared with Debussy's evocations of the East, yet they are striking. The finale depicts an ancient sunrise. Though less subtle than the unforgettable dawn of Ravel's *Daphnis and Chloë* (another Diaghilev promotion from 1912), its raw energy reminds us that, of all natural phenomena, dawn – that essential, daily re-creation of light (and time) in our lives – is among the things that music portrays best.

Nicholas Williams © BBC

Sergey Rakhmaninov (1873–1943)

For most of his life, Rakhmaninov led a dual career as pianist and composer. He graduated from the Moscow Conservatory with his first opera, *Aleko*, and also took to conducting after the disastrous premiere of his First Symphony in 1897 directed by Glazunov. The resulting three-year compositional silence was overcome by hypnosis, and Rakhmaninov soon wrote his highly successful Second Piano Concerto (1901). He made a lucrative tour of America in 1909 (for which he wrote his Third Piano Concerto), and after the Revolution in 1917 he lived in self-imposed exile, largely in the USA. His richly chromatic, broadly lyrical and unashamedly nostalgic style has found many critics, but has ensured his music's popularity among audiences. In addition to his three symphonies and two piano sonatas, he wrote two sets of *Études-tableaux* and *Préludes* for piano, a mighty Cello Sonata, three evocative symphonic poems and a rich setting of the Vespers (*All-Night Vigil*, 1915).

Symphonic Dances, Op. 45 (1940)

1 Non allegro
2 Andante con moto (Tempo di valse)
3 Lento assai – Allegro vivace

In the winter of 1939–40, the Philadelphia Orchestra gave five all-Rakhmaninov concerts in New York to mark the thirtieth anniversary of the composer's American debut (in 1909 he had premiered his Third Piano Concerto in New York, first with Walter Damrosch and then with Gustav Mahler conducting). Rakhmaninov appeared as pianist and conductor; the works played included the first three piano concertos, the *Rhapsody on a Theme of Paganini*, the Second and Third Symphonies, the symphonic poem *The Isle of the*

Dead, and the choral symphony *The Bells*. It was a great retrospective of Rakhmaninov's triple career as composer, pianist and conductor.

That career was now coming to an end. On 11 August 1939 Rakhmaninov had made his last appearance in Europe and shortly afterwards sailed for the USA, one of many artists driven from Europe by the approach of war. In the summer of 1940 he and his family rented an estate on Long Island, and there he composed what was to be his last work. On 21 August he wrote to Eugene Ormandy offering him and the Philadelphia Orchestra the first performance of three 'Fantastic Dances'; when the orchestration was completed two months later, the title had been finalised as Symphonic Dances. The work exists in two versions: for large orchestra, and for two pianos. Rakhmaninov, although an expert orchestrator, was always anxious to have the bowings and articulations of the string parts checked by a professional player, and in this case he enjoyed the assistance of no less a violinist than Fritz Kreisler.

Rakhmaninov was usually reluctant to talk about his music, so we know almost nothing about the background to the composition of the Symphonic Dances. We do know that other works of his owe their existence to some visual or literary stimulus – *The Isle of the Dead*, for example, or several of the *Études-tableaux* – and it seems likely that the composer invested the Symphonic Dances too with a poetic and even autobiographical significance that we can now only guess at. One clue is perhaps provided by the titles Rakhmaninov gave to each movement when playing the score to the choreographer Mikhail Fokine, who had devised a successful ballet to the music of the *Paganini Rhapsody* (Covent Garden, 1939) and had proposed a further collaboration. Rakhmaninov told Fokine that the three dances follow the sequence Midday–Twilight–Midnight.

The first dance ('Midday') is a three-part structure, with fast outer sections in C minor enclosing a slower episode in C sharp minor. It is marked by an extraordinary and at times even eccentric use of the orchestra. After the stamping opening section, with its use of the piano as an orchestral instrument and piercingly strident woodwind calls, the central section offers gently undulating woodwind lines against which appears a great Rakhmaninov melody given at first to a solo alto saxophone – an eerie, melancholy sound, unique in his works.

Towards the end of this first dance a calm spreads over the music, and with a change from C minor to C major comes a broad new theme in the strings against a chiming decoration of flute, piccolo, piano, harp and bells. Rakhmaninov would not have expected this to be recognised as a self-quotation, for it is the motto theme of his ill-fated First Symphony, withdrawn (and the score apparently lost) after its disastrous first and (in the composer's lifetime) only performance in 1897. The failure of this work had been a crippling blow to the young composer, who for some years afterwards had been incapable of further composition. There is no knowing what private significance this quotation now had for Rakhmaninov at the end of his life. Was it an exorcism, perhaps, or a recollection of the early love affair that had lain behind the symphony?

A snarl from the brass opens the second of the dances. This is a symphonic waltz in the tradition of Berlioz, Tchaikovsky and Mahler; and as in movements by those composers, the waltz, that most social and sociable of dances, at times takes on the character of a *danse macabre*. The composer's suggested title 'Twilight' is perfectly suited to this shadowy music, haunted by spectres of the past.

The first four notes of the motto theme from the First Symphony quoted in the first dance have a further significance that reveals itself in the third: they form the beginning of the *Dies irae* plainchant, that *memento mori* which stalks through so much of Rakhmaninov's music. This third dance ('Midnight') is, like the first, a three-part structure. The central section is imbued with a lingering, fatalistic chromaticism; the outer sections, by contrast, contain some of the most dynamic music Rakhmaninov ever wrote. Another significant self-quotation is the appearance of a chant from the Russian Orthodox liturgy which Rakhmaninov had set in his 1915 *All-Night Vigil* (usually referred to as the Vespers). This chant and the *Dies irae* engage in what is virtually a life-against-death struggle; and towards the end of the work, at the point where the *Dies irae* is finally vanquished by the Resurrection hymn from the Vespers, Rakhmaninov wrote in the score the word 'Alliluya' (Rakhmaninov's spelling, in Latin characters).

We cannot tell whether or not Rakhmaninov knew that the Symphonic Dances would be his swansong, but the self-quotations and the range of experience that they contain very much suggest that he did. The first performance was given on 3 January 1941 by the Philadelphia Orchestra under Ormandy. The work received a mixed reception, much as the Third Symphony had done five years before. Apart from the hardly relevant question of whether the musical language was too old-fashioned or not, what seems to have confused everyone at the time was a mysterious quality about the work, its ambiguity of aims and expression. With the passage of time the Symphonic Dances have gradually come to be recognised as one of Rakhmaninov's finest achievements, a work in which the high level of invention and the orchestral brilliance are only further enhanced by the deep sense of mystery that lies at its heart.

Maurice Ravel (1875–1937)

Ravel was a fastidious, perfectionist composer who produced some of the most enduring music of the early twentieth century. Born in the Basque region to a Swiss father and a Basque mother, Ravel studied at the Paris Conservatoire, where he consistently and controversially failed to win the prestigious Prix de Rome. Yet by the time of his final failure, in 1905, he had written impressive works such as *Jeux d'eau* (1901), the String Quartet (1902–3) and the orchestral song cycle *Shéhérazade* (1903). Often cast as an impressionist alongside Debussy, he was also drawn to the simplicity of classical dance forms (*Sonatine*, *Le tombeau de Couperin*), and other dances figure prominently in his output: waltzes (*La valse*, *Valses nobles et sentimentales*), and the *Boléro* (one of many works showing an Iberian influence). Always reclusive, he was deeply affected by the death of his mother, after which he seemed to abandon all close human contact. He conjured up a world of childhood innocence in the ballet *Mother Goose* and the opera *L'enfant et les sortilèges*. He wrote little after his two piano concertos (1929–31), and died a week after a brain operation in December 1937.

Alborada del gracioso (1904–5; orch. 1918)

There may be, as Sibelius said, no statues to critics – unless you count Bernard Shaw – but the critic M. D. Calvocoressi will surely have taken more pride in being the dedicatee of the *Alborada del gracioso* than in any marble effigy of himself. A French Greek active in Paris and later in London, Calvocoressi was an associate and early public champion of Ravel. 'His' piece was one of a set of five for piano, *Miroirs*, that upheld the somewhat controversial reputation Ravel had acquired in his early career, though more on the part of other pieces in the set, such as the enigmatic 'Oiseaux tristes'. The

Alborada is the most straightforward and has always had an independent life as a recital piece. Straightforwardness, all the same, is a relative matter with Ravel. The title implies a morning piece, designed to wake lovers, and performed by a jester. The music consists of a rhapsodic, extended song, preceded and followed by a bout of dance music. From the start, even in the piano version, the 'Spanish' rhythms are a touch exaggerated, the song parodistically mournful, and the conclusion – after a frantic wind-up – a kind of sarcastic laugh. But all that was to develop further when Ravel came to orchestrate the music.

The circumstances were that the ballet impresario Serge Diaghilev, who in the meantime had premiered Ravel's *Daphnis and Chloë*, decided to put together a new work for London to a mixed score: the *Menuet pompeux* by Chabrier, the Fauré *Pavane*, and the *Alborada*. He asked Ravel to make orchestral versions of the first and last pieces, and presented the ballet, *Les Ménines*, at the Alhambra Theatre in 1919. There had been an earlier try-out of the *Alborada* at a Pasdeloup orchestra concert in Paris. At first the music seemed – and seems – like a faithful transcription, full of Ravel's now-expected flair and brilliance, the bassoon taking on the singer's role and giving it an additional pathetic depth. But the more you hear it, the more different it sounds. Exaggeration and parody are much more dominant: surely this huge orchestra is an over-the-top treatment for a simple piano piece. The world, and Ravel, had changed. War (in which Ravel served) had intervened. His music was never the same again. This is the *Alborada* revisited by the composer of *La valse* and, as in that disturbing deconstruction of the Viennese waltz, there now lurks a dark despair beneath the scintillating surface.

Robert Maycock © BBC

Boléro (1928)

Ravel was surprisingly disparaging about his *Boléro*: he would say that the piece contained no music, he approved of the audience member who shouted 'Rubbish' at the première, and he didn't know why the conductor Ernest Ansermet liked it. All the same, he was angry when Arturo Toscanini conducted it, as he thought, too fast. There are all the signs of complex motivations here.

The circumstances were that Ravel had to change his plan late when responding to a commission for Ida Rubinstein and her dance company. He had intended to make orchestrations of piano music by Albéniz, and was annoyed to find that copyright restrictions prevented him. So he went off to see Rubinstein, and a few weeks later started telling people what he was up to instead, in a defensive way, as if the world might think the lack of key changes or symphonic elaboration in *Boléro* was a defect.

Perhaps Ravel just wanted to set himself a musical challenge by limiting his means; we can only guess. He was surprised that the music quickly became popular as a concert piece after its danced premiere at the Paris Opéra in November 1928 (with choreography by Nijinska, designs by Benois). Clearly that was for the 'wrong' reasons. Yet he had surely hit on something more fundamental than he expected, or even accepted.

On one level, all that happens in *Boléro*, apart from the big harmonic surprise at the end, is that a pulse continues unchanged, and alternating melodic lines return in changing orchestral colours. On another, Ravel lavished all his sophisticated skill on making a substantial, perfectly timed form out of these few dimensions. You just try making a crescendo build for ten minutes! He might have 'got away with it', but whether by accident or design he made the same discovery as the American minimalists: less can mean more.

Daphnis and Chloë, Suite no. 2 (1909–12)

1 Lever du jour –
2 Pantomime –
3 Danse générale

Sometimes dubbed the earliest known novel, Longus's prose pastoral *Daphnis and Chloë* was written in Ancient Greek some time in the third century of our era and widely translated in more recent times. The English edition that Penguin Classics published in the last century shows eloquently why. Not only is it a lightly teasing tale of two adolescent lovers who do not know how the opposite sex's body works, it is written with genuine charm and the merest hint of a gentle knowingness. Mikhail Fokine, chief choreographer of the Ballets Russes, which regularly visited Paris in the early twentieth century, suggested it to the company's impresario Serge Diaghilev in 1909, when Diaghilev was looking for scenarios to be set by leading French composers of the day. Ravel was already on the shortlist and Diaghilev decided that this was just the thing for him. After he introduced the two men, they were left to get on with it.

Ravel played his would-be collaborator some piano pieces; then Fokine, with the help of Léon Bakst as interpreter, talked him through the stage version he proposed. There were many discussions and meetings before Ravel went off to compose what needed to be an hour's worth of music. It was to be the biggest orchestral piece he ever wrote. Once it was ready, he played it through to Fokine, who loved almost every note except for one scene he wanted even longer, a raid by pirates that he would have preferred as a series of dances instead of a quick attack. Ravel kept things his way, though Fokine continued to regret not having been more insistent.

The composer had already taken great pains to get the music just right. He completed three sections right up to full score and had them tried out in a concert during 1911. They did not go down well and he temporarily lost interest. Then came the triumphant Ballets Russes premiere of Stravinsky's *Petrushka* later that year, and Ravel realised that international fame beckoned if he could only get this commission right. He extended the finale, which was one of the sections that had disappointed, and added more music to improve the score's proportions. The result, with designs by Bakst, conducted by Pierre Monteux and starring Nijinsky and Karsavina, duly scored its success at the premiere on 8 June 1912.

Since then *Daphnis and Chloë* has been a repertoire piece, though more for orchestras than for dance companies. Ravel never wrote a symphony, and this lavish, dramatic and broadly organised score fits the bill perfectly. Half of it has become even more familiar, to varying degrees, because Ravel made it into two concert suites of some fifteen minutes each, which are less demanding on rehearsal time.

The second suite, comprising the ballet's final scene, has three episodes: a sunrise, culminating in the lovers' reunion after an enforced separation; a symbolic pantomime involving the wooing of Syrinx by Pan; and a declaration of undying love followed by a general party during which, to judge by the rhythmic thrust of the final crescendo, Daphnis is able to show Chloë that he has spent his absence acquiring a little education.

On a musical level, surprisingly little is lost by not knowing what has gone before, apart from some cross-references to principal themes. The luminous sounds of dawn; the suave flute solo for Pan, which at its climax is cleverly shared by all the members of the orchestral family in rapid succession; and the cumulative excitement of the finale that Ravel quite rightly (for most imaginable reasons) made longer – all add up to a mini-symphony of their own that tells its story as clearly as anybody could wish.

Mother Goose, Suite (1908–10; orch. 1911)

1 Pavane of the Sleeping Beauty
2 Hop-o'-my-thumb
3 Little Ugly, Empress of the Pagodas
4 Conversation between Beauty and the Beast
5 The Fairy Garden

Until recently, any composer who restricted his expressive range to the exotic, precious and childlike, and, moreover, generally put forward his own musical ideas under the guise of borrowed styles, would have risked belittlement by modernistic critics. Yet, for whatever psychological reasons – and his private life remains the least scrutable of that of any of the great composers – Maurice Ravel managed to mediate through this oblique and defensive aesthetic some of the most perfectly resolved and unmistakably personal scores of the twentieth century.

The fairy tales of Charles Perrault and the other great French children's writers of the seventeenth and eighteenth centuries were, of course, an entirely legitimate inspiration for *Ma mère l'oye* (*Mother Goose*), the 'cinq pièces enfantines' for piano, four hands, which Ravel composed between 1908 and 1910 for the son and daughter of his friends the Godebskis – one of those cultivated, liberal, bourgeois families immortalised in the intimate canvases of Bonnard and Vuillard. But the 'Pavane of the Sleeping Beauty' is surely also a Ravelian transmutation of the kind of clavecin pieces that were later to inspire *Le tombeau de Couperin*; likewise, if less obviously, the patterns of wandering thirds in the second movement that depict 'Petit Poucet' – our Tom Thumb – following his trail of crumbs. Whether the Chinese 'Chopsticks' patterns on the black keys that portray the Empress 'Little Ugly' taking her bath derive from Debussy's *Pagodes* or from memories of the gamelan orchestras at the 1889 Exposition, the waltz for the 'Conversation between Beauty and the Beast' clearly echoes early Erik Satie – it has been called the fourth *Gymnopédie* – while the sumptuously unrolling four-part harmony of 'The Fairy Garden' sounds like an affectionate tribute to Ravel's teacher, Gabriel Fauré.

The orchestral version, scored in 1911, invokes yet a third means – besides stylistic imitation and the retreat to past times or distant places – which Ravel habitually deployed to maintain a distance between his audience and his own feelings: the idea of orchestration as a technical end in itself, complementary to the actual substance of the music. The score teems with innovations: the chirruping solo violin glissando harmonics that depict the marauding birds in 'Hop-o'-my-thumb', for instance, or the gong-like deployment of the lowest notes of the celesta in the middle section of 'Little Ugly'; the unprecedentedly wide-ranging and melodious contrabassoon for the Beast, or the almost intoxicatingly perfumed string and harp chord that blooms just before the end of the fourth piece. Yet the final wonder is the extent to which these sophistications actually enhance the unique purity and innocence of the original conception.

Pavane pour une infante défunte (1899; orch. 1910)

The house where Ravel was born in Ciboure is just across the river from the historic Maison de l'Infante in St-Jean-de-Luz. It was there, halfway between Madrid and Paris, that the Infanta Maria Teresa of Spain met Louis XIV before their wedding in 1660. This might well have nothing to do with the *Pavane pour une infante défunte* – Ravel once claimed that he chose the title simply because he liked the sound of it – but at least it is not contradicted by his later and more helpful description of the piece as 'a pavane that a little princess might, in former times, have danced at the Spanish court'.

Commenting on the work in the *Revue musicale* in 1912, thirteen years after it was written, Ravel was rather hard on it. 'From this distance I can no longer see its qualities,' he wrote.

'But, alas, I can certainly see its faults: the too flagrant influence of Chabrier and its weak construction.' On both counts, it is difficult to understand what he meant. True, it does bear some resemblance to the 'Idylle' in Chabrier's *Pièces pittoresques* but it is actually closer to the *Pavane* by Gabriel Fauré, his teacher at the Conservatoire at the time. In writing a piece for Parisian salon society – the original piano version is dedicated to the Princesse Edmond de Polignac – Ravel could have found no better model. His *Pavane* is less perfumed than Fauré's but conceptually and texturally the two works have much in common.

Apart from the Infanta of the title, there is nothing specifically Spanish about the *Pavane pour une infante défunte*. Italian in origin though it was, however, the pavane would certainly have been danced at the Spanish court 'in former times' – perhaps even, in Ravel's imagination, by the Infanta Maria Teresa as portrayed at the age of fourteen or fifteen by Velázquez in about 1653. Certainly Ravel could have invented nothing more evocative of some such scene than the opening bars of his *Pavane* with its stately and yet graceful melody on first horn floating over the lute-like accompaniment of pizzicato strings. As for the allegedly 'weak construction', its miniature rondo form – with a timely application of harmonic and dynamic pressure just before the final return of the main theme in enriched colours – seems perfectly well calculated.

© Gerald Larner

Rapsodie espagnole (1907–8)

1 Prélude à la nuit
2 Malagueña
3 Habanera
4 Feria

The *Rapsodie espagnole* dates from Ravel's so-called 'Spanish year'; three out of the four pieces he composed in 1907 were inspired by Spain and Spanish musical culture. The least substantial of the three was the *Vocalise-Étude en forme de Habanera*, which was probably an offshoot of his one-act opera *L'heure espagnole*, on which he worked in the first half of the year, while the third 'Spanish' piece, the *Rapsodie espagnole*, was itself in part based on a much earlier work, the 'Habanera' for two pianos from *Sites auriculaires*, written in 1895 when Ravel was only twenty.

It is not clear why 1907 in particular should have been dedicated to these various expressions of Ravel's fascination with Spanish rhythms (the habanera especially); although it coincided with Manuel de Falla's arrival in Paris, it is clear that Ravel had already been much influenced by Chabrier, reminiscences of whose own orchestral rhapsody *España* (1883) are to be found in the last movement of the *Rapsodie espagnole*, and who had also written a Habanera for piano in 1885.

Ravel's 1895 'Habanera' was in turn influential. Having heard a performance of *Sites auriculaires* in 1898, Debussy asked Ravel if he could borrow the score. Ravel was not best amused to find that several of its features – not only the habanera rhythm, but also the pervasive C sharp ostinato – later appeared in Debussy's 'La soirée dans Grenade' (one of his *Estampes* of 1903); all the more galling since, at the time, there was a tendency among critics to trace everything back to Debussy.

'Ibéromania' was certainly still much in vogue in Paris at the beginning of the twentieth century, a fashion no doubt given a new lease of life by the presence of Falla, Granados and other Spanish musicians. Ravel, for all that he had Basque blood in his veins, was composing at one remove; he was writing French music about Spain, rather than Spanish music. Yet it is interesting that the *Rapsodie espagnole* inhabits more the world of Falla's as-yet-unperformed opera *La vida breve* than that of Chabrier's *España* or Rimsky-Korsakov's *Capriccio espagnol*: the colour and élan are there, but more subtle, less blatant.

Except for the 'Habanera', the third of its four movements, the *Rapsodie espagnole* was apparently conceived specifically for orchestra, and marks a major advance in the composer's handling of orchestral scoring, although the reviews at the time criticised the work for, among other things, its 'strange sonorities'. All four movements are linked by Ravel's systematic exploration of the tritone C–F sharp.

© Tess Knighton

La valse, choreographic poem (1919–20)

After thinking about *La valse* for as long as thirteen years, Ravel finally got to grips with it towards the end of 1919. The stimulus to complete the long-cherished project had come from Serge Diaghilev who, against his better judgement perhaps, had commissioned the score for the Ballets Russes. Although the Russian impresario had no great faith in Ravel as a ballet composer – he never really appreciated the quality of *Daphnis and Chloë*, which Ravel had written for him in 1912 – he was persuaded that music intended as a celebration of the Viennese waltz could scarcely fail to suit his purposes. When the composer first played it to him, however, at a private audition in Paris in April 1920, it turned out to be something rather different from what he was expecting.

Francis Poulenc, who was present on that unhappy occasion, recalled what happened as Ravel played through the piece:

> I knew Diaghilev very well at that time. I saw his false teeth twitch, I saw his monocle twitch, I saw that he was very embarrassed and I saw that he didn't like it and that he was going to say 'No'. When Ravel had finished, Diaghilev said to him something which I thought was very true. He said, 'Ravel, it's a masterpiece, but it isn't a ballet. It's a portrait of a ballet, a painting of a ballet.

The problem was that, after a war in which he had served at the Front against the combined might of Germany and

Austria, Ravel's feelings about the Viennese waltz had inevitably changed. When he first conceived the work in 1906, he had thought of calling it 'Wien' (Vienna) and, as he said at the time, it was to be 'a grand waltz, a sort of homage to the memory of the great Strauss – not Richard, the other, Johann. You know how much I love those rhythms.' Thirteen years later he still loved the rhythms but he was also painfully aware of what Viennese waltz-time culture had in the meantime become.

Diaghilev was right. Ravel's 'choreographic poem' is indeed a masterpiece and it is true that it is not so much a waltz as a painting of a waltz – except that it is two paintings, those of an impressionist and an expressionist side by side in the same frame. It is, as the composer said, 'a kind of apotheosis of the waltz', but one inescapably linked in his mind with the image of 'a fantastic and fateful whirlpool'.

The impressionist first half of *La valse*, as it emerges out of the darkness of the rumbling basses in the opening bars, corresponds quite happily with the scenario Ravel published in the score:

> Clouds whirl about. Occasionally they part to allow a glimpse of waltzing couples. As they gradually evaporate, one can discern a gigantic hall filled by a crowd of dancers in motion. The glow of the chandeliers breaks out fortissimo. An Imperial Court about 1855.

But halfway through, at the height of a brilliant episode of virtuoso figuration on trumpets and woodwind, the chandeliers are extinguished and the dark rumblings are heard again.

The waltz is reassembled out of the same material but in no orderly sequence and with increasing vehemence, as the rhythmic and harmonic excesses characteristic of the genre are driven to extremes. The heavily percussive climax which finally explodes a once-civilised scene – the last two bars shattering the waltz rhythm itself – is a direct expression of the trauma experienced by the composer in the preceding few years.

Ottorino Respighi (1879–1936)

Respighi was born in Bologna, where he studied violin and viola at the Liceo Musicale. In 1900 he went to St Petersburg, where he studied with Rimsky-Korsakov – from whom he learnt his skill as a colourful orchestrator – and played viola in the Imperial Theatre orchestra. He also attended lectures by Bruch in Berlin and returned to Bologna before taking up a teaching appointment in Rome at the Liceo di Santa Cecilia. By the time he left the Liceo in 1926 Respighi had written the first two of his celebrated trilogy of orchestral picture postcards from Rome – *The Fountains of Rome* (1914–16) and *The Pines of Rome* (1923–4, which includes the recorded sounds of a nightingale); the last instalment, *Roman Festivals*, followed in 1928. Respighi's fascination with earlier music led him to produce a number of editions and arrangements, including a transcription of Monteverdi's *Orfeo* and the suite *Gli uccelli* ('The Birds', 1927) which uses baroque keyboard works. Though mainly an orchestral composer, he wrote a handful of operas, the last of which, *Lucrezia*, was completed by his widow Elsa, a composer in her own right, who championed Respighi's works until her death aged 101 in 1996.

The Pines of Rome (1923–4)

1. The Pines of the Villa Borghese (Allegretto vivace) –
2. Pines near a Catacomb (Lento) –
3. The Pines of the Janiculum (Lento) –
4. The Pines of the Appian Way (Tempo di marcia)

During the nineteenth century, the proper domain of the Italian composer was felt to be opera. Respighi – who also aspired, throughout his career, to recognition as an operatic composer – was much more versatile. In addition to copious chamber music, choral works and songs, he became one of the first Italians to be generally admitted to the concert repertoire, even if admiration for the brilliance of his scoring was sometimes tempered by reservations about substance and taste. Though he wrote many 'abstract' works, including a symphony and several concertos, he became most celebrated for his vividly colourful suites and symphonic poems – above all, for the 'Roman trilogy': *The Fountains of Rome* (1914–16), *The Pines of Rome* (1923–4) and *Roman Festivals* (1928).

Respighi's greatness as an orchestrator is proved not just by his original works but by his breathtaking orchestrations of Bach, Rakhmaninov, Rossini, Vitali and Italian lute works of the Renaissance. Like Rimsky-Korsakov (with whom he studied), and like Debussy and Ravel, he knew exactly what would sound well, be the aptest and most striking colour, and create a sonic metaphor for a visual impression. Open the score of *The Pines of Rome* anywhere and the sheer bravura of the instrumentation – in the quietest as well as the most grandiose pages – takes the breath away: the sovereignty of the imagination that guides the ear.

Critics who would like to consign Respighi to the status of a 'mere' orchestrator make much of his 'naive pictorialism'. But in seeking to summon up pictures in sound, he clearly belongs to a grand tradition of 'naive pictorialists' (Berlioz, Liszt, Mussorgsky, Rimsky-Korsakov, Richard Strauss). If his thematic invention is often simple, and the emotions direct, this doesn't mean his aims are unambitious. The 'Roman' poems are music as spectacle, and brilliantly successful at what they set out to do; much subtle compositional craft goes into the shaping of each movement, the placing of climaxes, the art of transition – which in Respighi's hands often becomes a kind of cinematic 'dissolve'.

Indeed his symphonic poems are often dismissed as 'like film music' (as if that was necessarily a criticism). It's truer to say that in them he created, to depict matters Roman, a distinctive idiom that film composers have gratefully imitated ever since when called upon to score some sword-and-sandals epic. Some have, in fact, directly plagiarised Respighi – two instances that come to mind are 'Caesar's March' in Miklós Rózsa's score for *Julius Caesar*, modelled to the point of reproduction on the march in the finale of *The Pines of Rome*, and the troika ride in the snow in Sergei Bondarchuk's *War and Peace*, which his composer, Vyacheslav Ovchinnikov, lifted wholesale from Respighi's first movement. If this music can be transferred from Roman urchins to Russian sleighs, what kind of 'pictorialism' are we talking about? It remains to add that in *Fantasia 2000*, the modern-day sequel to Walt Disney's *Fantasia*, Respighi's *The Pines of Rome* is used to accompany a sequence about a pod of humpbacked whales. Something in this music must exist beyond its programme.

The Pines of Rome was premièred to a packed audience at the Augusteo, Rome, on 14 December 1924, conducted by Bernardino Molinari, and was a tremendous success.

In the published score, Respighi supplied his own descriptive programme for each of the four linked movements:

The Pines of the Villa Borghese

'Children are at play,' Respighi writes, 'in the pine groves of the Villa Borghese; they dance round in circles, they play at soldiers, marching and fighting; they are wrought up by their own cries like swallows at evening; they come and go in swarms.' Respighi evokes the children's high-pitched excitement through prominent scoring for flutes and piccolo, harp, piano, celesta and glockenspiel. One tune is clearly a traditional children's singing game: this is taken up by the full orchestra, building to a climax of uproarious activity, at the peak of which three unison trumpets urgently break in upon the proceedings, their insistently repeated C in dissonance to the A major revelry.

Pines near a Catacomb

'Suddenly the scene changes and we see the shades of the pine trees fringing the entrance to a catacomb. From the depth rises the sound of mournful psalm-singing, floating through the air like a solemn hymn, and gradually and mysteriously dispersing.'

The catacomb location is the cue for Respighi to introduce the flavour of Gregorian chant – a resource of which he was very fond – to evoke the spirit of the early Christians. Muted horns hint at a plainchant fragment; then in the distance a solo trumpet (with celesta) instils a mood of rapt serenity. In the depths of the orchestra a chanting figure begins: Respighi marks it 'sotto voce' (*come una psalmodia*) – 'like psalm-singing'. On this figure he builds up a long crescendo, spreading through the orchestra as the psalm gains in ardour and intensity to a fervent climax, in counterpoint with the horn and trumpet themes. It subsides into the depths, and after a quiet coda Respighi transports us to the vicinity of the Janiculum Hill.

The Pines of the Janiculum

'A quiver runs through the air: the pine trees of the Janiculum stand distinctly outlined in the clear light of a full moon. A nightingale is singing.' The 'quiver' is a cadenza-like solo for piano; the moonlight is limned in a long-breathed clarinet solo. The pines rustle in *Rosenkavalier*-ish harmonies; an exquisite oboe and viola theme sounds over harp and celesta figuration, taken up ecstatically by violins in textures of dream-like insubstantiality. At the end, evocation gives way to a concrete phenomenon, thought very daring in 1924: the nightingale sings on a gramophone recording, nested among quietly shimmering strings. This literal birdsong falls silent, and a distant, heavy tramping makes itself felt.

The Pines of the Appian Way

'Misty dawn on the Appian Way: solitary pine trees guarding the magic landscape; the muffled, ceaseless rhythm of unending footsteps. The poet has a fantastic vision of bygone glories: trumpets sound and, in the brilliance of the newly risen sun, a consular army bursts forth towards the Sacred Way mounting in triumph to the Capitol.'

The Via Appia was the great military highway of classical Rome. In his depiction of Roman Imperial might, Respighi's quiet 'speaking' lines in the introductory section are notable, as of weeping and wailing, especially the cor anglais's plangent lament.

Stentorian fanfares arise: Respighi introduces a group of six saxhorns (or flugelhorns) to represent the sound of the *buccina*, the Roman army bugle. With a fine mastery of cumulative effect he builds up an overwhelming climax, with full brass, percussion and eventually organ contributing to the musical vision of the grandeur that was Rome.

Nikolay Rimsky-Korsakov (1844–1908)

Though his principal achievements were his fifteen operas, largely derived from Russian tales, among them *The Snow Maiden* (1881), *Sadko* (1896) and *The Golden Cockerel* (1908), Rimsky-Korsakov is better known for his equally colourful concert works, especially *Capriccio espagnol*, *Sheherazade* and the *Russian Easter Festival Overture* (all completed in 1888). He first began composing aged nine but was sent to naval college in St Petersburg and became a naval officer. Under Balakirev's strong guiding hand, he wrote his First Symphony (1865), which, along with his symphonic poem *Sadko*, based on a legend of the sea, led to his appointment, aged twenty-seven, as a professor of composition at the St Petersburg Conservatoire. He purposefully undertook a period of self-study to equip himself for the task, renewed when he became inspector of naval bands (1873–84). His reputation for orchestration rivalled that of Berlioz and, like the Frenchman, he wrote a valuable treatise on the subject. He became the most technically accomplished of the group of Russian nationalist composers known as 'The Five', and as a teacher influenced Lyadov and Glazunov as well as the later generation of Stravinsky and Prokofiev.

Capriccio espagnol, Op. 34 (1887)

1 Alborada –
2 Variazioni –
3 Alborada –
4 Scena e canto gitano –
5 Fandango asturiano

The 1880s were a relatively unproductive period for Rimsky-Korsakov in terms of his own compositions. In the early part of the decade he was absorbed with the legacy of unfinished works left by Mussorgsky; later, after the death of Borodin in 1887, he dedicated himself to the completion of his *Prince Igor*. In between, much of his time was taken up with his unofficial position as adviser to the publisher and concert promoter Belyayev and, from 1883, with his duties as assistant to Balakirev at the Imperial Chapel.

Rimsky-Korsakov's work on the unfinished operas of his two friends stood him in good stead for the operatic slant of the latter part of his career, but his time at the Imperial Chapel was also important, in a perhaps surprising way. As he himself said: 'My years at the Chapel developed in me a propensity for brilliant orchestration.' This 'propensity' resulted in some of his most colourful and enduringly popular works, including the symphonic suite *Sheherazade* as well as the *Capriccio espagnol*.

Towards the end of 1886, Rimsky-Korsakov had completed his *Fantasia on Two Russian Themes* for violin and orchestra, and the following year planned a companion piece based on Spanish themes. Just as Bizet had blazed the trail for Debussy and Ravel, so Rimsky-Korsakov did not need to cross the Pyrenees in order to write a 'Spanish' work; in this case, the pioneer was Glinka, whose extended visit to Spain in 1845–7 resulted in a number of pieces inspired by the melodic patterns and dance rhythms of the Iberian peninsula. Rimsky-Korsakov's *Spanish Fantasy* never materialised as such, but, rather, by the summer of 1887, it had been transformed into the brilliant exercise in virtuoso orchestration that is the *Capriccio espagnol*.

Hard on its heels came *Sheherazade* and then the *Russian Easter Festival Overture*, which Rimsky-Korsakov saw as closing 'a period of my work at the end of which my orchestration had attained a considerable degree of virtuosity and warm sonority without Wagnerian influence, limiting myself only to the normally constituted orchestra of Glinka'. Shortly afterwards, though, he heard Wagner's *Ring* in St Petersburg, and his compositional career changed direction.

The *Capriccio espagnol* falls into five movements: a lively

'Alborada' (or 'dawn song'); a more restrained set of orchestral 'Variations'; an elaboration of the 'Alborada', which recurs in cyclic fashion; a 'Scene and Gypsy Song', in which the brass imitate the Andalusian style of *cante jondo* (literally 'deep song'); and finally a foot-stamping Asturian 'Fandango', with a coda that recalls once more the theme of the opening 'Alborada'.

Rimsky-Korsakov saw the work's orchestration as the 'very essence of the composition and not its garb . . . The Spanish themes, of dance character, furnished me with rich material for putting in use multiform orchestral effects. All in all, the *Capriccio* is undoubtedly a purely external piece, but vividly brilliant for all that.' The work was an immediate success on its first performance in the Russian Symphony Concerts season of 1887, and has remained a staple of the repertory ever since.

Sheherazade, Op. 35 (1888)

1 The Sea and Sinbad's Ship
2 The Story of Prince Kalender
3 The Young Prince and Princess
4 Festival at Baghdad – The Sea – Shipwreck – Conclusion

Sheherazade was composed in 1888. It was a period when Rimsky-Korsakov was producing some of his best work: he had just finished the *Capriccio espagnol* and would follow *Sheherazade* with the *Russian Easter Festival Overture*. The legends of Old Russia and of the East had always been the chief inspiration of Rimsky's music. His first encounter with Eastern music, at Bakhchisaray in the South Crimea, left an indelible impression on him.

Sheherazade is based on the Arabian Nights, the famous collection of tales that were supposed to have been told by the Princess Sheherazade to her husband, the Sultan Shahriar.

He was accustomed to put his wives to death on the morning after the marriage had been consummated; but on her wedding night Sheherazade began telling him a story which so captivated the Sultan that she was able to prolong it for a thousand and one nights, at the end of which time she had succeeded in appeasing him. Like many other composers of descriptive music, Rimsky was anxious not to be too explicit: wishing *Sheherazade* to be appreciated in the first place as symphonic music, he even had the original titles of the movements withdrawn from the score. Nevertheless, it seems appropriate to give them here. Rimsky wrote in his autobiography, 'In composing *Sheherazade* I meant these hints [the titles] to direct but slightly the hearers' fancy on the path which my own fancy had travelled, and to leave more minute and particular conceptions to the will and mood of each.'

Rimsky also warns against interpreting the themes as leitmotifs: themes associated with one particular episode may reappear in quite another context. For instance, the main theme of the first movement, which one is tempted to call the 'sea' motif, is also used to depict the stern Sultan at the opening of the first and fourth movements; and when the Princess's theme in the third movement turns up again, in very different guise, as the second subject of the finale, we are not meant to suppose that the Princess is joining in the festivities at Baghdad! One theme, however, is definitely a leitmotif: the one that is played by the solo violin immediately after the brusque opening. It stands for Sheherazade herself, and its various appearances throughout the work, almost always cadenza-like and accompanied only by the harp (in the first movement it is cleverly interwoven into the orchestral texture), depict her in her role of tireless storyteller. She introduces three of the movements; she has an intermezzo to herself in the third; and in the finale, when storm and Sultan have been calmed, she has, appropriately, the last word.

Writing of the *Capriccio espagnol* in his autobiography, Rimsky indulged in some understandable self-congratulation over its orchestration:

> The opinion formed by both critics and the public – that the *Capriccio* is a magnificently orchestrated piece – is wrong. The *Capriccio* is a brilliant composition for the orchestra. The change of timbres, the felicitous choice of melodic design and figuration patterns, exactly suiting each kind of instrument, brief virtuoso cadenzas for instruments solo, the rhythm of the percussion instruments, etc., constitute here the very essence of the composition, and not its garb or orchestration.

These words are also true in every way of *Sheherazade*. There have been few composers more capable than Rimsky-Korsakov of translating their ideas so perfectly into instrumental sound.

Gioachino Rossini (1792–1868)

During the early decades of the nineteenth century Rossini came to dominate the Italian operatic scene, excelling in both comic and serious genres. Unusually precocious, at the age of twelve he wrote six sonatas for strings that are still heard today. After studying at the Liceo Musicale di Bologna, in 1810 he received his first operatic commission for a one-act *farsa* (*La cambiale di matrimonio*) for Venice, where three years later he scored a double triumph with the heroic *Tancredi* and the comic *L'Italiana in Algeri*, which spread his fame throughout Europe. As musical director of the San Carlo Theatre, Naples from 1815 to 1822 he produced a number of experimental works, ending his Italian career with *Semiramide* (Venice, 1823). Moving to Paris in 1824 he adapted to the French style two of his Neapolitan stage works before composing the newly minted *Le Comte Ory* (1828) and *Guillaume Tell* (1829), the latter among the grandest of Parisian grand operas. But he wrote no more for the stage: only a couple of liturgical compositions, the *Stabat mater* and *Petite messe solennelle*, and a miscellany of piano and vocal pieces.

Although by his own account classical by temperament, Rossini laid down the formal ground-rules of Italian romantic opera, to be followed by Bellini, Donizetti and the young Verdi. His reputation may have fluctuated over the years, but his comedy *Il barbiere di Siviglia* (Rome, 1816), described even by the severe Schumann as 'life-enhancing', has never left the repertoire.

Overture, *The Barber of Seville* (1816)

Why is the Barber of Seville Spanish? After all, the play *Le barbier de Séville* by Pierre-Augustin Caron de Beaumarchais, first produced at the Comédie Française in Paris in 1775, is based on a stock international plot: an elderly guardian wants to marry his pretty young ward, but is outwitted by her aristocratic lover with the help of a cunning valet. Perhaps Beaumarchais felt that the element of social criticism in the play would be more safely displaced to a country other than his native France; or perhaps he saw comic potential in a land where balconies abound for maidens to be wooed under, and where (as his opening stage direction says) 'every casement is barred'. Most probably, though, having visited Spain in the 1760s, he was attracted by the idea of infusing the story with some local colour, in the shape not only of a few Spanish words, but also of Spanish songs – because he initially conceived the piece as an *opéra comique*, with spoken dialogue interspersed with arias composed or adapted by himself.

With this background, it is hardly surprising that *The Barber of Seville* soon appeared in several operatic adaptations: notably that of the Neapolitan Giovanni Paisiello, first performed in 1782 in St Petersburg, and soon a favourite in Italian theatres. So popular was Paisiello's *Barber*, indeed, that when Rossini presented his new opera on the same subject in Rome in February 1816, with a libretto by Cesare Sterbini, he felt it necessary to circulate the news that the project had Paisiello's approval. This did not save the opera on the first night, which was cut short by the hostility of the audience. But the second performance was more successful, and *The Barber of Seville* was soon on its way to being recognised as – in the words of Rossini's great successor Giuseppe Verdi – 'the most beautiful *opera buffa* there is'.

Rossini composed the opera rapidly, in no more than a few weeks; and, to preface it, he pressed into service an overture previously unheard by the Roman audience. He had written it for the *opera seria Aureliano in Palmira* in Milan in 1813, and later also adapted it for *Elisabetta, Regina d'Inghilterra* in Naples in 1815. So there is no possibility that its themes could represent the characters of the opera, nor yet that the chirpy first theme of the main Allegro might have been intended to conjure up a Spanish atmosphere. The piece is simply a perfect appetiser for an evening's entertainment, with sparkling solo writing for woodwind and horn, and some sonorous tuttis (though not as noisy as in the 'traditional' rescored version once in widespread use). It begins with a slow introduction, leading to an Allegro vivo – in two similar halves, separated only by the briefest of transitions, each half ending in a stirring 'Rossini crescendo' – and a breathless coda at a faster tempo.

© Anthony Burton

Overture, *William Tell* (1829)

A popular joke once defined an intellectual as someone who could listen to the *William Tell* Overture without thinking of the Lone Ranger; and indeed the two have become as inextricably linked in the minds of a generation reared on the famous children's TV series; as Rakhmaninov and railway stations are for their parents. In fact, the world's best-loved overture first fell upon French ears – at the Paris Opéra on 3 August 1829, as the curtain rose on the thirty-seven-year-old composer's last opera. *William Tell* is a four-act marathon based on Schiller's play about Switzerland's thirteenth-century folk hero – the marksman who was happily able to distinguish his own son's head from an orange pippin at a distance of forty yards.

As with so many of Rossini's works, the new opera was not at first an unqualified success. The libretto, written by committee, was deeply flawed, and the composer himself realised that as it stood, *William Tell* was too long, even for Parisian audiences accustomed to four or five acts plus interminable ballets. Drastic cuts were soon administered to the score, a process which continued so systematically that one day, on being informed by the director of the Opéra that Act 2 would be performed that evening, the bitter composer retorted sarcastically: 'Ah! Really! All of it – the whole thing?' Although long inured to initial disappointments, this one proved too much for Rossini. *William Tell* (now regarded as one of his finest achievements, though still performed relatively infrequently) marked his retirement from the theatrical world.

The overture is indisputably one of Rossini's best. It begins with a slow introduction, featuring five solo cellos, which portrays a calm morning in the Alps. Then comes a storm, after which we hear the 'Ranz des vaches' (cowherd's call), introducing the famous Allegro. This is said to depict the call to arms, and the Swiss – led by William Tell – rising up against their Austrian oppressors.

Camille Saint-Saëns (1835–1921)

The classical simplicity of Saint-Saëns's music, and the fluency with which he produced it, may seem to contrast with his intellectual pursuits as a scholar, editor, student of archaeology and natural history, and writer of poems, plays and criticism. A prodigy of Mozartian facility (aged ten, he gave a concert in Paris which included piano concertos by Mozart and Beethoven) he studied at the Paris Conservatoire before winning the post of organist at La Madeleine in 1857. He taught piano at the École Niedermeyer, where Fauré was among his students. A predilection for travel, especially to North Africa, influenced a number of musical references, as in his first opera *La princesse jaune* (1871), the 'Egyptian' Piano Concerto (No. 5), Persian songs and the *Suite algérienne*. Of his thirteen operas, only *Samson et Dalila* is regularly staged. In a bid to preserve his reputation as a serious composer, Saint-Saëns banned the publication of his *Carnival of the Animals* (1886) until after his death.

Carnival of the Animals, grand zoological fantasy (1886)

1 Introduction and Royal March of the Lion
2 Hens and Cocks
3 Wild Asses (Speedy Animals)
4 Tortoises
5 The Elephant
6 Kangaroos
7 Aquarium
8 Personages with Long Ears
9 The Cuckoo in the Depths of the Wood
10 Aviary
11 Pianists
12 Fossils

13 The Swan
14 Finale

Early in 1886, the fifty-year-old Saint-Saëns went to Austria on holiday, and as relaxation embarked on a brief cello solo for the well-known performer Lebouc. But one thing led to another, and in a matter of days 'The Swan' had turned into a 'grand zoological fantasy' (though it has to be said that Saint-Saëns seems to have had a project of the sort in mind for some years).

Although 'The Swan' was duly published, the composer resolutely set his face against the other thirteen pieces being played during his lifetime outside a small circle of his friends, and the *Carnival* as a whole was not published until 1922, the year after his death. It could appear that he lacked confidence in the work, but the more likely explanation is that he recognised its quality all too well. From our vantage-point, looking back over the established reputations of composers such as Fauré, Debussy and Ravel, it is hard to appreciate the extent to which serious French composers a century ago were conditioned to glance nervously over their shoulders at German music, and at Wagner in particular. Saint-Saëns was one of the founders in 1871 of the Société Nationale de Musique, and the very fact that the society took the phrase 'Ars Gallica' as its motto indicated that its endeavours were implicitly to be measured against those of its Teutonic neighbour. French music had to be not only different, but also not inferior; and, for Saint-Saëns anyway, to be heard as such by audiences in Germany.

In 1886 he was, in fact, in a particularly delicate situation, since he had in the previous year published a series of articles in which he resisted the notion that 'no music at all existed before Wagner and none could exist after him'. This wholly reasonable resistance brought all Valhalla crashing round his head and, since he valued his German contacts both as composer and as concert pianist, it was certainly not the moment to appear as the perpetrator of a grand zoological fantasy.

The Carnival, therefore, led a quiet private life for over thirty years, brought out on the salon circuit for those who would appreciate it (such as Liszt on his last visit to Paris a few months before his death).

1 *Introduction and Royal March of the Lion*
This suggests that, while entitled to pride of place, the lion is not the subtlest of animals.

2 *Hens and Cocks*
What one might call 'Messiaen in the farmyard'.

3 *Wild Asses*
The French title 'hémiones' refers to Asiatic wild asses, subspecies of which include the Tibetan kyang and the Mongolian dziggetai. Here they bear the further description 'animaux véloces' and their wildness is further evidenced in their knowing practically nothing of harmony.

4 *Tortoises*
These tortoises crawl to the sounds, suitably modified, of the can-can and galop from Offenbach's *Orpheus in the Underworld*.

5 *The Elephant*
Here the chosen theme for parody is the waltz tune from the 'Dance of the Sylphs' in Berlioz's *The Damnation of Faust*.

6 *Kangaroos*
The two pianos alternate marsupially.

7 *Aquarium*
A more extended movement in which beauty shows itself for the first time.

8 *Personages with Long Ears*
The two violin sections indulge in a braying competition.

9 *The Cuckoo in the Depths of the Wood*
Off-stage effects were always popular in French opera. Here the cuckoo is heard from the corridor outside the salon.

10 *Aviary*
The aviary gives Saint-Saëns a chance to show off his command of Mendelssohnian delicacy.

11 *Pianists*
Strictly speaking, pianists are not animals that are found in captivity. Perhaps the composer felt it was never too late to start.

12 *Fossils*
A kind of pendant to the *Danse macabre*, which is duly quoted. Other tunes include the French folk songs 'J'ai du bon tabac' and 'Ah! vous dirai-je Maman', the patriotic air 'Partant pour la Syrie', and Rosina's aria 'Una voce poco fa' from Rossini's *The Barber of Seville*.

13 *The Swan*
One of the most widely arranged pieces of all time. The choreographer Fokine, who used it for Pavlova's famous dance 'The Dying Swan', learnt it on the mandolin. The ballerina's dying words were 'Prepare my Swan costume'.

14 *Finale*
A happy ending. How many reminiscences of the previous movements can you identify?

Erik Satie (1866–1925)

The poise and sparse expressiveness of Satie's well-known *Three Gymnopédies* and *Three Gnossiennes*, for piano, belie his position as one of the most eccentric and original composers in history. After seven unhappy years at the Paris Conservatoire he deliberately contracted bronchitis to reduce his period of military service. During his twenties he lived an impoverished, bohemian existence as a pianist in Montmartre cabaret clubs and embraced mysticism and the occult as a member of the Rosicrucian (Rose and Cross) Order. He then founded the Église Métropolitaine d'Art de Jesus Conducteur – of which he was the sole member – and after moving out into a Paris suburb, owing to financial exigency, took to walking daily the six miles into Paris, ducking into cafés along the way to compose. At thirty-nine, aware of his technical shortcomings, he took himself to study for three years at the Schola Cantorum. He became celebrated after his ballet for Diaghilev, *Parade* (1917), and became the iconoclastic figurehead of Les Six. His hypnotic repetitions led the way to minimalist music and his 'musique d'ameublement' (furniture music) paved the way for ambient music.

❧ ***Two Gymnopédies*** (1888), orch. (1896) by Claude Debussy (1862–1918)

1 No. 3: Lent et grave
2 No. 1: Lent et douloureux

Two French composers of the late nineteenth century were regularly cited by their colleagues and successors as models and inspirations: Emmanuel Chabrier and Erik Satie. That may surprise you if you are used to thinking of them as minor masters, but in both cases their originality, independence and quirky character, as much as their skill, won unstinting respect from people in the same trade who knew how rare and essential those qualities are. All the acquired technique in the world won't write you a set of *Pièces pittoresques* or a *Gymnopédie*.

Debussy, who first met Satie in 1891, gave him a score of his *Cinq poèmes de Baudelaire* on which he had written 'For Erik Satie, the sweet medieval musician who has strayed into this century for the joy of his very friendly Claude Debussy'. Satie had already written his *Three Gymnopédies* by then, in 1888, the same year that Joséphin Péladan founded the quasi-religious Ordre de la Rose-Croix Catholique du Temple et du Graal. Péladan, author of texts such as *Le vice suprême* and *L'androgyne*, was a strong influence on the young Satie, who became the order's house composer in 1891. So was Gustave Flaubert. Satie said that Flaubert's Carthaginian novel *Salammbô* was the direct inspiration for his *Gymnopédies*, though the fanciful title appears to allude to Ancient Greek athletes or dancing boys. At all events the result was music of astonishing simplicity: all three of these piano pieces use the same pulse and similar repeating harmonies, with a slow, seductive melody singing out above. The genius is in the daring: perfect proportions achieved with minimal means.

Debussy's orchestrations of 1896 grew out of the two composers' weekly meetings at the home of the Swiss conductor Gustave Doret – Monday evenings of 'wild gaiety', according to Doret. On one occasion Satie brought a printed score of the *Gymnopédies*, and sat down to play them, rather imperfectly.

Debussy then decided to show how the music really should go. According to Doret, it was his own idea that Debussy should orchestrate them, and Debussy did so almost immediately, choosing the first and third pieces, and placing them in reverse order. Doret conducted the first performance at the Société Nationale in February 1897. Together, they make a fascinating exercise in respecting simplicity while making subtle original contributions. In no. 3, strings (introduced by muted horns) accompany a solo oboe, handing over to flute from time to time, once doubled by a solo violin, while the main body of first violins provides the colour element midway. In no. 1, a harp carries the basic pulse, a second harp ornaments it, the melody passes from violins to oboe, and a quietly struck cymbal adds colour.

Robert Maycock © BBC

Franz Schubert (1797–1828)

Schubert is one of the greatest song composers; his gift for lyrical melody and poetic expression gave rise to the bedrock of the Lieder repertory. Along with dances, marches and other piano miniatures, these songs would be performed in social gatherings, or 'Schubertiades'. Born in Vienna, Schubert was taught by Salieri while a chorister at the imperial court chapel. He worked initially as a classroom teacher to appease his father, but left after two years. Following the success of two Rossinian overtures, he spent one summer as a music teacher at the country estate of Count Johann Karl Esterházy. His aspiration to break into opera remained unfulfilled after a handful of unsuccessful efforts but he wrote symphonies and piano sonatas which are increasingly part of the repertory. He contracted syphilis in 1822. The last years of his life brought the 'Great' C major Symphony (1825), the song cycle *Winterreise* (1827), and the three great late piano sonatas (1828).

Ballet music from *Rosamunde* (1823)

1 Allegro moderato – Andante un poco assai
2 Andantino

> On the 5th October 1867, I had the happiness to find myself for the first time in the city of Vienna. It was a place which I had looked forward to, almost hopelessly, as a kind of El Dorado, for years. I was with one of my best friends, and the object of my visit was as dear and congenial to me as possible.

The writer was George Grove, founder of the famous music dictionary; and the friend who accompanied him on his travels was the young Arthur Sullivan. The purpose of their trip was to obtain some of Schubert's unknown orchestral works, among them the complete incidental music to the play *Rosamunde*. Their first port of call was one Dr Schneider, the nephew and heir of Schubert's younger brother Ferdinand. Schneider brought out of a cupboard in the corner of his room the original manuscripts of no fewer than five of Schubert's earlier – and as yet unpublished – symphonies, as well as several dramatic works. But still the *Rosamunde* music eluded Grove's eager hands. Eventually, on a return visit, he ventured to ask whether he might look in the cupboard himself. Certainly, was the response – if he didn't mind being smothered in dust. And so it was that, while Sullivan engaged the good doctor in polite conversation, the begrimed Grove emerged triumphantly clutching the orchestral parts of *Rosamunde*, which had lain unused for more than forty years.

The romantic drama of *Rosamunde, Princess of Cyprus*, was written by the minor poet Helmina von Chézy. It opened, with Schubert's incidental music, on 20 December 1823 – and closed the following day. (Two months earlier, Chézy had been responsible for another theatrical disaster, Weber's *Euryanthe* – surely one of the greatest musical scores ever lavished on so poor a libretto.)

The text of *Rosamunde* has not survived, but its improbable plot was gleefully recounted by several critics present at the first night. On his deathbed, the Prince of Cyprus gives instructions that his daughter Rosamunde is to be raised as a shepherdess until she reaches the age of eighteen – at which time she is to marry Prince Alfonso of Candia. Summoned to Cyprus by a mysterious letter, Alfonso is shipwrecked off the coast, and, meeting Rosamunde by chance, he conceals his identity in order to test her constancy. Meanwhile, the Governor of the island has fallen in love with Rosamunde; and when she rejects his advances he first imprisons her, and then sends her a poisoned letter. Via a circuitous route the letter is eventually returned to its sender, who thus dies by his own hand. Rosamunde and Alfonso ascend the throne amid general rejoicing.

Schubert's incidental music for this concoction was put together in considerable haste, and he found himself having to raid his own cupboard. With no time to compose a new overture, he reused one he had written two years earlier for his opera *Alfonso and Estrella*. In addition, one of the entr'actes of the *Rosamunde* music shares a theme with the slow movement of Schubert's great String Quartet in A minor, D804, written during the same period, and it is likely – if not certain – that the quartet movement came first. Either way, that same entr'acte incorporates an arrangement of a much earlier song, 'Der Leidende' ('The Sufferer').

It was Grove who first floated the idea that the dramatic B minor entr'acte which stands at the head of Schubert's *Rosamunde* score was the lost finale of the 'Unfinished' Symphony, and his theory has never been entirely disproved. Certainly, the piece is substantial enough to have served such a purpose, and Schubert uses its main theme again, in less symphonic form, to launch the first of the score's two ballet numbers. The latter half of that same number is much calmer in mood (Andante un poco assai – 'Andante slightly very much' – is Schubert's disarming tempo marking), and it forms a perfect transition to the second ballet number – a gentle march-like piece which has become one of the composer's most popular compositions.

Jean Sibelius (1865–1957)

Sibelius established himself early in his career as Finland's national composer, helped by his ability to convey the austere beauty of his country, his passionate adoption of themes from the Finnish folk epic the *Kalevala*, and his patriotic music such as *Finlandia* (1900). Born north of Helsinki, he initially intended to become a violinist, but studied composition in Vienna and Berlin between 1889 and 1891. His choral *Kullervo* Symphony and the tone poem *En Saga* (1892, both inspired by the *Kalevala*) preceded seven purely orchestral symphonies, ranging from the Tchaikovsky-influenced First (1900) to the enigmatically brief Seventh (1924). Supported by a government pension from the age of thirty-two, he effectively retired for the last thirty years of his life, writing no major works (though he started an eighth symphony, which he destroyed). His Violin Concerto, by turns introverted and highly virtuosic, remains among the most popular in the repertory.

Finlandia, Op. 26 (1899; rev. 1900)

'When we look at Sibelius's *Finlandia* and then at his Seventh Symphony, we may well agree with George Moore that art must be parochial in the beginning to become cosmopolitan in the end.' Constant Lambert's dictum in *Music Ho!* epitomises a certain *froideur* of well-bred disapproval towards this piece, which is also exhibited towards the composer's no less widely acclaimed *Valse triste*. Yet for the more robust palate it belongs to a repertoire of well-loved concert-hall standards – Tchaikovsky's *1812 Overture*, Elgar's *Pomp and Circumstance* March no. 1, Holst's 'Jupiter' from *The Planets*, Walton's *Crown Imperial* among them – that find themselves very much at home in the Albert Hall and capture something of the essential demagogic spirit of the Proms. As with all great popular tunes and patriotic hymns, it simply refuses to lie down.

Perhaps to classify *Finlandia* as a tone poem is something of a misnomer: Sibelius had already written a piece much more generically deserving of the title in *En saga*. The tone poems of Sibelius form a body of programme music that is rightly admired for its symphonic qualities – an organic yet improvisatory approach to large-scale musico-dramatic form that reached its summit in *Tapiola*. The present short piece – organically cohesive though it may be – makes no such claims on our attention. It is essentially gestural in its broad appeal, a direct march-cum-fanfare with a hymnal 'trio' (in which we can already hear that characteristic woodwind sound of Sibelius) that was meant to stir the Finnish patriot's heart. (Sibelius's biographer Erik Tawaststjerna notes that Sibelius had shown a great enthusiasm for Beethoven's *Egmont* music, the spirit of which is surely echoed here.)

It came into being as the finale of a set of six historical tableaux in which Sibelius collaborated in November 1899 on the occasion of 'The Press Pension Celebrations' in Finland. The scenes were: 1 Väinämöinen's Song; 2 The Finns are Baptised [which introduced a version of the hymn tune in *Finlandia*]; 3 Duke Johan at Abo Castle; 4 The Finns in the Thirty Years War; 5 The Great Unrest; 6 Finland Awakes!

Shortly afterwards Sibelius was persuaded to contribute something for the Helsinki Philharmonic Orchestra to play at the Paris World Exhibition in March 1900 – the last leg of an extended tour that was to take in Sweden, Holland and Germany – and instead of writing a new piece he offered the music of the sixth tableau under a new title. Together with the First Symphony, *Finlandia* set off on its travels abroad.

When it finally reached Paris – where Sibelius acquired the sobriquet of 'the Finnish Grieg' – it scored a great success under the circumspect title of *La Patrie*, winning (as the composer recorded) 'a splendid review in *Le Figaro* from Alfred Bruneau'. Sibelius's pride in the popular success of what he once described as 'this relatively insignificant piece' never left him. Ten years later, after a Berlin performance conducted by Nikisch, he noted in his diary: 'Why does this tone poem catch on with the public? I suppose because of its *plein air* style. The themes on which it is built came to me directly. Pure inspiration.'

Karelia Suite, Op. 11 (1893)

1 Intermezzo
2 Ballade
3 Alla marcia

Following the ecstatic Helsinki reception accorded to his epic *Kullervo* Symphony of 1891–2, Sibelius found himself thrust very much into the national spotlight almost overnight. So when, in the spring of the following year, students at Helsinki University were looking for someone to provide the incidental music for their forthcoming series of tableaux depicting various scenes in the history of the Finnish province of Karelia, Sibelius was the natural first choice. Pageants such as this played a focal role in the rising tide of Finnish nationalism; indeed, it is worth remembering that Sibelius's contribution for a similar event six years later eventually yielded the fervently patriotic *Finlandia*.

In the particular case of Karelia, there was increasing concern about the gradual Tsarist Russianisation of the province, and it was intended that the money raised by the event would fund projects designed to try and prevent any ensuing cultural isolation. What is more, Karelia would have held happy memories for Sibelius, for he had spent his honeymoon there the previous summer and, at the same time, had even briefly immersed himself in a study of that region's oral folk tradition. The gala itself took place on 13 November 1893 with the composer himself conducting. Sibelius's music went down exceedingly well, even if, as he observed in a letter to his brother, 'not much of it was audible as everyone was either applauding or shouting'. After successfully presenting eight of the numbers in the concert hall six days later, Sibelius eventually refashioned just four, publishing the substantial Overture separately as his Op. 10, and assembling three others into this popular suite.

Ear-tickling tremolando strings and magically evocative horn calls launch the opening Intermezzo. Out of this fragmentary material there emerges a stirring march, first heard on the trumpets, then joined by violas and trombones. After a magnificent climax, Sibelius's majestic processional recedes once again into the far distance and the movement ends as mysteriously as it began. This sequence originally accompanied the third tableau in the students' production, which depicted the Karelian hunters coming to pay their tributes to a Lithuanian prince.

By contrast, the central 'Ballade' exudes a cosy, fireside warmth. The fifteenth-century scene is Viipuri Castle, where the deposed king, Karl Knutsson, listens to the song of a minstrel. After a brief introduction given to pairs of clarinets and bassoons, strings intone a ruminative A minor melody, itself soon gently underpinned by running cello counterpoint. As the tune is repeated, clarinets and oboes join the strings in some delightful canonic interplay, before the music dies away with hesitant violins and violas over tremolando cellos and basses. The strings enter once again, this time with a proud, stately tune in C major which, in the words of that foremost Sibelius scholar Erik Tawaststjerna, 'seems to recall past glory and power'. Lastly, after an extended pause, a lonely cor anglais delivers the haunting minstrel's song (in the original incidental music, this was sung by a tenor), and the movement ends with a brief reprise of the opening melody.

The concluding 'Alla marcia' finds Sibelius in his most good-humoured, extrovert vein. This infectiously jaunty 'call to arms' was in fact designed to accompany a portrayal of the siege of Käkisalmi Castle, and the vivid sense of spectacle both here and in the first movement is due in no small measure to the inclusion (unusual for this composer) of such various percussion 'extras' as triangle, tambourine, cymbal and bass drum. There are just two contrasting ideas: the swaggering violin tune heard at the outset, and a fanfare-like motif first given to trumpets and clarinets. In the closing stages especially, Sibelius subjects the main theme to some splendidly lusty imitative treatment, before the work ends with one final, rousingly affirmative flourish.

© Andrew Achenbach

Night Ride and Sunrise, Op. 55 (1907)

For human beings everywhere, the rising of the sun is a potent symbol. Some ancient religious rites apparently derive from a fear that the sun might not rise again – that mankind might be left in darkness, deprived of the primal source of life. Inevitably such fears would be particularly powerful among peoples who lived close to the Arctic Circle, where for part of the year the sun is a feeble, or a virtually non-existent presence.

In Sibelius's native Finland the sustained darkness of the winter presents problems even today. The condition known as SAD (Seasonal Affective Disorder) – depression caused by lack of sunlight – affects many Finns, and there is strong evidence that Sibelius himself was a sufferer. One can imagine how emotionally charged the image of sunrise would have been for him, as for many of his countrymen. A few years before his death, Sibelius told his secretary, Santeri Levas, about how he had taken a horse-driven sleigh ride to Helsinki around the turn of the century. Just before his arrival in the city, he'd experienced one of those spectacular sunrises, like a vast, slow-motion firework display, so common in extreme Northern latitudes: 'The whole heavens were a sea of colours that shifted and flowed producing the most inspiring sight until it all ended in a growing light.'

It's easy to relate those words to the second half of *Night Ride and Sunrise*, to trace the slow return of the light: thin and eerie at first, but with growing warmth and depth. Yet Sibelius was worried that listeners would think of *Night Ride and Sunrise* as purely illustrative music. Like Beethoven in his

'Pastoral' Symphony, he told a friend, he was more concerned with the 'inner feelings' of the spectator than with the spectacle itself. We hear the galloping horses clearly enough (persistent dotted string and percussion rhythms), and later there are suggestions of uncanny noises or movements within the trees (woodwind and horns). But direct programmatic elements gradually fade as we begin to sense the rider's awe at the stillness at the moment of dawn (impassioned hymn-like writing for strings), and his inward gratitude – and perhaps relief – as colour and warmth slowly return to what had been, only moments before, a dark, unsettling forestscape.

Stephen Johnson © BBC

The Oceanides, Op. 73 (1914)

In 1913 Sibelius was approached by the American composer Horatio Parker with an exciting proposition. A wealthy American patron named Carl Stoeckel was offering Sibelius $1,000 for a new orchestral work to be performed at a festival that he and his wife ran in Norfolk, Connecticut. Furthermore, they wanted Sibelius to come and conduct the premiere for an additional fee of $1,200 – ample inducement for a perennially cash-strapped composer.

In March 1914, Sibelius completed, and dispatched to America, a work called *Rondeau der Wellen* (*Rondo of the Waves*). This was in fact a reworking of the finale of a recently composed three-movement orchestral suite (of which only the second and third movements now survive). Self-critical as ever, Sibelius had no sooner sent it off than he decided to rewrite it again, simplifying textures and transposing the whole piece from the difficult key of D-flat major to the much more player-friendly D major. In May 1914, Sibelius set sail for America, continuing to make modifications even during the voyage.

Despite its auspicious beginnings, with a specially assembled orchestra comprising players from the finest American orchestras, *The Oceanides* has never achieved the popularity of, say, *Finlandia* or *Tapiola*. The piece is rather difficult to programme successfully because, though brief, it makes musical and technical demands equal to those of Sibelius's larger tone poems. This has implications for the amount of rehearsal the work can receive relative to the rest of the programme. Additionally, it is uncharacteristic of Sibelius's tone poems in taking its subject-matter not from Nordic legend but from Greek mythology: the Oceanides were the four thousand daughters of Oceanus, the origin of all rivers and seas. This shift in location is perhaps reflected in the work's luminous orchestration. It is no exaggeration to say that *The Oceanides* inhabits a sound-world unique in Sibelius's output.

Two particular instrumental features stand out: the quiet rumble of two sets of timpani suggesting fathomless oceanic depths; and swirls of colour from two harps that evoke the swell and spray of the sea's restless surface. This has frequently led to the work being described as 'impressionistic'. In so far as this word has any meaning when applied to music, it often implies something unstructured and more concerned with texture and colour than with symphonic discourse. This is no more true of Sibelius's *The Oceanides* than it is of Debussy's supposedly impressionistic *La mer*. What truly unites these superficially similar masterpieces is that their composers' iron grip on the musical material never relaxes.

The 'exposition' reveals two distinct, but profoundly related sections: the first dominated by arabesques for two flutes, the second introduced by a broader clarinet theme. The two sections are then repeated, but greatly expanded and embellished. Such a bald summary, however, cannot remotely convey the subtlety of the thematic relationships, nor the power and majesty of the work's final climax.

John Pickard © BBC

En saga, symphonic poem, Op. 9 (1892; rev. 1902)

'Many things are now clear to me: really I am a tone painter and poet,' Sibelius wrote to his wife Aïno in 1894. 'Liszt's view of music is the one to which I am closest. Hence my interest in the symphonic poem.' So far, however, he had hedged his bets as far as the Lisztian specifics of a programme were concerned. In his first major work, the *Kullervo* Symphony of 1891–2, an opening movement giving only the rugged outline of the hero's personality in strict sonata form is followed by a brooding sketch of Kullervo's unhappy childhood, again without narrative details; when Sibelius does choose to tell a story, in the third movement, it is with chorus and operatic soloists as well as orchestra. At the encouragement of the composer-conductor Robert Kajanus, he followed up *Kullervo* with a purely orchestral work which he called a 'symphonic poem'; this time the programme – if indeed Sibelius ever thought it through at all – was withheld altogether.

Image-makers can have a field day with the bracing mysteries of *En saga*, which both in Swedish and Finnish translates as 'A Fairy Tale'. There are tantalising clues in Sibelius's own words. Its prototype, he wrote, was a sequel to the 'Ballet Scene' he had composed in Vienna, and an octet – which has never been unearthed – contained the 'germ of *En saga*'. He also told his friend Adolph Paul that, in composing *En saga*, he thought of the German symbolist painter Arnold Böcklin, celebrated for *The Isle of the Dead* but not always so lugubrious in his choice of subject-matter. ('He paints the sky too bright, far too bright,' Sibelius commented, and the airy flurries of flutes and upper strings near the start of the work suggest exactly this.) In old age Sibelius claimed that the atmosphere of the tone poem was closer to the Eddas of Norse mythology – major sources for Wagner's *Ring* cycle – than to the *Kalevala*, and he also told his secretary that it was a revelation of his own character. If so, this is a journey of a soul through a supernatural landscape. Sibelius was later dissatisfied with the organisation of his 1892 thoughts, and thoroughly revised *En Saga* in 1902; although the original occasionally appears on disc and (rarer still) in concert, it is the revision we usually hear.

The introduction paints the magical scene in muted string

arpeggios punctuated by hints of themes to come: a woodwind song of narrow compass, but far removed from the runic style adopted in parts of *Kullervo*, and an epic narration launched by bassoons which eventually propels us into the Allegro proper. Our hero has two melodies of a vigour to match Kullervo's in the symphony, but of a different cut: a rhythmically charged viola theme, and a fiercely accented string chant with what sound like Moorish inflections. The forward propulsion of the piece gives it the sensation of always being in a state of development, and Sibelius further enhanced its symphonic status in the 1902 revision by cutting out a lyrical central episode and replacing it in part with the tense *sul ponticello* (on the bridge) passage for strings before the pace slackens and mysterious chamber-musical variations on the two 'hero themes' gather in the dark. The epic narrative returns for its turbulent high noon, careering towards disaster in the manner of Strauss's *Don Juan* (Sibelius had been much impressed by that work's Berlin première in 1889). Then the clarinet turns it into a trance-like threnody before a last, rhythmical reminder of the heroic light so abruptly snuffed out.

The Swan of Tuonela, Op. 22 no. 3 (1893; rev. 1897 and 1900)

In April 1892 Sibelius's *Kullervo* received its triumphant premiere. At a stroke, this vast choral symphony established Sibelius beyond question as Finland's greatest composer. It also placed a burden of expectation upon him regarding his next major project.

The music of *Kullervo* proved innately dramatic, so an opera seemed the obvious choice. As for subject-matter, the *Kalevala*, the Finnish national epic from which Sibelius had taken the story, seemed ripe for further plundering. Sibelius set to work, fashioning a libretto on the subject of Väinämöinen – a sort of *Kalevala* equivalent to Wagner's *Siegfried* – giving the project the working title 'The Building of the Boat'.

At the time, Sibelius was immersed in Wagner's music. Perhaps this ultimately proved inhibiting; perhaps public anticipation of the new opera grew burdensome. Whatever the reasons, after several years' struggle Sibelius eventually abandoned the opera.

However, it seems he managed to salvage some of the musical sketches. According to Sibelius, the projected overture eventually became what we know today as *The Swan of Tuonela*, one of the four orchestral tone poems he composed between 1893 and 1896 around the strange story of Lemminkäinen.

In the *Kalevala* legend, Lemminkäinen descends to Tuoni, the Kingdom of Death, to kill the swan that swims on the black waters of the Lake of Death. Lemminkäinen is attacked and torn apart by the Son of Death, but rescued by his mother, who magically stitches his dismembered body together again.

The sound-world of *The Swan of Tuonela* is quite unique – a lonely cor anglais solo floats across a lake of slowly shifting string chords, with bass clarinet, low brass and bass drum adding their darkly glowing colours. Every detail in this short masterpiece seems pared down to its essence, the prevailing austerity paradoxically emphasising the profound emotional impact of the whole.

Tapiola, symphonic poem for orchestra, Op. 112 (1926)

Tapiola was Sibelius's last major work, following the Seventh Symphony (1924) and incidental music for *The Tempest* (1925). (Although he started an eighth symphony, he destroyed what he had written.) Tapio is the Finnish god of the forests, and Sibelius's score is prefaced with these lines:

Wide-spread they stand, the Northland's dusky forests,
Ancient, mysterious, brooding savage dreams;
Within them dwells the Forest's mighty God,
And wood-sprites in the gloom weave magic secrets.

Early in 1926 Sibelius was asked by the conductor Walter Damrosch to write a symphonic poem for the New York Symphony Society. The choice of subject and the form were left to the composer, and only the length, between fifteen and twenty minutes, was stipulated. Sibelius wrote to the upper limit, a long span for a piece with no declared narrative programme and no preconceived form. Yet, compared with the time it took his Sixth and Seventh symphonies to evolve, *Tapiola* was swiftly completed, by the same summer, which is perhaps why, at first, Sibelius had misgivings about it. After the first performance on 26 December 1926, Damrosch reassured him in a letter which sums up the work, if any words could, very aptly:

> I consider *Tapiola* to be one of the most original and fascinating works from your pen. The variety of expression that you give to the one theme in the various episodes, the closely knit musical structure, the highly original orchestration, and, above all, the poetic imagery of the entire work, are truly marvellous. No one but a Norseman could have written this work. We were all enthralled by the dark pine forests and the shadowy gods and wood-nymphs who dwell therein. The coda with its icy winds sweeping through the forest made us shiver.

It was, however, Serge Koussevitzky's performances with the Boston Symphony Orchestra a few years later which launched *Tapiola*'s real success. The early critics had complained, as critics are wont to do, that the sixty-year-old Sibelius had lost his powers of invention, and that the new piece was more manner than substance. Their reaction was understandable, for *Tapiola* is based on only one, bald idea – the short phrase heard, like a text for a sermon, at the very beginning. It sounds unpromising, but its very simplicity, or ordinariness, makes it ideal for endless transformations. The motto theme is hardly a 'theme' at all, if we understand that as something distinctive; it's more like a source, which can disguise itself in different figurations, or rise to the surface at rare moments of emphasis. Most of *Tapiola* moves in cautious steps, as befits the mystery of its inspiration, and is underpinned by long-held pedal notes or the slow rise and fall of parallel thirds, like deep breathing. Sibelius's language is partly modal, partly chromatic; acutely sensitive to degrees of harmonic tension, he has an exquisite ear for dissonance, which is carefully planned as a result of individual strands in the texture moving as they must, and the sense of inevitability is confirmed by the final 'Amen' cadence.

Bedřich Smetana (1824–84)

Born in eastern Austrian-occupied Bohemia, the son of a brewer, Smetana was educated in German (only learning Czech as an adult). He decided on a musical career at the age of sixteen after hearing a concert given by Liszt, and worked as a piano teacher before taking up a teaching job in Sweden. By the time he returned in 1861 he had written three symphonic poems on nationalist themes, in the manner of Liszt. A connection with the Provisional Theatre in Prague (where he was principal conductor from 1866 to 1874) enabled him to secure performances there, beginning with *The Brandenburgers in Bohemia* and the comic folk opera *The Bartered Bride*. His patriotism is also fervently displayed in his series of six tone poems *Má vlast* ('My Country', 1872–9), celebrating the Czech landscape, its cities and heroes. During this period he lost his hearing through the effects of syphilis; the anguish of his deafness is depicted in his autobiographical String Quartet no. 1, 'From My Life'. He died in an asylum in 1884 but left a legacy of Czech nationalism to Dvořák, Janáček, Martinů and others.

Má vlast (1879–94)

1 *Vyšehrad*
2 *Vltava*
3 *Šárka*
4 *From Bohemia's Woods and Fields*
5 *Tábor*
6 *Blaník*

For many people during the nineteenth century, nationalism took the place of collective religion – not, be it said, the aggressive, acquisitive nationalism that has been the curse of our own age, but rather the ideal of a free society united by a common cultural heritage and no longer divided by caste or subject to foreign domination. Nowhere was this spirit more alive than in Czechoslovakia (then Bohemia) during the mid-century; and in Bedřich Smetana it found its chief spokesman in music.

Ever since his return from Sweden in 1861 he had devoted himself to Czech themes, literary and musical. In 1872 he completed his fourth stage work, *Libuše*, which he described as a 'sacred festival picture', to be performed, he later told a friend, only 'on festivals which touch the whole Czech nation'. Such an occasion did not present itself until 1881, when the National Theatre in Prague was finally inaugurated, by which time the composer had become totally deaf. But in the meantime a further seed had been sown. More oratorio than opera, *Libuše* ends with a succession of tableaux in which the heroine, who with her peasant husband founded the first Czech dynasty and the city of Prague, prophesies momentous events in the nation's history. From this sprang the idea of a cycle of symphonic poems that should evoke Bohemia past and present, on a larger scale and without the encumbrance of a vocal commentary.

The cycle, to be entitled *Má vlast* ('My Country'), was written over seven years, from 1872 to 1879, during which time Smetana's health was fast deteriorating. Although they share only a single, tenuous motif there has never been any doubt that *Libuše* and *Má vlast* are firmly linked. As František Bartoš observes in his introduction to the score of the latter in the Collected Edition, 'both works are ideologically similar in their glorification of the country and its people, dictated by the period of their origin' – that is, the time of the Czech struggle for independence. 'Their stressed national tendencies,' he continues, 'resulting naturally from such circumstances, their conflicts and ardent optimism, indicating a great future for the nation, are the reason why both works are fully understood and appreciated only by Smetana's countrymen.' There is a touch of exaggeration here; for while *Libuše*, with its wealth of pageantry and argument and its total lack of drama, may indeed be scarcely exportable, *Má vlast*, whether performed whole or in part, has proved itself one of the classics of the concert hall. The entire cycle was first introduced to Proms audiences by Sir Henry Wood in 1909.

Nationalism in music is traditionally conveyed by the use of folk melody. But that was not Smetana's way, nor in Bohemia was it necessary: for though the country possessed its own dances – such as the polka and the furiant, on whose rhythms Smetana, like Dvořák, freely drew – the national idiom was too close to that of Austria or Germany to offer those salient characteristics that mark out the music of Spain, Hungary or Russia. Smetana himself declared that no national style could be built up on a mere imitation of folk melodies. 'The essence of his Czech spirit', his biographer Nejedlý wrote, 'was thought; not playing with notes.' But how is one to define 'thought' in this case? Possibly as no more than the ability, possessed by Smetana in ample measure, to touch a common denominator of national feeling through the language that came most naturally to him, coupled with a simple clarity of vision that could make the most well-worn ideas seem newly minted.

Nor is there any conflict here, as sometimes in Dvořák, between head and heart. Smetana could harness complex techniques to his musical thought without impairing its spontaneity. For all such qualities *Má vlast* has rightly been called epic. Although its six components are obviously planned as a cycle, each is so constructed as to make a satisfying statement on its own. The one linking theme, which appears in three of the poems, is associated with the fortress Vyšehrad that dominates the city of Prague – a musical ideogram that never loses its identity no matter how variously developed (one can well understand why Smetana's enemies should have accused him of Wagnerism!). It forms the basis of the opening poem (*Vyšehrad*), surfaces again towards the end of *Vltava* and winds up the entire cycle on a note of triumph.

Vltava, which evokes the rise and progress of Bohemia's principal river, is the second poem of the cycle and the most popular. No matter if its programme is as naive as a cinema travelogue of the 1950s. Threads of flute and clarinet touched in by harp and pizzicato strings suggest the tiny rivulets that gather into a single stream, conveyed by a broadly flowing melody that has all the directness of a folk song without any of its primitiveness (in fact, scholars have attempted to trace its provenance from countries as far afield as Holland, Sweden and Slovenia, but without success, since it is far more subtly wrought than any folk song could possibly be). As the texture thickens, rousing horn flourishes conjure up a hunt in the woods. Next we pass a country wedding, whose strains recall vague memories of *The Bartered Bride*. As they fade into the distance night descends and we are offered a musical vision of naiads dancing on the moonlit river. The calm of the waters is disturbed as they plunge into the turbulence of St John's Rapids (now no longer in existence, since the dam which produced them has been destroyed). Finally we reach the walls of Prague. And so (it is tempting to conclude) we say farewell to the River Vltava, as it flows past the mighty fortress of Vyšehrad on its journey to the Elbe.

Šárka recounts the legend of a Czech maiden who, jilted by her lover, has dedicated herself to the destruction of the male sex. Her companions bind her to a tree in the forest, where she waits for the knight Ctirad to pass by with his train. Overwhelmed by her beauty Ctirad is all too ready to play the knight errant. He frees Šárka and he and his men accept her invitation to join her in a drinking bout, little knowing that their wine has been drugged. No sooner have they sunk into sleep than Šárka summons her maidens with a blast on the horn; they fall upon the knights and stab them to death.

Alone among the tone poems, *From Bohemia's Woods and Fields* has no specific programme; rather it corresponds to Beethoven's description of his 'Pastoral' Symphony as 'mehr Ausdruck der Empfindung als Malerei' ('more an expression of feeling than painting'). We are free to interpret the powerful opening as we please whether as forest trees tossed by a high wind or merely a vast expanse of rolling landscape. To

Smetana the first major-key melody suggested a naive country girl, and the central fugato the twittering of birds (surely the only case in Romantic music of counterpoint in an avowedly pastoral context); and we can hardly go wrong in taking the 'Allegro quasi polka' to represent peasant merry-making.

The penultimate movement is *Tabor*, named after the main stronghold of the Hussites in southern Bohemia. Like the final movement, its musical material is derived from a popular chorale-like melody, 'Ye who are God's warriors!', which evokes the struggles of the Hussites during the Reformation period. Smetana wrote of their 'resolute will, perseverance and stubborn inflexibility', and the music expresses to the full this spirit of determination.

Blaník, the last poem, is inspired by the Hussite wars of the fifteenth century, as is its predecessor, *Tábor*. The Protestant leader Jan Hus was as much a symbol of national identity to the Czechs as Luther was to the Germans. Legend has it that after his execution in 1436 his followers withdrew to Mount Blaník where, wrapped in deep slumber, they await their country's call in some future emergency (shades of *Drake's Drum*!). In the tone poem they are symbolised by the Hussite chorale 'Ye who are God's warriors'. After their retreat to the mountain fastness there is a pastoral intermezzo during which a shepherd boy plays on his shawm. A stormy episode depicts the sufferings of the Czech people and is followed by the return of the Hussites, who restore peace and glory to the land.

Johann Strauss II (1825–99)

The eldest of the sons of Johann Strauss (1804–49), Johann II, along with brothers Josef and Eduard, was discouraged by his father from becoming a musician. He learned the violin, however, with his mother's encouragement, and when only eighteen made his debut as director with his own orchestra, in competition with his father. He assumed directorship of a merged Strauss Orchestra following his father's death in 1849, and toured assiduously. He wrote more than 160 waltzes, which contributed greatly to the popularity of the dance in Vienna, and also composed hundreds of other dances, marches and potpourris. He became Vienna's Imperial music director for balls, 1863–71, and then began writing successful operettas. Of his stage works, *Die Fledermaus* (*The Bat*, 1874) and *Der Zigeunerbaron* (*The Gypsy Baron*, 1885) have proved the most enduring. Among his most famous waltzes are *An der schönen, blauen Donau* (*By the Beautiful, Blue Danube*, Op. 314), *Geschichten aus dem Wienerwald* (*Tales From the Vienna Woods*, Op. 325) and *Frühlingsstimmen* (*Voices of Spring*, Op. 140).

~ ***By the Beautiful, Blue Danube*, waltz, Op. 314** (1867)

The 'Waltz King' wrote his first choral waltz, *An der schönen, blauen Donau* (*By the Beautiful, Blue Danube*), for a Carnival-time song programme given by the Wiener Männergesang-Verein (Vienna Men's Choral Association) on 15 February 1867 in the Dianabad-Saal, Vienna. The waltz, commissioned by the Association, also bears a dedication to them. Since the composer was already committed to conducting the Strauss Orchestra at the Imperial Court that evening, the premiere instead featured the orchestra of the 'König von Hannover' (King of Hanover) Infantry Regiment, with the members of the Wiener Männergesang-Verein under the baton of their chorus-master, Rudolf Weinwurm.

In contrast to the widespread myth of the waltz's initial failure, many newspapers reported the extraordinary success of the premiere. *Die Presse*, for example, commented on 17 February: 'The lovely waltz, with its catchy rhythms, ought soon to belong among the most popular of the prolific dance-composer.' Nevertheless, Josef Weyl's original text, exhorting peasants, landlords, artists and politicians to forget their sad lot by joining in the carnival festivities, was largely unsuited to non-carnival occasions. Thus, in 1890, Franz von Gernerth, a member of the Association, provided this most famous of waltzes with a completely new text in which, for the first time, appear the words: 'Donau so blau . . .' ('Danube so blue'). The waltz is usually heard, however, in the version for orchestra alone.

© Peter Kemp

Emperor Waltz, Op. 437 (1889)

In autumn 1889, Johann Strauss II conducted five concerts in Berlin at the newly opened Königsbau concert hall. Prior to his departure for Germany, the Viennese press reported that he had sent his Berlin publisher a new waltz, entitled 'Hand in Hand'. This title referred to a toast made in August 1889 by the Austrian Emperor, Franz Joseph I, on the occasion of his visit to the German Kaiser, Wilhelm II, in which Austria had extended 'the hand of friendship' to Germany. It was Johann's astute German publisher, Fritz Simrock, who suggested that the composer change the title to *Kaiser-Walzer* (*Emperor Waltz*), and that by not specifically dedicating the work to either monarch, the vanity of both men would be satisfied.

It was under the now familiar title of *Kaiser-Walzer* that the Waltz King's magnificent composition was first performed in Berlin on 21 October 1889 – though it should be noted that the illustrated title-page of Simrock's original piano edition is emblazoned with the *Austrian* Imperial crown.

© Peter Kemp

Roses from the South, waltz, Op. 388 (1880)

Even after the Waltz King, Johann Strauss II, had become a full-time stage composer at the beginning of the 1870s, he maintained a strong presence in ballrooms and bandstands by arranging melodies from his theatre works into orchestral dances and marches. The abundantly tuneful score of his 1880 operetta *Das Spitzentuch der Königin* (*The Queen's Lace Handkerchief*) yielded six such pieces, of which the best-known remains the waltz *Rosen aus dem Süden* (*Roses from the South*). This delightful number began its conquest of the world when the composer's youngest brother, Eduard, conducted it for the first time at his Sunday concert in the 'Golden Hall' of the Vienna Musikverein on 7 November 1880.

The first melody of the second waltz section was to gain fresh and lasting popularity with British audiences when an arrangement of it became the signature tune of the BBC's long-running radio series *Grand Hotel*.

Richard Strauss (1864–1949)

Strauss composed from his early years (his first two published works were written when he was ten), and also developed a conducting career alongside his success in composition: 1886 saw not only the premiere of his First Horn Concerto, but also a conducting post at the Munich Court Opera. In the same year, influenced by Liszt, he produced *Aus Italien*, the first of a string of brilliantly orchestrated tone poems extending through the 1890s, among them *Don Juan*, *Till Eulenspiegel* and *Also sprach Zarathustra*. Strauss was also inspired by Wagner, and went on to write some of the twentieth century's finest operas: in 1905 he shocked the operatic world with *Salome*. *Elektra* (1909, another fiercely powerful portrait) marked his first collaboration with the poet Hugo von Hofmannsthal, a partnership that bore four further operas, including the comedy *Der Rosenkavalier* (1911). His operatic output continued through the turbulence of the Nazi years, and he also wrote successful orchestral works in a generally late-Romantic idiom. He died on 8 September 1949, several months before the first performance of his *Four Last Songs*.

Also sprach Zarathustra, tone poem for large orchestra, freely after Friedrich Nietzsche, Op. 30 (1895–6)

Even before Stanley Kubrick's 1968 film *2001: A Space Odyssey* brought the introductory fanfares of *Also sprach Zarathustra* to the attention of a new generation, the opening of the work was already celebrated as one of the most arresting in the entire repertory of Western music. Nor did Kubrick do violence to the composer's programmatic intention, which had been stated thus: 'I meant to convey in music an idea of the evolution of the human race from its origin, through the various phases of development, religious as well as scientific, up to Nietzsche's idea of the Superman.' Indeed, it is rather this latter concept – with its misleading twentieth-century overtones of Aryan supremacy and brutal totalitarianism – that has caused nervousness in some quarters, and even led Strauss commentators to 'protect' their man by suggesting that he was indifferent to Nietzsche's philosophy.

The truth is that he was attracted, at least as a young man, by aspects of Nietzsche's thunderous challenge to civilisation. Strauss read Nietzsche – and in particular the newly published *Also sprach Zarathustra* (*Thus Spake Zarathustra*) – while convalescing from an illness contracted in 1892. He doubtless relished the text's many incidental Wagnerian references, though *Zarathustra* is in fact, as has convincingly been demonstrated, a sustained counterblast to *The Ring* and *Parsifal*. But Strauss also responded to Nietzsche's fervent attack on the Church and all its works, and to his espousal of a new morality based on egoist principles rather than those of Christianity – or indeed of socialism. The 'Superman' (*Übermensch*) was Nietzsche's embodiment of the ideal human spirit: fearless, self-sufficient, rejoicing in its strength and unfettered by the false values of conventional morality. Barely a decade after the crystallisation of this concept in *Also sprach Zarathustra*, Nietzsche's most ambitious work, it was given unforgettable musical expression in the opening bars of Strauss's eponymous tone poem.

On the basic level of pictorialism, the work's opening depicts Zarathustra's high-flown salute to the rising sun, with which the score is prefaced: it is thus, as Strauss himself indicated, a representation of a spectacular sunrise. But it is no less evidently, at the same time, a Nietzschean celebration of all that is strong and noble in spirit. Strauss by no means embraced Nietzsche's philosophy wholeheartedly or without qualifications. His tone poem is a personal response to it, and can perhaps best be viewed as a free commentary on the model.

At the centre of Strauss's conception is a confrontation between Nature (represented by the C–G–C motif heard at the outset on the trumpets) and Mankind, whose questing spirit is represented by a similar motif – but a four-note one and generally in B minor or major – first heard low down on pizzicato cellos and basses soon after the initial clamour has died away. The scrubbing in the basses and the growling brass that immediately follow the blaze of C major, however, are headed 'Von den Hinterweltlern', an untranslatable pun combining the senses of 'Afterworldsmen' (that is to say, believers in an after-life) and 'Backwoodsmen' (beings with a naive, primitive intellect). Then, after the hesitant appearance of humanity, is heard a snatch of the plainchant theme associated with the Credo, mockingly intoned on muted horns. The consolatory balm experienced by the 'sickly people who invent fables and long for God' is depicted in the ensuing passage for richly divided strings with quiet organ accompaniment; so intensely does the lyricism glow that the composer himself seems momentarily to have succumbed to the comforts of religion.

A solo viola line leads to the next section, 'Of the Great Longing', which depicts the struggle of humanity to free itself from the false, superstitious promises held out by religion. The clash of principles involved in this process is symbolised by the pungently polytonal effect of the C major Nature motif being sounded forthrightly in a B major context. But the blandishments of religion – depicted by the returning Credo theme as well as the opening notes of the traditional Magnificat chant heard on the organ – are vigorously swept aside by Zarathustra, initiating the uninhibited sensuality of the next section, 'Of Joys and Passions'. So wild are the passions that they seem to provoke a reaction: the theme proclaimed on the trombones at the climax of this section is usually known as the 'Disgust' or 'Satiety' motif. The latter theme is interesting in that its augmented and diminished intervals, themselves redolent of profanity, cause it to inhabit an ambivalent tonal area somewhere between B and C major.

The more subdued tones of a darkly orchestrated B minor establish themselves for the following section, 'The Song of the Grave'. There are, however, more exalted moments, notably when the Nature motif rings out on a trumpet. The same motif forms the basis for the theme of the fugue that launches the next section, 'Of Science'. Strauss evidently relishes this depiction of dry academicism, generating a theme that uses all twelve notes of the chromatic scale and which emerges from the murky depths of the orchestra. Or perhaps it would be more accurate to say that he enjoys parading such oppressive pedantry chiefly in order to be able to soar above it, as the spirit of humanity clearly does before long.

A forceful resumption of the fugue brings us to 'The Convalescent', a key section for Strauss, as it was for Nietzsche. In the latter's poem, the hero undergoes an agonising psychic transformation at this point, springing up from his bed in the cave like a madman, and crying out with a terrible voice, before sinking down as though dead, remaining without food or drink for seven days. Zarathustra's invocation 'Up, abysmal thought, up from my depths!' indicates that this section is a parody of the scene in Act 3 of Wagner's *Siegfried* where Wotan (the Wanderer) summons the earth mother Erda from sleep for a portentous colloquy before allowing her eventually to return to her rest; the parody is at its most malicious when Zarathustra observes: 'It is not my way to awaken great-grandmothers from sleep in order to bid them – Go back to sleep!' The centrality of this episode to Nietzsche's conception – a fact confirmed by its direct confrontation with Wagner's masterpiece – was recognised unfailingly by Strauss, who matched it with a passage which, in Norman Del Mar's words, is 'one of the most remarkable in the orchestral repertoire from the point of view of sheer colouristic virtuosity'.

The drama and tension gradually accumulate until the hero is ready to revel in his 'Dance Song'. It is sometimes suggested that the latter is merely a light-hearted diversion, but this is to misapprehend and diminish (perhaps intentionally) the nature of Strauss's philosophical inspiration. The 'Dance Song', on the contrary, is in fact a wholly Nietzschean expression of Dionysiac ecstasy: 'I would believe only in a god who knew how to dance,' proclaims Zarathustra. The climax is reached in the last section with the tolling of the midnight bell, after which a radiant epilogue in B major appears to leave no doubt of humanity's ultimate self-sufficiency – until the very last bars, that is, when the discordant reassertion of the C major motif low down on the bass strings intimates that the struggle between humanity and nature must go on.

Don Juan, tone poem after Nikolaus Lenau, Op. 20 (1887–8)

At first sight the traditional character of Don Juan, or Don Giovanni – created by the Spanish Renaissance dramatist Tirso da Molina in his play *El burlador de Sevilla* (The Joker of Seville) – might appear the archetype of the male chauvinist pig: all those conquests, all those broken promises and quick departures. But there is something beyond this sexual equivalent of trainspotting or butterfly-collecting which Mozart captured (perhaps more than his librettist, Lorenzo da Ponte), which the nineteenth century treasured as the epitome of Romanticism, and which retains its fascination even in this tentatively emancipated age. What motivates Juan, and with what degree of sincerity does he carry on his adventures?

According to the verse play by Nikolaus Lenau (1802–50), Juan is genuinely in love with all of his 'victims', seeking with each of them one isolated moment of perfect bliss: 'Passion is always and only the new passion; it cannot be carried from this one to that, it must die here and spring anew there, and when it knows itself, then it knows nothing of repentance . . . Forth and away, then, to triumphs ever new, so long as youth's fiery pulses race!' (The translation is by Norman Del Mar, from his authoritative study of Richard Strauss.) When Lenau's Juan dies, it is not as an act of supernatural revenge for impiety, but of his own volition, in a mood of despair and disillusion; he allows himself to be killed in a duel, because he finds victory as tedious as the rest of life.

It was on this interpretation that Strauss based his tone poem, completed in 1888 and first performed in Weimar in 1889 under his own direction. It is the first work of his to survive in the standard repertoire, and an early example of the mastery of large orchestral forces that was to be a hallmark of his entire career.

Like many works of its kind, Strauss's *Don Juan* can be interpreted as being in a modified version of traditional symphonic first-movement form. It is in E major, with a second subject in the 'regular' key of B major, a development section, a recapitulation, and a coda. However, since many other features stem directly from the programme which Strauss derived from Lenau's play, it makes more sense to summarise the progress of the piece in terms of the action depicted.

The work begins, then, with some impetuous flourishes and a more sustained string theme, together depicting 'youth's fiery pulses' racing in Juan. A broader theme, with distinctive crotchet triplets in its second bar, soon makes a first brief appearance: it represents Juan in the role of seducer, and the object of his attentions is portrayed by slightly coquettish little sighing figures. This is obviously very much a casual encounter, from which Juan turns away in a descending chromatic phrase. With the next affair, however, the music becomes more tranquil and sweetly romantic, and the seductive theme returns in full flood in an extended love scene. The scene ends, though, in sudden collapse; the opening flourish returns marked 'senza espressione' (without expression), and with a continuation developing the themes associated with Juan: the lady is forgotten already.

But passion 'must die here and spring anew there': a new love sparks off a new melody of seduction, on violas and cellos, 'molto appassionato'. The response of this new object of Juan's attentions is at first characterised by hesitant two-note woodwind phrases, but eventually blossoms into an extended and expressive oboe melody. The idyll this time is without the passionate urgency of the previous love scene, but correspondingly more tender, more intimate and ultimately deeper. And with its calm close, we reach the crux of the score: after these two contrasting scenes, what is Juan – what is Strauss – to do next?

Strauss's answer is a masterstroke: the first appearance, at this late stage, of 'Don Juan's horn call'. It symbolises the noblest and most idealistic side of Juan's nature, and leads the music away from amorous intimacy and back into the public arena – or, more prosaically, out of its lyrical interlude and into a resumption of the development section, in which the horn call is joined by Juan's opening themes. The music dashes away into an episode which is a little reminiscent of the carnival music in Berlioz's *Benvenuto Cellini*, and which can possibly be identified with a masked ball in Lenau's *Don Juan*. This ends suddenly, however, and over a long-held pedal B there are nostalgic reminders of all three of the affairs in the first half of the score.

The opening flourishes return, ushering in a full-scale recapitulation of the first theme and the horn call, which are worked up together into a scene of mounting excitement and bravado as Juan takes up the challenge of a duel. And then comes the most sudden and complete of the work's several abrupt collapses: a long pause, then a quiet minor chord to indicate Juan's sudden resignation, and a stab from the trumpets as his opponent's sword finds its mark; and in a few quiet bars everything is over.

Ein Heldenleben, Op. 40 (1897–8)

The Hero – The Hero's Adversaries – The Hero's Helpmate – The Hero's Battlefield – The Hero's Works of Peace – The Hero's Escape from the World and Transfiguration

In recent years, Strauss has enjoyed such a vigorous revival of the operas which dominated his creative work for nearly forty years that one can easily forget the extent to which his reputation was built on concert music, and specifically on the genre of the symphonic poem. By the turn of the last century, when he was thirty-six, he had composed only a single opera (*Guntram*, staged at Weimar in 1894), but no fewer than eight substantial tone poems, of which all but (at most) two remain in the standard orchestral repertoire to this day.

Wherever one places the operas, the tone poems are in all respects ninteenth-century works. They sprang initially from Strauss's introduction to the music of Liszt and Wagner by the Meiningen violinist Alexander Ritter in the mid-1880s, before which Strauss had been subjected to a conservative musical upbringing by a musician father who lined up emphatically with the Brahmsians against the Wagnerites. Ritter persuaded Strauss that 'new ideas must search for new forms – this basic principle of Liszt's symphonic works, in which the poetic idea was really the formative element, became henceforward the guiding principle for my own symphonic work'.

In fact there was nothing particularly new about the notion of the form-giving poetic idea, which harked back a good fifty years to Berlioz and the young Liszt. But in Germany it had become mixed up with the (not wholly artistic) controversy surrounding the music of Wagner, and had bred a reaction which, specifically through the works of Brahms, retained its vigour right up to Schoenberg and the twentieth century. Strauss's real achievement was not that he became overnight the latest hired gun of the Music of the Future, but that he absorbed its expressive concepts into an unflinchingly classical attitude to compositional technique. It is only a slight exaggeration to say that *Macbeth* (1886–8) and *Don Juan* (1888–9) were the first symphonic works on the progressive wing that were technically beyond reproach even by the crusty standards of German academics. They established Strauss as a major figure on both the national and international scenes, long before Mahler's symphonies were more than a dot on the central European horizon. It is against this background that Strauss's last great tone poem, *Ein Heldenleben*, has to be understood.

Ein Heldenleben ('A Hero's Life') was the largest of Strauss's tone poems to date, and it was also the boldest and most original in its approach to harmony, counterpoint and orchestration. It used to be thought a damning indictment of the score that it offered a heroic portrait of its own composer, and correspondingly Strauss's advocates considered that they could vindicate the work by discrediting this particular criticism. The result was (and sometimes still is) that a great deal of attention is paid to the somewhat raw narrative structure which Strauss attached to the work. We are invited to admire the exploits of a composer-hero (identified by the 'Eroica' key of E flat: first-subject group) who is attacked in print by music critics (second group), reassured and for a time restrained by his wife (third group), but who finally rides out to battle (development), routs his critics (recapitulation: first group), takes stock of his life (second group), and rides into the sunset of a heroic retirement and honoured death (coda). The long section of quotations from Strauss's earlier scores (the so-called 'Works of Peace' section before the coda) always attracted particular notice, because it proved to the work's disparagers that Strauss was indeed the intended hero, while giving its admirers a chance to show their erudition by identifying the sources of the quotations. What all this nonsense argues in respect of the autonomous work of art is a matter for conjecture. It certainly does not tell us much about Strauss's music.

As a forty-minute single movement, *Ein Heldenleben* ranks with the first movement of Mahler's Third Symphony (1896) among late-Romantic symphonic blockbusters. But its universe is really very different. Whereas Mahler's approach to form is in large measure empirical, Strauss's is in outline academic. In proportion, sequence and broad tonal design the piece conforms with classical principles (notice, for instance, how 'correct' the recapitulation sounds: and this is a property of the theme and key, not of the story).

Stylistically, though, the message is as daring as Mahler's, and hardly less individual. Everything grows from the enormous opening theme, with its blend of simple triadic figures (as in Beethoven's 'Eroica') and ornate arabesques. What starts as a unison melody ranging across the entire orchestral register soon proliferates into a dense polyphony of such figures, always expressing a fairly simple, slow-moving harmony, but sounding complicated because each line is so freely embellished. In the second section Strauss uses the same technique with much spikier and expressively more restricted material (not just because critics are such mean people but because they never agree with each other). And in the Battlefield (development) section, he throws everything in together, binding it all with an ostinato rhythm and a pedal harmony, but allowing the noise to accumulate without particular limit.

Such music must have sounded devastatingly modern when it was first played under the composer's baton in Frankfurt in March 1899, though it was very soon eclipsed by the more organic counterpoint of early Schoenberg and the more volatile expressionism of Strauss's own operas *Salome* (1905) and *Elektra* (1909). *Ein Heldenleben* remains a Romantic score not least in its dependence on the long melodic line, and its consistent use of a huge orchestra to make a great deal of noise. Even in the gentler music of the love scene (third section) and the serene coda with its cor anglais *ranz des vaches* (cow-call), the scoring is full and eventful, while as for the famous violin solo which personifies the hero's gentle (and somewhat over-persuasive) wife, it would be hard to imagine a more archetypal Romantic image.

For Strauss, *Ein Heldenleben* was decidedly the end of an era. The operas he was about to write would call for a much more flexible and less formal approach to musical portraiture. Meanwhile, it was fairly clear that the expansion of symphonic narrative could not go much further. Strauss did in fact make one more attempt to personalise the genre, in the *Symphonia domestica*. But that is another story.

Till Eulenspiegels lustige Streiche, Op. 28 (1894–5)

As a young man, Richard Strauss was hailed as a modernist, champion of Wagner and the so-called New Music and composer of a series of demanding orchestral tone poems, vivid and immediately accessible monuments of late-Romantic music. The young Strauss's early appreciation of musical form and orchestration was greatly influenced by the conservative tastes of his father, a horn player in the Munich Court Orchestra. However, the twenty-four-year-old successfully outraged the musical establishment and impressed audiences with his first tone poem, *Don Juan*, a forward-looking score that deeply offended the powerful Viennese critic Eduard Hanslick. Strauss, lamented Hanslick, was like 'a routined chemist who well understands how to mix all the elements of musical-sensual stimulation to produce stupefying "pleasure gas"'.

Strauss's marriage in 1894 to the singer Pauline de Ahna eased his bitter disappointment at the failure of his first opera *Guntram* earlier that year, and appears to have inspired him to create one of his wittiest, most inventive tone poems, *Till Eulenspiegel*. Strauss christened his new score in full as 'Till Eulenspiegel's merry pranks, after the old rogue's tale, set for large orchestra in rondo form'. A telegram from Strauss to the work's first conductor suggested that he could not explain its literary 'programme': 'Analysis impossible for me. All wit spent in notes.' However, he later provided a narrative to fit the music based on the exploits of the mischievous villain of German folklore:

> Merry Till cavorts through life, his jaunty progress charted at first by a carefree tune for solo horn. The anti-hero enjoys poking fun at mankind's pretensions, religious hypocrisy and the world of academia; he disrupts a village market, unsuccessfully attempts to find true love, impersonates a priest, and continues whistling on his way. An

ear-splitting roll on the side drum signals that Till must answer for his 'crimes', brought before judge and jury yet unwilling to observe the trial in silence until the death sentence is announced. Trumpets and drums herald Till's journey to the scaffold, where his merry pranks are ended.

Andrew Stewart © BBC

Igor Stravinsky (1882–1971)

Stravinsky's unrivalled impact on the course of twentieth-century music was originally brought about by the complexity and originality of his first ballets, on Russian themes, for Diaghilev's Ballets Russes: *The Firebird* (1910), *Petrushka* (1911) and *The Rite of Spring* (1913), though we now know how much they owe to the Russian folk-music tradition. With his move to Paris and another ballet, *Pulcinella* (1920), came a shift to the sharp-edged clarity of the neoclassical style, which also characterises the Octet (1923) and Piano Concerto (1924). In the eight months to June 1939, Stravinsky suffered the loss of his daughter, wife and mother in turn and, with war impending, decamped to the USA, where he undertook numerous conducting tours, and composed *The Rake's Progress* (1951). In the 1950s, ever in tune with the times, Stravinsky made another compositional change, in which he embraced serialism (the ballet *Agon*, 1957; the cantata *Threni*, 1958). He made many recordings of his own music, as both conductor and pianist.

Agon, ballet for twelve dancers (1953–7)

1 Pas de quatre – Double pas de quatre – Triple pas de quatre –
2 Prelude – First pas de trois: Saraband-Step – Gailliarde – Coda –
3 Interlude – Second pas de trois: Bransle simple – Bransle gay – Bransle double –
4 Interlude – Pas de deux – Four Duos – Four Trios

The idea of completing a trilogy of ballets on classical subjects only came up after Stravinsky had composed *Apollo* (1927–8) and *Orpheus* (1946–7), both choreographed by Stravinsky's Russian-American compatriot, George Balanchine.

For the final ballet of the trilogy Stravinsky suggested to Balanchine a scenario based on the meeting of Odysseus and the Princess Nausicaa in the *Odyssey*. Balanchine resisted, and put forward his own suggestion of 'the enormous finale of a ballet to end all the ballets the world has ever seen'. This met with a characteristic Stravinskyan response: 'Well, limits are precisely what I need and am looking for in everything I compose . . . I will compose a "Concerto for the dance".'

The score of *Agon* materialised only after the completion of several other works, including *Canticum sacrum* (1955). By then Stravinsky's neo-classical idiom of the three preceding decades had begun to move steadily closer to the twelve-note serial procedures of Schoenberg and Webern. *Agon*'s beautifully designed and balanced form is therefore a compendium of Stravinsky's magpie-like musical interests over a period where his style – though not his personal voice – was changing in a radical and unexpected way.

Besides the references to the Baroque models so loved by Stravinsky, and his new-found fascination with Webern, *Agon* also draws on dance forms unearthed by the insatiably omnivorous master-composer in a classic seventeenth-century manual (François de Lauze's *Apologie de la danse* of 1623). The ballet's Greek title means 'contest'.

The musical incident of *Agon*'s twelve dances – four groups of three – is highly compressed. So without the presence of the dancers themselves to make the work's shape easily clear to the eye, a few signposts may be helpful to the ear. The indications in square brackets, as given in the score, are Stravinsky's.

Pas de quatre [As the curtain rises, four male dancers are aligned across the rear of the stage with their backs to the audience.]
Crisp trumpet-and-horn fanfares and restless cellos and basses meet a cooler response from mandolin and harp; the ideas are combined and extended.

Double pas de quatre [Eight female dancers]
Busy string figures accompany chattering woodwind; swooping glissandos on violas and cellos offer roguish contrast.
Triple pas de quatre [Eight female and four male dancers]
The previous section elaborated.

Prelude
An insistent timpani figure sets off a swirl of surrounding figuration, leading towards a graceful arabesque for double-bass harmonics, flutes and bassoons.
First pas de trois: Saraband-Step [Male dance solo]
A slow dance in triple time, scored for the startlingly unlikely combination of flamboyant, Baroque-style solo violin, solo xylophone and two trombones – plus two fragments of blink-and-you'll-miss-it commentary from the cellos.
Gailliarde [Two female dancers]
More instrumental alchemy: delicate harp and mandolin tracery flows between high, ethereal chords on flutes and double-bass harmonics, and low ones on solo viola and cellos.
Coda [One male and two female dancers]
Loping triple-time rhythms, with prominent solo violin.

Interlude
The same timpani-led music as the Prelude (above), slightly elaborated.
Second pas de trois: Bransle simple [Two male dancers]
Two trumpets chase each other in close canon (playing identical music in different phases).
Bransle gay [One female dancer]
Castanets click along in an unchanging three-beat rhythm; meanwhile the metre of the music played by pairs of flutes, bassoons and clarinets is both irregular in itself, and constantly changing.
Bransle double [Two male and one female dancers]
An angular violin line is counterpointed by solo trombone and trumpet; contrast comes in repeated piano-and-woodwind chords.

Interlude
The timpani-led material again, elaborated further.
Pas de deux
The kernel of the work, scored at first for solo violin and strings only. The music's poised gravity recalls the Baroque, while its rhythmic suppleness and spare, wide-stretching melodic shapes evoke the serial world of Webern. Yet the detached sensuality of the result is the purest Stravinsky. A central episode introduces horns and piano in canon [Male dancer], then an elegant trio of flutes [Female dancer] and a restatement of the canon [Male dancer – refrain]. Then comes a fast, incisive Coda [Both dancers].
Four Duos [Male and female]
Quick-striding unison material for pizzicato strings and trombones leads straight into . . .
Four Trios [Male and two females]
. . . an equally terse development of this material (on bowed strings), and then on into a final Coda [All the dancers], where the work's opening music returns. [The female dancers leave the stage. The male dancers take their position as at the beginning – backs to the audience.]

Apollo, ballet in two scenes (1927–8)

Birth of Apollo – Apollo's Variation – Pas d'action – Calliope's Variation – Polyhymnia's Variation – Terpsichore's Variation – Apollo's Variation – Pas de deux – Coda – Apotheosis

Composed in 1927 and completed in January 1928, *Apollo* was the first ballet Stravinsky wrote for a company other than Diaghilev's (to Diaghilev's intense annoyance). It was also the first work he ever wrote to a commission from the USA. The invitation came from the Library of Congress, and specified a pantomime for three or four dancers and small orchestra on a subject of the composer's own choice, to which

Stravinsky responded with what amounts to the first of his abstract (or plotless) ballets, and his first ever work for string orchestra. When he started composing the music, in July 1927, Stravinsky seems to have envisaged parts for harp and piano as well, and he already knew the subject-matter, if not the details of the scenario – which, indeed, seem never to have assumed great importance for him, if we are to believe his remark in a Paris interview of 1935 to the effect that *Apollo* contains no 'argument' and that 'this is the key to the mystery of Terpsichore'.

Those who commission works of art usually have some mental picture of what might result, and no doubt such preconceptions are more often disappointed than not. But *Apollo* must surely have come as one of the biggest artistic surprises in history. Here was the great bogeyman of modern music, still best known for the barbarisms of *The Rite of Spring* but with a recent reputation among the culturally up-to-date for steely formalism backed up by an arid theoretical anti-expressionism, suddenly coming up with a melting and graceful score for strings that sounded suspiciously like an attempt to revive the French Romantic ballet as cultivated by Léon Minkus, Adolphe Adam and Delibes. At the time of the commission *Oedipus rex* was nearing completion but had not yet been played; would this astonishing mixture of Handel and Verdi have made *Apollo* any easier to predict? No easier, perhaps, than to have predicted Stravinsky's next work, *The Fairy's Kiss*, a Hans Christian Andersen ballet on themes by Tchaikovsky, after hearing *Apollo*.

Technically, if not aesthetically, *Apollo* fits well enough into the period which began with *Mavra* (1921–2) and the Octet (1922–3), a period which from the first concerned itself, self-consciously, with the relation between form and expression. The very subject-matter of the ballet, such as it is, amounts to a dramatised version of this issue. Apollo, the leader of the Muses and god of formal perfection and ideal classical beauty, is born, grows to maturity, and enters Parnassus at the head of the nine muses (represented in the ballet by Calliope,

Polyhymnia and Terpsichore: the muses of poetry, mime and dance). In between, he and they perform a series of statuesque but vigorous dances, modelled on the general formulae of French Romantic ballet, but plainly arguing the virtues of classical restraint and artifice in the modes of intellectual, emotional and physical expression.

Stravinsky claimed that the rhythms of *Apollo* were based on the idea of versification. Each dance is supposed to be a variation on an iambic pattern, perhaps in the manner of Valéry's *vers donné*, where a whole poem may be made out of minute fluctuations against an unvarying background metre. Such variations had always been basic to Stravinsky's rhythmic technique; but the whole point of *Apollo* is that they occur discreetly, without the violent emphasis of his earlier ballets, drawing attention to the subtle refinement of the device rather than its strangeness or barbarity. This careful presentation of method is very typical of his synthetic, or neoclassical, phase. He also claimed that *Apollo* was important for its sense of long line, which is already a feature of *Mavra* and the Octet, but is accentuated here by the sustaining powers of the string orchestra. And while this chiefly has to do with 'top-line' melody, it also breeds rich counterpoint, notably in the four-part canon of the 'Pas d'action'.

The Firebird, Suite (1909–10; arr. 1945)

1a Introduction –
b Prelude and Dance of the Firebird –
c Variations (Firebird) –
2 Pantomime 1 –
3 Pas de deux (Firebird and Ivan Tsarevich)
4 Pantomime 2 –
5 Scherzo (Dance of the Princesses) –
6 Pantomime 3 –
7 Rondo (Khorovod)
8 Infernal Dance –

9 Lullaby (Firebird) –
10 Final Hymn

Stravinsky composed *The Firebird* with almost defiant speed between November 1909 and May 1910, to a commission from Serge Diaghilev, the legendary impresario, which was originally intended for Lyadov. As it happened, however, there was a deadline that the older, indolent Lyadov was unlikely to be able to meet. So Stravinsky, who had already caught Diaghilev's ear with some arrangements of Chopin piano pieces, got his chance and, with the work's first performance in Paris on 25 June 1910, launched a career as a ballet composer that was long to outlast his association with both Diaghilev and the Ballets Russes.

The Firebird was scored for a large orchestra, which the young Stravinsky exploited with great brilliance and not a little originality. The year after its premiere, he produced a suite of five excerpts that retained those orchestral forces, including quadruple woodwind and extensive percussion. In 1919, however, he revised the score so that it could be performed by smaller orchestras (with only double woodwind and less percussion). And finally, in 1945, he produced a new, definitive version of the suite, revising his reduced orchestration and inserting five extra items – or rather two extra items with linking transitions (the Pantomimes) – between the first and second movements of the 1919 suite. The music in the 1945 suite illustrates all the principal characters involved in a plot that at times seems like a blend of *The Magic Flute* and *Parsifal.* First there is an atmospheric Introduction depicting the magic garden of the sorcerer Khaschei. Then the Firebird herself appears, with the young Prince Ivan in pursuit. The Firebird's solo dance follows (Tempo giusto), and ends with her capture by the Prince.

After a brief linking Pantomime, the couple dance a romantic, exotic Pas de deux, in which the Firebird pleads for her freedom (Adagio), and the Prince eventually agrees, extracting a feather as payment. Then follows another short

Pantomime, after which thirteen bewitched Princesses appear: a scherzo section accompanies their dancing.

After the third Pantomime comes the Rondo (Moderato), starting with a simple, folk-like melody on the oboe. The Prince inevitably falls in love with one of the Princesses, and the demon Khaschei, sensing a threat to his power, appears suddenly and launches an Infernal Dance (Vivo). This flexes those unmistakably Stravinskyan muscles whose violent energy would be fully unleashed two years later in *The Rite of Spring*.

At the end of the Infernal Dance, Prince Ivan destroys Khaschei's evil kingdom with a flourish of the magic feather. His Princess is freed, and the last two sections of the suite, Lullaby and Final Hymn, celebrate the couple's emergence from the infernal regions and their triumphant betrothal.

Fireworks (1908)

Stravinsky's early scores, many of them composed under the supervision of his beloved teacher Rimsky-Korsakov, include a full-blown Tchaikovskyan piano sonata, a four-movement symphony (dedicated to his teacher) and a handful of brief orchestral works. The lessons initially consisted in Stravinsky orchestrating piano sonatas by Beethoven or the short scores of pieces by Rimsky-Korsakov himself, exercises that the young student found particularly useful. Rimsky-Korsakov subsequently advised him on the orchestration of his early original works, in which the influence of the older man is clearly discernible – as is the pervasive influence of Dukas, whose *Sorcerer's Apprentice* is almost literally quoted in *Fireworks*.

Stravinsky composed *Fireworks* in 1908, while on vacation at his country estate at Oustiloug, and sent the score to his teacher, intending it as a celebration piece for the wedding of Rimsky-Korsakov's daughter. 'A few days later,' Stravinsky recalled, 'a telegram informed me of his death, and shortly afterwards my registered packet was returned to me: "Not delivered on account of death of addressee".'

The piece was performed the following year, and the course of twentieth-century music was changed irrevocably when the Russian ballet impresario Serge Diaghilev heard the music. He immediately asked Stravinsky to write some orchestrations of Chopin for his recently formed Ballets Russes company, subsequently commissioning the series of remarkable ballet scores that includes *The Firebird*, *Petrushka* and *The Rite of Spring*.

From the pianissimo woodwind opening, these orchestral *Fireworks* develop, through a series of ostinatos and canonic repetitions, into a highly colourful pyrotechnical display.

Brendan Beales © BBC

Petrushka (1910–11)

1 The Shrovetide Fair – Showman's Scene – Russian Dance
2 In Petrushka's Cell
3 In the Blackamoor's Cell – Dance of the Ballerina – Waltz
4 The Shrovetide Fair (Evening) – Nursemaids' Dance – Dance of the Coachmen – The Masqueraders – Petrushka's Death

Stravinsky's ballet *Petrushka* was composed between *The Firebird* and *The Rite of Spring* and thus forms part of a logical progression in his early compositional career. *The Firebird*, Stravinsky's first collaboration with Diaghilev and the Ballets Russes, was first performed in June 1910 and was an instant success. Almost immediately the composer had an idea for a new project, a ballet based on pagan rites in prehistoric Russia, but, having gone to Switzerland on holiday with the intention of beginning work on what was to become *The Rite of Spring*, he found another piece rapidly taking shape in his mind.

At first he envisaged it as a 'Konzertstück' for piano and orchestra, but, as he began to compose, the image of a puppet that came to life dominated his thoughts, a puppet that, as he put it, kept 'exasperating the patience of the orchestra with diabolical cascades of arpeggios. The orchestra in return retaliates with menacing trumpet-blasts. The outcome is a terrific noise which reaches its climax and ends in the sorrowful and querulous collapse of the poor puppet.' He quickly completed this piece, and then struggled to find a title, eventually alighting on *Petrushka*, the name given in Russia to the ridiculous puppet figure common throughout Western culture under the various names of Punch, Harlequin or Guignol.

The idea appealed strongly to Diaghilev, and Alexandre Benois was chosen to do the scenario and decor. Stravinsky worked closely with Benois in the winter and spring of 1910–11, and rehearsals began at the Paris Opéra in April, with Mikhail Fokine, who had choreographed *The Firebird*, working overtime with the dancers. The constantly shifting rhythmic patterns of *Petrushka* proved a challenge to the company, but excitement about the new work mounted, and its status as a masterpiece was immediately established by its first performance (conducted by Pierre Monteux, with Karsavina, Nijinsky, Orlov and Cecchetti in the four principal roles) at the Théâtre du Châtelet on 13 June 1911.

The work is now so familiar that it is difficult to imagine how strange it must have sounded in the early part of the last century. Russian folk melodies and dances permeate the score, whose 'patchwork' quality – a mixture of narration and set-piece dances (mirrored in the choreography by free pantomime and closed forms) – is enhanced by the interlocking musical tableaux, and the way in which Stravinsky combines the musical themes associated with each character or situation. Already Stravinsky's highly individual handling of melodic material, and the novel metrical patterns and brilliance of the orchestral scoring, were paving the way for the *succès de scandale* of the century – *The Rite of Spring* – which as yet lay two years in the future.

1 *The Shrovetide Fair*
A brief prelude sets the frosty, bustling scene – the snow-covered Admiralty Square in St Petersburg, about 1830. A Russian Easter folk song accompanies the parading, jostling crowd. After street dancers have entertained them (two popular tunes, suggesting organ-grinder and musical box), ominous drum rolls introduce a Showman from a booth, his flute solo intimating that he has magic powers. He presents three dolls – a Ballerina, a Blackamoor and Petrushka – who display their movements in a 'Russian Dance' which incorporates another folk-song theme, followed by a sudden blackout and a thud of drums.

2 *In Petrushka's Cell*
The sad, white-faced puppet is kicked into his room by the Showman's boot. Sobs on bassoon express his suffering, and he rails against his fate with a *furioso* passage for full orchestra. The Ballerina enters; Petrushka wildly and grotesquely tries to convey his love for her, but succeeds only in frightening her away, leaving him to lonely rage and despair.

3 *In the Blackamoor's Cell*
Magnificent but stupid, the Blackamoor accepts his fate idly and contentedly. A solo trumpet heralds the Ballerina, who dances with the Blackamoor to the strains of a waltz (incorporating two tunes by Johann Strauss I's rival, Joseph Lanner). Distant cries announce Petrushka, angry with jealous rage. They quarrel and chase each other until the Ballerina collapses and Petrushka is roughly thrown out.

4 *The Shrovetide Fair (Evening)*
Back among the crowd outside, the revelry is in full swing. A traditional dance by Imperial Nursemaids; a performing bear; gypsies with tambourines; coachmen and grooms dance with a heavy, stamping rhythm, and then with the Nursemaids. Carnival masqueraders intrude among them, and the revelry increases until interrupted by Petrushka's cries from the booth behind. He rushes out, pursued by the Blackamoor,

who fells him with his scimitar (the sound of a tambourine let fall on the floor). The Showman is sent for, picks up the 'corpse' and shakes it at the crowd to show that it is merely sawdust. Suddenly Petrushka's mocking call high on the trumpet is heard: his ghostly figure is cocking a snook from the roof of the booth. The music drops from the key of C to an enigmatic, unresolved F sharp, ending the ballet with a deliberate question mark.

Pulcinella, ballet in one act (1919–20; rev. 1965)

According to Stravinsky, *Pulcinella* was his second ballet to have been based on an idea furnished by Serge Diaghilev (the first having been *The Firebird*). This time, though, in September 1919 (not spring, as Stravinsky wrongly recalled), the motive was more complicated. For some years Stravinsky had been trying to achieve a final form of his ballet *Les noces* – emphatically a Diaghilev project, and one to which the impresario was deeply attached. But meanwhile there had been other works for other patrons: *Renard* had been commissioned by the Princesse de Polignac, though not yet performed, and *The Soldier's Tale* had been put on in Lausanne with money provided by the Swiss industrialist Werner Reinhart. Diaghilev was jealous of these works ('I know', Stravinsky reports him as saying, 'that you are much taken by your Alpine colleagues') and had various schemes for enticing Stravinsky back into his own sphere of influence. He planned a revival of *The Rite of Spring*, and a ballet called *The Song of the Nightingale*, which Stravinsky had originally extracted from his opera *The Nightingale* at Diaghilev's suggestion in 1917. But he was also desperate for new work and, with *Les noces* no nearer completion, Diaghilev's idea for a Neapolitan ballet based on pieces by Pergolesi provided a useful stopgap. Diaghilev had originally planned to commission the work from Manuel de Falla. But Falla was heavily involved that summer in an operetta based on pieces by Chopin. So it was purely fortuitous that, at the end of the summer, Diaghilev had the project to offer to Stravinsky.

Pulcinella was in fact one of several ideas that had originated with Diaghilev's latest protégé, the dancer and choreographer Léonide Massine. Diaghilev had bought Massine a set of seventeenth- and eighteenth-century dance manuals with choreographic notations that Massine had attempted to decipher and recreate. The immediate product of these researches was a ballet based on Goldoni's comedy *The Good-Humoured Ladies*, for which Vincenzo Tommasini orchestrated some Scarlatti, and Massine choreographed according to the old manuals. Next, in August 1919, Diaghilev and Massine found a large quantity of music in Pergolesi's name (much of it, as it happens, misattributed) in the library of the Naples Conservatory, and Massine also dug up a number of eighteenth-century *commedia dell'arte* scenarios, some of which were still being played by Neapolitan puppet theatres.

'During that summer in Naples,' Massine wrote (though it probably was not the same but an earlier summer):

> I went often to watch the puppet plays in which Pulcinella played the chief part. I delighted in his ever-changing gestures, his dangling legs and his hook-nosed mask, with one side of the face laughing and the other crying . . . I bought an authentic Pulcinella mask . . . put it on, and began trying to reproduce Pulcinella's gestures and movements.

In fact, Diaghilev had also found some trio sonatas (which he believed to be by Pergolesi but were in fact by Domenico Gallo) in the British Museum in September 1918, and had even had them copied out. These copies, and others from Naples, were what he handed to Stravinsky in Paris a year later. 'I looked,' Stravinsky later told Robert Craft, 'and I fell in love. My ultimate selection of pieces derived only partly from Diaghilev's examples, however, and partly from published editions.' (Actually, all the *Pulcinella* material was published, though only about half of it was by Pergolesi.) Stravinsky completed the score the following April, and *Pulcinella* reached the stage in the Ballets Russes season at the Paris Opéra, with designs by Picasso, on 15 May 1920.

'A stylish orchestration was what Diaghilev wanted,' Stravinsky recorded, 'and my music so shocked him that he went about for a long time with a look that suggested the Offended Eighteenth Century.' Since the two had been quarrelling bitterly over royalty payments for a year or more, one might cynically suggest that Diaghilev was as much shocked by the financial, as by the artistic, implications of Stravinsky's re-compositions (rather than straight arrangements). But if he had been more in touch with the composer's recent music, he might at least have been less surprised. For instance, the flirtations with ragtime, of which the *Piano Rag Music* was only the latest of several, hardly suggest virtuous obedience to a received idiom. Diaghilev did know some of Stravinsky's little piano pieces, among which there is a polka inspired by Diaghilev himself in the guise of a circus ringmaster, and it might even be thought curious that he made no suggestion for a ballet based on such material. But such a ballet was already to hand in Satie's *Parade*. And from Stravinsky was still expected, above all, the quintessentially Russian *Les noces*. *Pulcinella* was plainly conceived as a follow-up to *The Good-Humoured Ladies*. But what emerged was subtly, yet profoundly, different.

In the various synthetic, or referential, pieces Stravinsky had been writing – whether based on ragtime, or folk music, or old dance types – his idea seems always to have been to think himself into the manner in question, then to compose in the usual way. The only difference with the Pergolesi material was that the restrictions were tighter and more specific. Throughout *Pulcinella*, Stravinsky sticks in essence to the existing melody and bass, but adds inner voices which show that he was hearing the harmony as a kind of sound-field. The extra notes are nearly always part of the scale (that is, not harshly dissonant), and they are the same kind of smooth discord that Baroque music throws up in the normal way. Stravinsky's rhythmic thinking is also much in evidence. As he was writing the ballet, he said, he had begun to look through Pergolesi for 'rhythmic' rather than 'melodic' numbers – 'I did not go far, of course, before discovering that this distinction does not exist . . . eighteenth-century music is, in one sense, all dance music.'

But here, too, he could not resist extra-stylistic additions. Occasionally the rhythms and barrings are subtly distorted by added or subtracted values, mostly quite discreet, but sometimes (as in the finale) more drastic – as if the music had been cut into pieces, then repasted with one or two bits missing or displaced. There is no better illustration in Stravinsky of the now-accepted fact that his method and attitude to his material never really varied, however un-Stravinskyan the raw materials.

All the local girls, runs the synopsis in the score, are in love with Pulcinella. The boys are so jealous that they plot to kill him. When they imagine they've succeeded, they borrow his costume to show to their lovers. But the crafty Pulcinella has put a double in his place, and the double has only feigned death under his enemies' blows.

Pulcinella disguises himself as a magician and resuscitates the double. Just as the boys, thinking themselves rid of him, come in search of their betrotheds, the real Pulcinella appears and arranges all the weddings. He himself marries Pimpinella, with the blessing of his double, Fourbo, who now in turn appears as the magician.

The Rite of Spring (1911–13)

Part 1: The Adoration of the Earth
Introduction – Auguries of Spring: Dances of Adolescent Girls – Game of Capture – Round-Dances of Spring – Games of Rival Tribes – Procession of the Sage – The Sage – Dance of the Earth
Part 2: The Sacrifice
Introduction – Mysterious Circles of Adolescent Girls – Glorification of the Chosen One – Evocation of the Ancestors – Ritual Dance of the Ancestors – Sacrificial Dance of the Chosen One

Stravinsky's account of how he conceived *The Rite of Spring* has almost the character of religious witness: 'I saw in imagination a solemn pagan rite: wise elders, seated in a circle, watching a young girl dance herself to death. They were sacrificing her to propitiate the god of spring.' This vision came to him just as he was finishing *The Firebird* and before he wrote *Petrushka*. He knew he needed more time for *The Rite*, so he wrote *Petrushka* first; he also needed a detailed scenario, which he requested from the painter and expert in Russian folklore, Nicholas Roerich.

To most people, the details of the ritual that Roerich worked out probably seem academic. The meaning is clear, cruel but true: something (someone) must die for life to go on. Besides, although it had its famously scandalous premiere as a ballet for Serge Diaghilev's Ballets Russes company – with radical choreography by Vaslav Nijinsky emphasising earthiness rather than airiness – *The Rite* rapidly won a place in the concert hall, and, unlike Stravinsky's other ballets, there has never been a suite of extracts: it is almost always played complete.

In his poem 'Concert-Interpretation (*Le sacre du printemps*)', Siegfried Sassoon satirised the quick switch in public response following the riot that greeted the score's Paris premiere in 1913:

The audience pricks an intellectual Ear . . .
Stravinsky . . . Quite the Concert of the Year!

Forgetting now that none-so-distant date
When they (or folk facsimilar in state
Of mind) first heard with hisses – hoots – guffaws –
This abstract Symphony (they booed because
Stravinsky jumped their Wagner palisade
With modes that seemed cacophonous and queer),
Forgetting now the hullabaloo they made,
The Audience pricks an intellectual ear.

Bassoons begin . . . Sonority envelops
Our auditory innocence; and brings
To Me, I must admit, some drift of things
Omnific, seminal, and adolescent.
Polyphony through dissonance develops
A serpent-conscious Eden, crude but pleasant;
While vibro-atmospheric copulations
With mezzo-forte mysteries of noise
Prelude Stravinsky's statement of the joys
That unify the monkeydom of nations.

This matter is most indelicate indeed!
Yet one perceives no symptom of stampede.
The Stalls remain unruffled: craniums gleam:
Swept by a storm of pizzicato chords,
Elaborate ladies re-assure their lords
With lifting brows that signify 'Supreme!'
While orchestrated gallantry of goats
Impugns the astigmatic programme-notes.

In the Grand Circle one observes no sign
Of riot: peace prevails along the line.
And in the Gallery, cargoed to capacity,
No tremor bodes eruptions and alarms.
They are listening to this not-quite-new audacity
As though it were by someone dead, – like Brahms.

But savagery pervades Me; I am frantic
With corybantic rupturing of laws.
Come, dance, and seize this clamorous chance to function
Creatively – abandoning compunction
In anti-social rhapsodic applause!
Lynch the conductor! Jugulate the drums!
Butcher the brass! Ensanguinate the strings!
Throttle the flutes! . . . Stravinsky's April comes
With pitiless pomp and pain of sacred springs . . .
Incendiarise the Hall with resinous fires
Of sacrificial fiddles scorched and snapping! . . .

Meanwhile the music blazes and expires;
And the delighted Audience is clapping.

from *Siegfried Sassoon: Collected Poems*

For Stravinsky, the symbolic idea of *The Rite* coincided with a turning-point in his music. Just as, he recalled, 'the violent Russian spring was like the whole earth cracking', so he was to give music new life by breaking up its past. At least, some of its past; for he based many of the melodies, or bits of melody, on folk tunes, the most famous being the Lithuanian melody that the bassoon plays at the very beginning. (Stravinsky once joked that it ought to be transposed up each year as players got used to the high register, since a sense of strain was essential.) The harmonies, too – and they are harmonies, however dissonant – are based on recognisable chords, though disguised by shocking superimpositions, as in the opening crunch of the final 'Sacrificial Dance', where D grinds against E flat.

Stravinsky composed at the piano, and said that he could play this whole movement before he worked out how to write it down – 'I had only my ear to guide me.' In fact, he revised the notation of the rhythm thirty years after the first performance, changing the unit of beat. Earlier, in 1921, he revised other parts of the score, shortening bars to make it easier to conduct. In two early commercial recordings, both made in

1929, under Stravinsky himself and under Pierre Monteux, the asymmetrical rhythms of *The Rite* still proved an insurmountable challenge, and in the 'Sacrificial Dance' the unpredictable juggling of short–long–long and short–short–long–long, with short–short–long–long–long and short–long–long–long thrown in for bad measure, proved altogether too much and had the orchestras floundering.

Neither pounding motor rhythms nor shifting, asymmetrical metres were Stravinsky's invention – Bartók and Prokofiev had both already used them – but his unpredictable syncopations, breaking rhythm up into the tiniest motifs, have been a model for all kinds of composers. Equally influential was Stravinsky's defiance of the traditional idea of continuity in 'classical' music. After the tangled elaboration of the 'Introduction', which is rather like an improvisatory free-for-all, *The Rite* is a succession of blocks, of contrasts between ideas that are perpetuated rather than developed or taken anywhere, and in that sense it fulfils its title – a 'rite' that admits no argument or discussion, but asserts an irresistible power.

Pyotr Ilyich Tchaikovsky (1840–93)

After study at the School of Jurisprudence and four years working in the Ministry of Justice, Tchaikovsky enrolled at the newly founded St Petersburg Conservatory (1862–5). He came into contact with 'The Five', whose leader, Balakirev, supervised the younger composer's *Romeo and Juliet* overture (1869), which already displayed a gift for tragic lyricism. Despite his homosexuality, he married a young admirer of his music in 1877, which proved disastrous after a matter of weeks. That year also saw the beginning of a fourteen-year relationship with Nadezhda von Meck: though they never met, she acted as Tchaikovsky's benefactress and soulmate by correspondence, and the ballet *Swan Lake*, the Fourth Symphony and the opera *Eugene Onegin* were the results of her support. A fallow period followed the successful Violin Concerto (1878), lasting until the *Manfred* Symphony (1884). Between 1890 and 1892 he wrote two further ballets, *The Sleeping Beauty* and *The Nutcracker*, demonstrating a skill and seriousness of purpose in the medium unusual for a composer principally renowned for his symphonies. He died, possibly through suicide, within ten days of conducting the premiere of his Sixth Symphony.

Francesca da Rimini, symphonic fantasia after Dante, Op. 32 (1876)

No subject meant more to Tchaikovsky than that of doomed or illicit love: the stories of Romeo and Juliet, Onegin and Tatyana, Manfred and Astarte, Hermann and Lisa, all drew from him some of his most personal music. It was towards the end of 1875, when he was casting about for a suitable opera libretto, that he first seems to have been attracted by the story of Francesca da Rimini. In the fifth Canto of Dante's *Inferno* the poet tells of his meeting with Francesca, condemned to an eternity of torment for yielding to a forbidden love for her husband's younger brother Paolo. The strength of Francesca's passion and Dante's pity at her frightful punishment must have struck a profound chord in Tchaikovsky, similarly gnawed by passions he had to conceal from the world, and living in constant fear of gossip and exposure.

Nothing came of the projected opera, but during the following months Tchaikovsky's mind kept returning to the subject. In July 1876, while staying in Switzerland, he complained of a depression that stifled any desire to compose. His brother Modest, hoping to stimulate him into working again, suggested possible subjects for musical treatment: *Hamlet*, *Othello*, Lermontov's *Tamar*, and again *Francesca da Rimini*, not as an opera, but as an orchestral piece. Tchaikovsky could not at first make up his mind, but the following month, while on a train to Paris, he reread Dante 'and was inflamed with a wish to write a symphonic poem on *Francesca*'.

Before he could begin the composition, he had to go to Bayreuth to review the first complete performance of Wagner's *Ring*. His articles were respectful, but privately he was unenthusiastic. 'At least I'm not bored,' he wrote to Modest, 'though in no way can I say that I'm enjoying myself.' And later, 'taken all in all it's killingly boring! How many hundreds of thousands of times nicer is [Delibes's] *Sylvia*!'

Back in Russia his depression deepened, and increasing shame and anguish drove him towards the fateful decision which he first announced to his brother: 'I am now living through a very critical moment in my life. When an opportunity occurs I'll write to you about it in rather more detail, but meanwhile I'll just say: I have decided to marry. I cannot avoid this.'

So it was that at the very time he determined to banish 'illicit love' from his own life he began to compose the symphonic poem about the forbidden love of Paolo and Francesca. When he had finished drafting it he commented unemotionally:

> I have written it with love, and the love seems to have come out respectably. As far as the whirlwinds are concerned it would have been possible to make something corresponding more with Doré's illustration, but it didn't come out as I wanted. On the other hand a reliable judgement on this piece is inconceivable while it remains unscored and unperformed.

When it was performed the following year, some listeners thought they detected a Wagnerian flavour in the music, and Tchaikovsky himself confessed:

> The remark that I wrote under the influence of the Nibelungen is quite correct. I myself felt this while I was at work. If I'm not mistaken, it's especially noticeable in the introduction. Isn't it odd that I should have submitted to the influence of a work of art that in general is extremely antipathetic to me?

But in spite of Tchaikovsky's admission, very little in *Francesca*, apart perhaps from the introduction, with its descending tritone figure and sombre brass chords, can be traced to his stay in Bayreuth. Countless lesser composers fell under the spell of Wagner's storms and love music, but Tchaikovsky's individuality was strong enough for him to withstand such temptations.

The form of *Francesca da Rimini* is essentially very simple: a large ternary structure with an introduction. The opening depicts the eerie darkness of the Inferno; there follows the whirling storm which drives the souls of the lovers before it; the long central section expresses the love of Paolo and Francesca; and the piece ends with a return to the music of the storm. The formal simplicity of *Francesca* stands out when we compare it to Tchaikovsky's two preceding symphonic poems, *Romeo and Juliet* and *The Tempest*. Both are very rich in themes, drawing as they do on different episodes and characters from the Shakespeare plays. *Francesca*, on the other hand, is more single-minded. It is not concerned with dramatic narrative, but confines itself obsessively to the stark contrast between irresistible love and its subsequent punishment. The idea and the title are drawn from Dante, but if the work is in any sense a character study, the character in question is unmistakably Tchaikovsky's own.

© Andrew Huth

Fantasy-Overture, *Romeo and Juliet* (1869; rev. 1870, 1880)

Andante non tanto quasi moderato – Allegro giusto – Moderato assai

Immediately after graduation from Anton Rubinstein's recently founded St Petersburg Conservatory at the end of 1865, Tchaikovsky was approached by Rubinstein's brother Nikolay to teach theory at the brand-new Conservatory in Moscow, of which Nikolay was to be the first Director. For several years Tchaikovsky resided in the home of his boss, and though he chafed at the awkward working conditions there, he enjoyed being so close to the cultural levers of power.

His burgeoning talent soon came to the attention of Mily Balakirev, who had very different ideas from the Rubinsteins about the future of Russian music – in a nutshell, Balakirev held that it should be more nationalist than internationalist, and founded more on instinct than on professional craft. There is evidence that Balakirev would willingly have co-opted Tchaikovsky into the 'Mighty Handful' (so dubbed by the publicist and man of letters Vladimir Stasov, in 1867) of which he himself was the senior composer and guiding light. At any rate, Balakirev saw fit to suggest various musical projects to Tchaikovsky, just as he did to his fellow members of the 'Mighty Handful', to the point of specifying programmes, musical forms and even specific keys for the various sections.

This was the case with the *Romeo and Juliet* Fantasy-Overture. Balakirev first proposed the subject-matter, then, when Tchaikovsky confessed that musical inspiration was failing him, outlined a sonata form with a dark introduction evoking Friar Laurence in his cell, a fast main theme in B minor suggesting the feuding Montagues and Capulets, and a love theme in the remarkably distant key of D flat major for the second subject. In Tchaikovsky's first version of the piece, completed in November 1869, he followed those suggestions to the letter. He also responded positively to Balakirev's criticisms after the coolly received premiere the following March. But it was only ten years later, in 1880, and with the experience of the Fourth Symphony just behind him, that Tchaikovsky undertook a second revision, which produced the version we know today.

To reach that definitive state, Tchaikovsky completely recast his Friar Laurence introduction, basing it on a freshly composed chorale theme for clarinets and bassoons, to which the strings respond with mournful fragments. The longer these ideas are spun out, the more the tension builds up, and it takes not one but two accelerations before the eventual release into the Allegro giusto, with its graphic depiction of the Montagues and Capulets. This dramatic, surging music, and the great love theme – magically scored for cor anglais and muted violas – remained more or less unchanged from Tchaikovsky's original through to his final revision. Even before the first performance, Balakirev had confessed to being thrilled by the love theme, and Rimsky-Korsakov agreed: 'What ineffable beauty, what burning passions!' he wrote. 'It is one of the finest themes in all of Russian music!'

Instead of his original, rather dry fugal development section, Tchaikovsky's revision came up with tense interchanges between elements of Friar Laurence's chorale and the Montagues' and Capulets' swordfight music. Finally, after a passionate consummation of the love theme and an intensified version of the development section, the music sinks to rest in a magnificent coda, reflecting on all the moods of the preceding drama and keeping the final outcome uncertain until the last moment.

Michael Tippett (1905–98)

Tippett studied at the Royal College of Music, but he was unhappy with his early works and withdrew them. He sought a period of further study – of counterpoint with R. O. Morris – which prepared the ground for his first mature works, the String Quartet No. 1 (1935; rev. 1944) and the Piano Sonata No. 1 (1936–7). His moral and political convictions pervaded his life and music: he conducted in Oxted, Surrey, in the 1930s, then organised the South London Orchestra of Unemployed Musicians, and was imprisoned for three months in 1943 for refusing to comply with military exemption requirements. After the war he was a leader of the revival of early music at Morley College. His first public success was the oratorio *A Child of Our Time* (1939–41), a public statement against persecution, which included settings of Negro spirituals. He wrote five operas, also to his own texts, as well as four concertos, four piano sonatas, five string quartets, and two major choral works concerned with Man's relationship to Time, *The Vision of St Augustine* (1965) and the vast, eclectic *The Mask of Time* (1980–2).

Fantasia Concertante on a Theme of Corelli (1953)

In 1953 Tippett was commissioned by the Edinburgh International Festival to compose something commemorating the tercentenary of the birth of Arcangelo Corelli. He wrote the work quite rapidly, and conducted the premiere himself with the BBC Symphony Orchestra in Edinburgh's Usher Hall that August. Since the Italian composer's most famous achievement was his twelve Concerti Grossi, Op. 6, published in 1712, Tippett constructed his Fantasia Concertante as a kind of expansion and commentary on the concerto grosso medium, taking a 'theme' from one of

Corelli's concertos and elaborating it through a series of variations that time-travel between Corelli's idiom and his own.

Except that what Tippett calls a 'theme' in his title is not a single melody. Corelli's Concerto Grosso, Op. 6 no. 2, in F, has an unusually extended first movement in several sections: Tippett fashioned a two-part subject that consists of a mellifluous contrapuntal Adagio segment followed by a sprightly homophonic Vivace. (In Corelli's original, the Vivace does indeed follow the Adagio, but it also precedes it, being a kind of ritornello, or refrain, rather than the second limb of a two-part structure.)

Tippett used a string orchestra (instead of Corelli's strings and harpsichord) but divided this body into three: a 'concertino' of two solo violins and solo cello; a 'concerto grosso' made up of about half the remaining strings; and a 'concerto terzo' comprising the rest. Although this last corresponds in some respects to Corelli's continuo, the effect is more that Tippett's Fantasia is conceived for three soloists and double string orchestra, with plentiful opportunities for antiphonal effects.

At the outset, Corelli's theme is presented comparatively simply and straightforwardly by concertino and concerto grosso, accompanied by the concerto terzo. But as soon as this first statement is over, Tippett presents a floridly decorated variation. The decorations grow out of the elaborate flourishes of Baroque ornamentation, but rapidly assume the character of the highly decorated style which Tippett was cultivating at this period (he had just composed his opera *The Midsummer Marriage*). In Corelli's original Adagio Tippett saw an archetype of Italianate lyricism through the ages – he once remarked that Corelli's bass had only to be put into the relative major and somewhat extended to sound like pure Puccini, and he does exactly this at one point in the Fantasia. Yet the result is one of the unassailable classics of the English string repertoire. If Elgar (composer of one of the others, the Introduction and Allegro) was right in maintaining to Herbert Howells and Bernard Shaw that the English mastery of the string medium derives not only from Purcell but also from Handel – who derived it partly from Corelli – there is no paradox here.

As the variations proceed, the concertino becomes progressively more independent, the polyphonic textures ever richer and more involved. Meanwhile, the concerto grosso and concerto terzo gradually lose their separate roles, to the point where they fuse into a single entity in a deeply lyrical Andante espressivo.

This rapt point of greatest unanimity serves as introduction to an elaborate fugue, Allegro moderato, in which all three bodies are now treated as a single orchestra, but of course divided into the many constituent voices of the fugal argument. Tippett includes within its swirling, closely worked counterpoint a transcription of the first twelve bars of J. S. Bach's Fugue on a Theme of Corelli, BWV 579 (now thought to be of doubtful authenticity).

At the incandescent climax of the fugue, the string orchestra re-divides into its original three groupings, and the final variation unfolds as an ecstatic pastoral with florid ornamentation of hallucinatory intensity. (This music is closely related to the evocation of dawn in the final scene of *The Midsummer Marriage*.) A sudden recollection of Corelli's Vivace alternates with a reminiscence of Tippett's first decorated version of the Adagio, the Vivace bringing the work to a crisp formal close.

Ralph Vaughan Williams (1872–1958)

Unlike Elgar before him, Vaughan Williams received a traditional musical education at the Royal College of Music in London, but he also studied abroad – in Berlin with Bruch and in Paris with Ravel. Soon after his return came the *Fantasia on a Theme by Thomas Tallis* and *A Sea Symphony* (1910); he became active as a collector of folk music and edited *The English Hymnal* (1906). After completing his second symphony, *A London Symphony* (1913), he joined the army. As well as choral works such as *Sancta civitas* (1925) and *Serenade to Music* (1938), he wrote a Mass and made many choral arrangements of English folk songs. Apart from *The Lark Ascending* for violin and orchestra, his concerto-type works – for viola (*Flos campi*), piano, oboe and tuba – remain rarely performed. After the death of his first wife, he remarried aged eighty, and produced two more symphonies before his death.

Fantasia on a Theme by Thomas Tallis (1910; rev. 1913 and 1919)

The sound of the string orchestra has often brought out the best in English composers. Elgar's Introduction and Allegro, Britten's Variations on a Theme of Frank Bridge, Tippett's Concerto for Double String Orchestra and Fantasia Concertante on a Theme of Corelli are among the high points of the British orchestral repertoire. And Vaughan Williams's Fantasia on a Theme by Thomas Tallis is perhaps the finest of them all.

The Fantasia is so well known and loved today that it is hard to imagine a time when it could have been found 'difficult' or 'modernist'. But at the first performance, in Gloucester Cathedral (as part of the 1910 Three Choirs Festival), the Tallis Fantasia seems to have baffled most of its audience. The organist of Gloucester Cathedral, Herbert

Brewer, summed up its composer (then in his late thirties) as 'a queer, mad fellow from Chelsea'. But for the young composers Herbert Howells and Ivor Gurney the Tallis Fantasia was a revelation – a pointer to a new path, leading away from the German Romantic models followed by Elgar and his generation.

What was it about the Tallis Fantasia that was so new? Granted, Vaughan Williams wasn't the first British composer to look to the music of the Elizabethan period for inspiration. But what he finds in his chosen theme – Thomas Tallis's psalm tune, 'Why fumeth in fight?' – is more than quaint olde-worlde colouring. Tallis's tune is based on the old church 'Phrygian Mode' (try imagining a scale of E on the keyboard using only the white notes), and there are strikingly abrupt major–minor contrasts. These elements are reflected again and again in the themes and harmonies of Vaughan Williams's Tallis Fantasia. There is also the division of the string orchestra into contrasting 'choirs': a string quartet, an ensemble of nine stringed instruments, and a larger string ensemble. Modern listeners may hear echoes of Tallis's atmospheric use of separately placed groups of singers in his great choral motet *Spem in alium* for eight five-part choirs.

But while the Fantasia on a Theme by Thomas Tallis partly evokes the music of the English Renaissance, and through it the spirit of the so-called 'Age of Faith', there is also something about it that marks it out as a product of the modern age. Tallis's theme isn't heard right away in its original form. It emerges slowly, in fragments, as if from the shadows (lower strings, pizzicato), after five hushed chords for full strings – the first of which has a luminous, serene quality that, once heard, is hard to forget. As the music builds to its magnificent climax, there is a growing sense of restlessness, of impassioned searching – as if the music were striving to recapture that fleeting ethereal sound from the very beginning. The end brings a kind of resolution, but that serene opening chord, along with the vision it seems to encapsulate, never quite returns in its original form.

A friend once half-jokingly described Vaughan Williams as 'The Christian Agnostic'. There is an important truth in that jest. Vaughan Williams knew there was some kind of spiritual truth in age-old faith, but there was also plenty of room in his mind for twentieth-century doubt. Both sides find expression in his music – but never with greater power and subtlety than in the Fantasia on a Theme by Thomas Tallis.

Overture, *The Wasps* (1909)

Vaughan Williams was a relatively late maturer: not until his mid-thirties did he finally begin to discover his own musical personality. A brief period of study in Paris with Ravel had refined his orchestral technique, while his work as a folk-song collector and editor of the *English Hymnal* had, he felt, put him in touch with his musical roots. In 1908 he was delighted to be asked to supply some incidental music for the following year's Greek play at Cambridge University, his own alma mater. The play in question was Aristophanes's lively comedy *The Wasps*, a satire on the Athenian system of trial by mass jury. The 'wasps' are certain citizens of Athens who have become addicted to paid jury service. The central character, Philocleon, is one of the most obsessive: he quarrels incessantly with members of his own family, and even goes so far as to indict his own dog on a charge of stealing some cheese!

For the Cambridge production in November 1909, Vaughan Williams supplied an overture and seventeen pieces of music. He later reorganised the music into a suite of five numbers, which was first performed by the New Symphony Orchestra, conducted by the composer, at a royal gala concert at the Queen's Hall in July 1912. The overture has since established itself as one of Vaughan Williams's best-known and most frequently performed short orchestral pieces. Although its arresting opening, depicting the angry buzzing of the 'wasps', takes us straight into the Athenian courtroom, the heat and choler of Attic politics soon give way to a spacious central section, influenced by the cooler climate of Vaughan Williams's own 'green and pleasant land'.

Richard Wagner (1813–83)

One of the most significant composers in the history of opera, Wagner weathered widespread rejection, but ultimately triumphed in winning a group of supporters – ideological and financial – and building a new theatre in Bayreuth (1876) as a temple to his vision of the musico-dramatic form. He was born in Leipzig and soon wrote his first opera, *Die Feen* (*The Fairies*, 1833–4). With *Der fliegende Holländer* (*The Flying Dutchman*, 1841), *Tannhäuser* (1843–5) and *Lohengrin* (1847) he developed opera's expressive range. After initial failure in Paris and an appointment at the Dresden court he went into exile in Zurich, where he theorised on the 'art-work of the future' and propounded the notion of a *Gesamtkunstwerk* (complete art-work), a fusion of poetry, music and drama. The embodiment of his theories was the monumental four-opera cycle *Der Ring des Nibelungen* (*The Ring of the Nibelung*), whose libretti he had written by 1853. By the time of the cycle's completion in 1874 Wagner had composed the highly chromatic and erotically charged *Tristan and Isolde* and the 'comic' opera *Die Meistersinger von Nürnberg*. Controversial in his waywardness with money, his personal affairs, his anti-Semitism, his egotism and his theories on art, no other composer has so vigorously polarised the reactions of audiences and academics alike.

'Good Friday Music', from *Parsifal* (1877–82)

However one interprets the spiritual aspect of *Parsifal* – as a religious experience in its own right or as a symbolic enactment of higher truths in sacred garb – there is no denying the powerful influence exerted by the imagery on the composer. Wagner liked to recall how he had conceived his last opera one Good Friday, in 1857: having woken in his new home, the Asyl, to the sound of birdsong, he felt inspired to pen a sketch based on Wolfram von Eschenbach's epic poem *Parzival*. The actual chronology belies such a poetic rewriting of history – Wagner was not living in the Asyl on Good Friday 1857 – but the story shows just how pregnant with meaning the concept of that most sacred day in the Christian calendar was for the composer.

The notion of compassion, of fellow-suffering, is central to the work and, in the sublime passage from Act 3 known as the 'Good Friday Music', the young knight Parsifal observes that the whole of nature seems on that day to weep in sympathy with Christ on the Cross. Parsifal has returned to the domains of the Grail at the beginning of Act 3, after many years wandering, bearing the sacred, healing spear. His feet are bathed and anointed and, gazing on the beautiful meadows, he proclaims that on Good Friday every living thing should only sigh and sorrow. The veteran knight Gurnemanz replies that on this day repentant sinners rejoice at the Redeemer's act of self-sacrifice and nature herself is transfigured.

The 'Good Friday Music' may be one of the best-known passages in *Parsifal*, but it is in no way unrepresentative of it. Indeed, as a poignant meditation on the chief themes of the opera – suffering, compassion and redemption – it reaches to the very heart of the work.

Overture to *Tannhäuser* (1845)

It may seem surprisingly naive of Wagner, the composer most irredeemably associated with sexual excess, that he should ever have contemplated calling his opera 'The Mount of Venus' (*Der Venusberg*). But it was not until it was pointed out to him that ribald jests were likely to be made that he was persuaded to call it *Tannhäuser* instead. Even then he professed to be disgusted.

Tannhäuser is indeed concerned with sexual excess, or, more precisely, with the rival claims of sensual and spiritual love –

the former personified by the love goddess Venus, the latter by Elisabeth, the niece of the Landgrave. At the beginning of the opera, the minstrel Tannhäuser, surfeited with the sensual pleasures of the Venusberg (identified by Wagner and others with the Hörselberg in Thuringia), begs Venus to release him. He returns to the virtuous company of the Wartburg court, from which he has long been absent, and to Elisabeth, who loves him with a sacred love. But when it comes to the famous song contest (based on a real historical event), Tannhäuser blots his copybook. Hearing the other minstrels extol the virtues of 'pure', holy love, he retorts that they know nothing of the joys of true love. He shocks the company further by hymning the praises of Venus and only narrowly escapes summary execution. Filled with remorse, on account of his betrayal of Elisabeth, he joins a pilgrimage to Rome. The Pope refuses to absolve him, but Elisabeth struggles successfully with Venus for his soul, albeit at the cost of her life.

Tannhäuser was first staged in Dresden in 1845. In the early 1860s came an invitation from Emperor Napoleon III to stage the work at the Paris Opéra – an invitation that led to one of the most notorious debacles in the annals of opera. The genteel members of the Jockey Club, a powerful cabal at the Opéra, were not in the habit of seeing works through from the beginning: rather they decamped from their dining tables, in leisurely fashion, in time for the traditional second-act ballet. It was not that they appreciated the finer points of choreography any more than those of music, but rather that this enabled them to renew acquaintance with the ladies of the *corps de ballet*.

To introduce a ballet into the second act of *Tannhäuser* would, Wagner insisted, be a dramatic absurdity. Courageously, he refused to pander to the cabal or surrender to the Opéra management – even though it jeopardised his long-desired debut in one of the world's leading musical capitals. He did, however, compromise to the extent of expanding the music of the Venusberg scene, which had previously opened Act 1, into a wild Bacchanal, the better to depict the excesses from which Tannhäuser wishes to escape. The members of the Jockey Club were unimpressed and took ruthless revenge. With prolonged aristocratic baying and blasts on their dog-whistles, they disrupted not only the premiere (13 March 1861) but also two further performances. The production, which had taken 164 rehearsals to bring to the stage, was finally withdrawn at Wagner's request.

The central polarity of *Tannhäuser* – between sacred and sensual love – is projected unequivocally in the Overture. It begins with the solemn chant of the pilgrims, intoned on clarinets, horns and bassoons. But even before the theme can be developed, the lower, and then the upper strings enter with a yearning, chromatic idea that presumably alludes to the temptations of the flesh. The chant is taken up again and rings out on a trio of trombones (unison, fortissimo) against a scurrying figure on the strings and repeated triplets from the rest of the orchestra. The tempo changes to Allegro as the earthly delights of the Venusberg are scented, and eventually an ebullient melody – later to become Tannhäuser's 'Hymn to Venus' – is pounded out on the full orchestra.

A passage intended to depict Tannhäuser languishing amid the delights of the Venusberg builds to another forthright statement of the 'Hymn to Venus'. The music boils over at the climax, dissolving into the excited string figure that previously accompanied the Pilgrims' Chant. Sure enough, the chant itself returns, heard as at the beginning, first on winds, then interrupted by yearning lower strings, and finally blasted out on three trombones, now joined for good measure by a trio of trumpets.

'Prelude and Liebestod', from *Tristan and Isolde* (1857–9)

It is well known that the dramatic situation of Wagner's opera *Tristan and Isolde* paralleled a comparable situation in the composer's own life, whereby a passionate (though in this case probably platonic) relationship between Wagner and Mathilde Wesendonck was mirrored by that of Tristan and Isolde, with Mathilde's husband Otto being cast in the renunciatory role of King Marke. And it was the psychological pressure of the unfolding of this new chapter in Wagner's emotional life that precipitated what can only be called a compositional crisis. Wagner was at this time (early 1857) immersed in the composition of *Siegfried* (the third instalment in his epic four-part *Ring* cycle), but by the time he moved into the little house adjoining the Wesendoncks' villa, called the 'Asyl' ('Refuge') – the Wesendoncks moved in shortly afterwards – he had long since had the idea for an opera on the *Tristan* subject, and had even begun to make sketches for it. For a time, he pressed on with *Siegfried*, but some of the musical ideas now occurring to him were obviously better suited to the *Tristan* conception and eventually he abandoned *Siegfried* in order to concentrate on the new work.

Love and passion are only a part of the conceptual nexus of *Tristan*, of course. It also deals with the notion that death and oblivion represent the only state in which erotic longing can truly be consummated. And it dramatises the Schopenhauerian ideal of the merging of individual identities in the realm of the single, undifferentiated noumenon (symbolised in the opera by 'night'). 'Oblivion' was understood by both Wagner and Schopenhauer in the Buddhist sense of nirvana, as the state obtaining when all earthly striving has ceased: the quietus following the pacification of the 'will-to-live'.

In a letter to Mathilde Wesendonck, Wagner later discussed the idea of nirvana in specific connection with the rising four-note chromatic phrase that dominates *Tristan* and which is first heard on the oboe in the Prelude's second bar. So central is that chromatic phrase to the melodic and motivic fabric of the work, to its emotional colouring, and to the nature of its discourse, that it initially comes as something of a shock to discover that it was presaged (together with the famous '*Tristan* chord' itself – the first chord to be heard in the Prelude) by composers as diverse as Mozart, Spohr, Liszt and Gottschalk. A less well-known, but more immediate source is Hans von Bülow's symphonic poem *Nirwana*, which Wagner had been studying at the time he had made his first prose sketch for *Tristan* three years earlier. *Nirwana* contains not only the rising chromatic phrase but even a sublimation of it at the close of the work – exactly parallel to that in *Tristan*, right down to the tonality.

The final section of *Tristan*, in which Isolde, having hastened to her mortally wounded lover, ecstatically embraces the oblivion of death before falling lifeless over his body, is known – perhaps irreversibly – as the 'Liebestod' ('Love-Death'). Wagner, however, referred to it as 'Isolde's Transfiguration', reserving the title 'Liebestod' for the Prelude itself, as if to make clear the conceptual content of the opera from the start.

The desirability of appending the closing section of the work to the Prelude for concert performance has frequently been questioned, but the idea was Wagner's own. 'Isolde's Transfiguration' is given sometimes with the vocal part, sometimes without. It is not true that the vocal part is redundant, as occasionally stated, but on the other hand the music scarcely suffers from a purely orchestral performance, so richly complex are the textures and so opulent the scoring. On the final point, we have the testimony of Richard Strauss – himself no mean orchestrator – for whom the concluding radiant B major chord was 'the most beautifully scored final chord in the history of music'.

Siegfried Idyll (1870)

Birthdays in the Wagner household were not events to be taken lightly. In 1878, for example, Wagner's wife, Cosima, commissioned a play and coached the children (the girls were dressed as Erda and the Three Norns, characters from the

Ring cycle) for several months beforehand; incidental music was taken from Wagner's works and flowers strewn around his bust. Cosima's own birthday was actually on 24 December, but it was given increased resonance by being celebrated on Christmas Day (to be fair, there were probably practical considerations too). And on Christmas Day 1870 she woke to the strains of the *Siegfried Idyll*, written specially for the occasion and now performed on the staircase so that the music could waft into her room.

When it had finished, Wagner, who had been conducting, entered Cosima's bedroom with the five children and put into her hands the score of the 'Symphonic Birthday Greeting'. The entire household was said to be in tears. After breakfast, the orchestra was reassembled and gave another performance, followed by the 'Bridal March' from *Lohengrin* and Beethoven's Septet. The *Siegfried Idyll* was then given for a third time.

As the tone of the relevant entry in Cosima's diary confirms, the work both reflected and set the seal on the couple's new-found domestic bliss. After years of uncertainty and misery they were at last happily, and legally, united at Tribschen on Lake Lucerne – Cosima had finally moved in on 16 November 1868, but they had not been able to marry until 25 August 1870. The *Idyll* was at the same time a retrospective celebration of the birth of their son, Siegfried (on 6 June 1869), and of the composition of Act 3 of *Siegfried*, also the previous year. The private significance of the work for the couple caused them to resist publication as long as possible, but financial necessity eventually made it inevitable: 'the secret treasure is to become public property,' Cosima wrote in her diary (19 November 1877).

In spite of its intimacy, the *Siegfried Idyll* was not intended for a small chamber ensemble: the size of the band for the first performance (probably fifteen players rather than the oft-cited thirteen) was dictated more by the width of the staircase at Tribschen than by aesthetic considerations. For a later private performance in Mannheim on 20 December

1871, Wagner requested a considerably larger body of strings: six or seven first violins, seven to eight second violins, four violas, four cellos and two or three double basses (there had been eight string players altogether at the first performance). And in her diary (14 January 1874) Cosima reports a later intention of Wagner's (not realised) to arrange the *Idyll* for 'a large orchestra'.

In spite of the presence of music familiar from Act 3 of *Siegfried*, the *Idyll* is characterised by gentle lyricism, pastoral pedal points and an original lullaby first noted down by Wagner in his so-called 'Brown Book' on New Year's Eve 1868.

'Wotan's Farewell and Magic Fire Music', from *Die Walküre* (1852–6)

Wagner's attitude to the concert performance of extracts from his stage works – 'bleeding chunks', as they have come to be known – was a pragmatic one. Naturally he would have preferred complete performances of his music dramas, but in the absence of the artistic and political conditions that would make that possible, he occasionally allowed concerts to be promoted for the purposes of disseminating his music and raising revenue. And, in fact, several of these excerpts make effective concert pieces in their own right.

A favourite candidate for separate performance has always been 'Wotan's Farewell' from *Die Walküre*, the second instalment in Wagner's great four-night epic *Der Ring des Nibelungen*. This music forms the opera's finale and it is the Valkyrie of the title, Wotan's daughter Brünnhilde, to whom the god (sung by a bass or baritone) bids his reluctant and loving farewell. She has earlier disobeyed his express command by trying to shield his mortal son (and her half-brother) Siegmund from death at the hands of his enemy Hunding. Even though Brünnhilde was in fact acting in accordance with Wotan's own innermost wishes, she has to be punished by banishment from Valhalla. Wotan at first sentences her to be put to sleep on a mountain-top, to be woken and won by the first man that finds her; but then, softening under her entreaties, he agrees to surround her with a circle of fire that will at least deter all but the most fearless of heroes.

Wotan's passionate leave-taking of his favourite daughter is in two parts. The first extends from his opening repeated sighs of 'Farewell!' to the promise 'For only one shall win the bride, one freer than I, the god!' – a prophecy significantly accompanied by the motif for Siegfried (Siegmund and Sieglinde's as-yet-unborn son), which rings out heroically on the brass. As Brünnhilde sinks ecstatically into her father's embrace, a richly scored orchestral passage eloquently conveys the heartbreak experienced by Wotan as he accepts the course of destiny.

In the extract's second part, the god addresses Brünnhilde's radiant eyes, which shone at him in the darkest moments of his hopelessness, and which he now closes with a prolonged kiss that takes away her godhead. After another orchestral passage during which he lays Brünnhilde down on a low mossy mound, Wotan summons the fire-god Loge. His flickering presence is evident in every bar as the rocks are encircled by a sea of flame and Wotan sorrowfully departs.

William Walton (1902–83)

Born in industrial Lancashire, Walton made an early escape to Oxford, becoming a chorister at Christ Church Cathedral, then staying on at Christ Church as an undergraduate. Here he had the good fortune to fall in with the literary Sitwell family (Edith, Sacheverell and Osbert), who supported him for ten years as well as introducing him to leading artists of the day. His *Façade* (1922) – a chic, jazzy entertainment for reciter and ensemble, to texts by Edith – caused a stir. The Viola Concerto (1928–9) soon followed, as did the cantata *Belshazzar's Feast* (1929–31), which quickly became a staple of choral societies. During the 1940s he produced film scores for, among others, Olivier's *Henry V* and *Hamlet*. Following his marriage in 1949 he and his wife Susana moved to Ischia, off the Naples coast. He also wrote concertos for violin (1938–9) and cello (1956–7), and showed a flair for occasional music, displayed in the marches *Crown Imperial* and *Orb and Sceptre* written for the coronations of George VI and Elizabeth II respectively.

Crown Imperial, Coronation March (1937)

Many British composers have responded positively to the ceremonial splendours of royal occasions – the rituals which are part of our national heritage. Purcell, Handel, Parry, Elgar and Bliss have all in their time written excellent examples of ceremonial music, without being false to their normal style of composing; and Walton also did so, despite the gibes of his friend Constant Lambert to the effect that he was becoming an 'Establishment' composer.

Crown Imperial was the result of a BBC commission for a march originally for the Coronation of Edward VIII, then diverted, after his abdication, to that of King George VI and Queen Elizabeth in May 1937. It was first broadcast from a

London studio three days before the Coronation; and then, on the day itself, it was played in Westminster Abbey for the entry of Queen Mary, the new King's mother, before the beginning of the Coronation Service. The BBC Symphony Orchestra (playing as the 'Coronation Orchestra') was conducted by Adrian Boult.

The title *Crown Imperial* comes from William Dunbar's celebratory poem 'In honour of the City of London', which Walton had recently set as a cantata: London is described as 'the flower of cities all . . . in beauty bearing the crown imperial'. For his setting of Dunbar's poem, Walton had found a rhetorical and ceremonial style which matched exactly that of the poet – the outward pageant and the genuine feelings that lay beneath. In purely musical terms, also, this aspect of Walton's personality had already been expressed in the finale of the First Symphony. So when, in 1937, he was asked to write a *pièce d'occasion* – a coronation march – he could do so without inconsistency, and with the example of Elgar behind him. Like everything else that Walton wrote, even a march was a very personal utterance, with the composer's fingerprints all over it. In form, Elgar's *Pomp and Circumstance* pattern was followed: a stirring march section contrasting with an expansive flowing melody, noble in character. The rhythmic textures, the astringent harmonies, the tensions, the resplendence of the coda – in all this, the real Walton is unmistakably present.

© David Cox

Orb and Sceptre, Coronation March (1953)

When King George VI died in 1952 and the nation, after a suitable period of mourning, began to look eagerly ahead to the Coronation of Queen Elizabeth II, Walton was a natural choice to provide a new march for the occasion. His reputation as the post-Elgarian master musician of 'pomp and circumstance' had been both launched and sealed with *Crown Imperial*, the march commissioned by the BBC.

For Queen Elizabeth II's Coronation on 2 June 1953, Walton composed both a *Te Deum* and a march. He found the new march's title, *Orb and Sceptre* in the famous speech in Shakespeare's *Henry V* which, as he liked to point out, contained enough potential titles to keep him in business in this way for some time to come. ('Bed majestical', he suggested, would come in useful one day.)

Orb and Sceptre's short fanfare-like introduction for trumpets leads at once into the swaggering main theme for full orchestra, with its sonorous, Elgar-like pendant on horns and second violins. The key changes from E major to C major for the quieter central section, where the strings (soon joined by the horns) present one of those classic English march tunes that had by now become a Walton trademark. This is repeated fortissimo before the opening theme returns and is further extended. A grand reprise of the central tune, now in E major, leads to a resounding, brass-dominated conclusion.

Chronology of Works

*c.*1717	Water Music	Handel
1749	Music for the Royal Fireworks	Handel
1776	Serenade in D major, K250, 'Haffner'	Mozart
1779	Serenade in D major, K320, 'Posthorn'	Mozart
1787	*Eine kleine Nachtmusik*, K525	Mozart
1806	Overture, *Leonore* no. 3, from Op. 72	Beethoven
1810	Overture, *Egmont*, from Op. 84	Beethoven
1816	*The Barber of Seville*	Rossini
1823	*Rosamunde*	Schubert
1826	*A Midsummer Night's Dream*, overture, Op. 21	Mendelssohn
1829	*William Tell*	Rossini
1830	Overture, *The Hebrides*, Op. 26 (revised 1832)	Mendelssohn
1842	*Ruslan and Lyudmila*	Glinka
1843	*A Midsummer Night's Dream*, incidental music, Op. 61	Mendelssohn
1844	Overture, *Le corsaire*, Op. 21 (rev. 1852)	Berlioz
1844	Overture, *Roman Carnival*, Op. 9	Berlioz
1845	*Tannhäuser*	Wagner
1846	*The Damnation of Faust*, Op. 24	Berlioz
1852–6	*Die Walküre*	Wagner
1856–8	*The Trojans*	Berlioz
1857–9	*Tristan and Isolde*	Wagner
1867	*Night on the Bare Mountain* (arr. Rimsky-Korsakov, 1881–6)	Mussorgsky
1867	*By the Beautiful Blue Danube*, Op. 314	J. Strauss II
1869	Fantasy-Overture, *Romeo and Juliet* (revised 1870, 1880)	Tchaikovsky

1870	*Siegfried Idyll*	Wagner
1873	Variations on the St Anthony Chorale, Op. 56a	Brahms
1873–5	*Carmen*	Bizet
1874	*Pictures at an Exhibition* (orch. Ravel, 1922)	Mussorgsky
1875	*Prince Igor*	Borodin
1876	*Francesca da Rimini*, Op. 32	Tchaikovsky
1877	Symphonic Variations, Op. 78	Dvořák
1877–82	*Parsifal*	Wagner
1879–94	*Má vlast*	Smetana
1880	*Roses from the South*, Op. 388	J. Strauss II
1880	*Academic Festival Overture*, Op. 80	Brahms
1883	*España*	Chabrier
1886	*Carnival of the Animals*	Saint-Saëns
1887	*Pavane*, Op. 50	Fauré
1887	*Capriccio espagnol*, Op. 34	Rimsky-Korsakov
1887–8	*Don Juan*, Op. 20	R. Strauss
1888	*Sheherazade*, Op. 35	Rimsky-Korsakov
1888	*Two Gymnopédies* (orch. Debussy, 1896)	Satie
1889	*Emperor Waltz*, Op. 437	J. Strauss II
1891	Overture, *Carnival*, Op. 92	Dvořák
1892	Serenade for Strings, Op. 20	Elgar
1892	*En saga*, Op. 9 (revised 1902)	Sibelius
1892–4	*Prélude à 'L' après-midi d'un faune'*	Debussy
1893	*Karelia Suite*, Op. 11	Sibelius
1893	*The Swan of Tuonela*, Op. 22 no. 3 (revised 1897 and 1900)	Sibelius
1894–5	*Till Eulenspiegels lustige Streiche*, Op. 28	R. Strauss
1895–6	*Also sprach Zarathustra*, Op. 30	R. Strauss
1897	*The Sorcerer's Apprentice*	Dukas
1897–8	*Ein Heldenleben*, Op. 40	R. Strauss
1898	*Pelléas and Mélisande*, Suite, Op. 80 (orch. 1901)	Fauré
1899	Variations on an Original Theme ('Enigma'), Op. 36	Elgar

1899	*Pavane pour une infante défunte* (orch. 1910)	Ravel
1899	*Finlandia*, Op. 26 (rev. 1900)	Sibelius
1900–1	*A Village Romeo and Juliet*	Delius
1900–1	Overture, *Cockaigne*, Op. 40	Elgar
1901	*Pomp and Circumstance* March no. 1	Elgar
1902–5	*La mer*	Debussy
1903–4	Overture, *In the South*, Op. 50	Elgar
1904–5	Introduction and Allegro for Strings, Op. 47	Elgar
1904–5	*Alborada del gracioso* (orch. 1918)	Ravel
1907	*Brigg Fair*	Delius
1907	*Night Ride and Sunrise*, Op. 55	Sibelius
1907–8	*Rapsodie espagnole*	Ravel
1908	*Fireworks*	Stravinsky
1908–10	*Mother Goose* (orch. 1911)	Ravel
1909	Overture, *The Wasps*	Vaughan Williams
1909–10	*The Firebird* (revised 1945)	Stravinsky
1909–12	*Daphnis and Chloë*	Ravel
1910	Fantasia on a Theme by Thomas Tallis (revised 1913, 1919)	Vaughan Williams
1910–11	*Petrushka*	Stravinsky
1911–13	*The Rite of Spring*	Stravinsky
1912–13	*Falstaff*, Op. 68	Elgar
1914	*The Oceanides*, Op. 73	Sibelius
1914–17	*The Planets*, Op. 32	Holst
1915	*Love, the Magician*	Falla
1915	*Scythian Suite*, Op. 20	Prokofiev
1915–18	*Taras Bulba*	Janáček
1916–19	*The Three-Cornered Hat*	Falla
1919–20	*Pulcinella* (revised 1965)	Stravinsky
1919–20	*La valse*	Ravel
1920	*Le boeuf sur le toit*, Op. 58	Milhaud
1923	*Pacific 231*	Honegger
1923	*La création du monde*, Op. 81	Milhaud
1923	*Les biches*	Poulenc
1923–4	*The Pines of Rome*	Respighi

1926	Sinfonietta	Janáček
1926	*Tapiola*, Op. 112	Sibelius
1927–8	*Apollo*	Stravinsky
1928	*An American in Paris*	Gershwin
1928	*Boléro*	Ravel
1932–6	*El salón México*	Copland
1935–6	*Romeo and Juliet*, Op. 64	Prokofiev
1936	Adagio for Strings, Op. 11 (arr. 1938)	Barber
1936	Music for Strings, Percussion and Celesta	Bartók
1937	*Crown Imperial*, Coronation March	Walton
1938	*Billy the Kid*	Copland
1940	Symphonic Dances, Op. 45	Rakhmaninov
1942	*Fanfare for the Common Man*	Copland
1943	Concerto for Orchestra	Bartók
1943	Symphonic Metamorphoses on Themes of Weber	Hindemith
1945	*Peter Grimes*	Britten
1945	*The Young Person's Guide to the Orchestra*, Op. 34	Britten
1945	*Appalachian Spring*	Copland
1953	Fantasia Concertante on a Theme of Corelli	Tippett
1953	*Orb and Sceptre*, Coronation March	Walton
1953–7	*Agon*	Stravinsky
1956	*Candide*	Bernstein
1957	*West Side Story*	Bernstein
1999–2000	'Pluto, the Renewer'	C. Matthews